Human Well-Being Research and Policy Making

Series Editor
M. Joseph Sirgy, Department of Marketing, Virginia Polytechnic Institute & State University, Blacksburg, VA, USA

This series includes policy-focused books on the role of the public and private sectors in advancing quality of life and well-being. It creates a dialogue between well-being scholars and public policy makers. Well-being theory, research and practice are essentially interdisciplinary in nature and embrace contributions from all disciplines within the social sciences. With the exception of leading economists, the policy relevant contributions of social scientists are widely scattered and lack the coherence and integration needed to more effectively inform the actions of policy makers. Contributions in the series focus on one more of the following four aspects of well-being and public policy:

- Discussions of the public policy and well-being focused on particular nations and worldwide regions
- Discussions of the public policy and well-being in specialized sectors of policy making such as health, education, work, social welfare, housing, transportation, use of leisure time
- Discussions of public policy and well-being associated with particular population groups such as women, children and youth, the aged, persons with disabilities and vulnerable populations
- Special topics in well-being and public policy such as technology and well-being, terrorism and well-being, infrastructure and well-being.

This series was initiated, in part, through funds provided by the Halloran Philanthropies of West Conshohocken, Pennsylvania, USA. The commitment of the Halloran Philanthropies is to "inspire, innovate and accelerate sustainable social interventions that promote human well-being." The series editors and Springer acknowledge Harry Halloran, Tony Carr and Audrey Selian for their contributions in helping to make the series a reality.

Dong-Jin Lee • M. Joseph Sirgy

Organizational Strategies for Work-Life Balance

For Whom, Why, and Under What Conditions

Springer

Dong-Jin Lee
School of Business
Yonsei University
Seodaemun-Gu, Korea (Republic of)

M. Joseph Sirgy
Dept. of Marketing
Virginia Tech
Blacksburg, VA, USA

ISSN 2522-5367 ISSN 2522-5375 (electronic)
Human Well-Being Research and Policy Making
ISBN 978-3-031-56313-3 ISBN 978-3-031-56314-0 (eBook)
https://doi.org/10.1007/978-3-031-56314-0

This Springer imprint is published by the registered company Springer Nature Switzerland AG
The registered company address is: Gewerbestrasse 11, 6330 Cham, Switzerland

This book is dedicated to all professionals, organizational executives, and HR directors who care about employee wellbeing; to management consultants who are in the business of helping their clients develop and implement effective work-life balance programs; and to academics and scholars who have committed to doing research and writing on this very important topic of quality of life.

Preface

This book provides a systematic review of the research literature related to the effectiveness of organizational policies and programs on work-life balance (WLB). It discusses policies, programs, and practices related to workload management, flex-time, flexplace, alternative job arrangements, and family care. Based on the evidence, the authors make specific recommendations to organizational executives and HR directors to design and implement work-life balance policies and programs to maximize their effectiveness and help employees achieve their optimal level of work-life balance. Specifically, the authors discuss how to: (1) identify employees with greater need for WLB programs, (2) evaluate environmental circumstances for WLB programs (3) design effective WLB policies and programs, (3) facilitate effective implementation of WLB policies and programs, (4) provide management support for WLB policies and programs, and (5) evaluate performance of WLB policies and programs.

This volume provides professional executives, HR managers, and management consultants with rich material to help them develop and implement effective work-life balance policies, programs, and practices. The volume is also written for academics and scholars interested in doing research on this very important quality-of-life topic, namely work-life balance.

Seoul, Republic of Korea — Dong-Jin Lee
Blacksburg, VA, USA — M. Joseph Sirgy

Contents

Part III Epilogue

About the Authors

Dong-Jin Lee is Professor Emeritus at the School of Business, Yonsei University, Seoul, Korea. He received his Ph.D. from Virginia Tech and has published extensively in quality-of-life studies. Before joining Yonsei University, he was on the faculty of the University of Western Australia (1996–1999) and the State University of New York at Binghamton (2000–2002). He served as Vice President for Academic Affairs, Vice President for Publication, and Program Area Chair for the International Society for Quality-of-Life Studies (ISQOLS) in 1997–1999, 2007–2009, and 1997–1998, respectively; he was Section Editor of Applied Research in Quality of Life (ARQOL) from 2009 to 2011; and Dean of Sangnam Management Institute at Yonsei University from 2017 to 2018. He won the best paper award from ARQOL in 2021. He is currently a member of the Board of Directors of the Management Institute for Quality-of-Life Studies (MIQOLS).

M. Joseph Sirgy is a management psychologist (Ph.D., U/Mass), Virginia Tech Real Estate Professor Emeritus of Marketing at Virginia Polytechnic Institute and State University (USA), and Extraordinary Professor at the WorkWell Research Unit at North West University – Potchefstroom Campus (South Africa). He has published extensively in marketing, business ethics, and quality of life (QoL). He co-founded the International Society for Quality-of-Life Studies (ISQOLS) in 1995, served as its Executive Director/Treasurer from 1995 to 2011, and as development Co-Director (2011-present). In 1998, he received the Distinguished Fellow Award from ISQOLS. In 2003, ISQOLS honored him as the Distinguished QOL Researcher for research excellence and a record of lifetime achievement in QOL research. He also served as President of the Academy of Marketing Science (2002-04) from which he received the Distinguished Fellow Award in the early 1990s and the Harold Berkman Service Award in 2007 (lifetime achievement award for serving the marketing professoriate). In the early 2000s, he helped co-found the Macromarketing Society and the Community Indicators Consortium and has served as a board member of these two professional associations. He co-founded the journal, Applied Research in Quality of Life, the official journal of the International Society for Quality-of-Life Studies, in 2005. He also served as editor of the QoL section in the

Journal of Macromarketing (1995–2016) and is its editor-in-chief (2020 onwards). He received the Virginia Tech's Pamplin Teaching Excellence Award/Holtzman Outstanding Educator Award and University Certificate of Teaching Excellence in 2008. In 2010, ISQOLS honored him for excellence and lifetime service to society. In 2012 he was awarded the EuroMed Management Research Award for outstanding achievements and groundbreaking contributions to well-being and quality-of-life research. In 2019 the Macromarketing Society honored him with the Robert W. Nason Award for extraordinary and sustained contributions to the field of macromarketing. He previously edited several collaborative ISQOLS/Springer book series and is currently the series editor of Human Well-Being and Policy Making (2015-present). He also serves as Executive Director of the Management Institute for Quality-of-Life Studies (MIQOLS). This institute received the Award for the Betterment of the Human Condition by ISQOLS in 2023.

Part I
Organizational Policies and Programs of Work-Life Balance

In Part I of the book, we try to accomplish the following:

- Introduce the concept of work-life balance (WLB),
- Provide the reader with established definitions of the concept,
- Describe a typology of WLB practices,
- Discuss the impact of these practices on both employees and the organization, and
- Provide the reader with information about the established theories that delineate the psychological mechanisms associated with these practices.

Chapter 1
Introduction

"I've learned that you can't have everything and do everything at the same time"—Oprah Winfrey (https://teambuilding.com/blog/work-life-balance-quotes)

Abstract In this chapter, we first describe the evidence related to positive outcomes of work-life balance (WLB) practices and explain the purpose of this book. This book is designed to answer the following question: for whom, why, and under what conditions are WLB strategies most effective? In answering this question, we first review the literature related to conceptual definitions, theories, antecedents, and consequences of each organizational strategy of WLB. Then, we review theoretical mechanisms of each strategy's effect on employee and organizational wellbeing. Finally, and most importantly, we identify the moderating conditions (individual, program, organizational, environmental, and cultural characteristics) that facilitate the efficacy of each strategy. The end goal is to provide recommendations to further develop WLB policies and programs to increase their effectiveness.

In response to various societal factors such as a greater number of women in the workforce, an aging population, changes in family structures, longer working hours, and the growing influence of information technology, many organizations have developed and implemented family-friendly practices (e.g., Bidwell, 2013; Boudreau & Jeppesen, 2015; Johnson & Ashforth, 2008; Kalleberg, 2012). These practices are designed to help employees manage work-life conflict and enhance their wellbeing.

Work-life balance (WLB) has also long been recognized as a key factor in creating and maintaining a sustainable, productive, and energized labor force—positively affecting individuals both at work and at home. WLB contributes significantly to organizational performance and personal wellbeing (Greenhaus et al., 2003; Sirgy & Lee, 2023). See Box 1.1 for signs of poor work-life balance. See Box 1.2

D.-J. Lee, M. J. Sirgy, *Organizational Strategies for Work-Life Balance*, Human Well-Being Research and Policy Making,
https://doi.org/10.1007/978-3-031-56314-0_1

concerning the increasing importance of WLB practices post-pandemic. In Box 1.3 we discuss WLB for Millennials and Generation Z.

Box 1.1 Signs of Poor Work-Life Balance

Work-life balance impacts all areas of an employee's life. It tends to show up differently for different people, however. Here are some "symptoms" that managers can keep in mind to "diagnose" poor work-life balance.

Employees can't stop thinking about work when they are not at work. They find it difficult to draw boundaries between work and life. Relationships with other co-workers are beginning to suffer. They may be easily irritated with coworkers. They complain about unexplained aches and pains. They may rarely have energy or find it difficult to focus when at work. When not at work, everything seems uninteresting or unimportant. They just don't feel like doing anything unless they must. They often turn down invitations, further isolating themselves from their colleagues and friends. They spend a lot of money outsourcing support for personal tasks. Household chores like laundry, dishes, and mail pile up. Their excuse is that they're waiting for the day when they "have time" to do these chores. They struggle to take time off when they are sick, mentally strained, or when they need to take care of personal matters. They don't remember their last vacation and they don't have plans to take one. They can't imagine doing what you do for the rest of their life. They always feel like no matter what they are doing, they should be doing something else.

Source: Adapted from https://www.betterup.com/blog/how-to-have-good-work-life-balance

Box 1.2 Work-Life Balance Policies and Programs Are Now More Important Than Ever

We now know, based on evidence, that corporate policies that support work-life balance promote productivity, reduce turnover, and improve employees' mental and physical health. Recently, Covid-19 demonstrated that firms could remain efficient while allowing employees more flexibility as to where and when they do their work: That is, employee productivity did not decline even though many companies have switched to flexible and remote work arrangements during the pandemic. But apparently many of the same companies did not learn much from this field experiment. As the pandemic faded, those companies reverted to their old policies related to office work. In contrast, two-thirds of Covid-era remote workers have reported that they don't want to return to the office. When forced to return, many opted to resign rather than go back to office work. Others who appreciate the pandemic-induced flexibility have negotiated to keep their newfound flexibility. Interestingly, in a recent survey 64% of employees at top companies hinted that they would forgo a $30,000 raise if it meant they didn't have to return to the office.

Source: Adapted from Kalev and Dobbin (2022).

Box 1.3 Work-Life Balance for Millennials and Generation Z
Millennials and Generation Z regard WLB as very important. They demand a good work environment, specifically work flexibility. The new generations have a different set of priorities. They expect a high level of autonomy and do not just work for the money. They value a flexible work environment. They expect to learn new skills. They demand opportunity to grow in the company.

Source: Adapted from Manpower Group (2016) and Sánchez-Hernández et al. (2019).

1.1 Work-Related Outcomes

Much research provides concrete evidence on the effects of WLB practices on organizational performance. In other words, WLB produces many positive work-related outcomes (see Table 1.1). Research has found that WLB increases job performance, job satisfaction, organizational commitment, career development and success. Research has also demonstrated that WLB reduces job malfunction, job burnout and alienation, absenteeism, and turnover intention (Allen et al., 2000; Anaton, 2013; Blazovich et al., 2014; Carlson et al., 2006, 2010; De Simone et al., 2014; Fisher et al., 2009; Frone et al., 1997; Konrad & Yang, 2012; Kossek & Ozeki, 1998; McNall et al., 2010; Sirgy & Lee, 2018; Wayne et al., 2004; Whiston & Cinamon, 2015).

Table 1.1 Impact of work-life balance policies and programs

Type of outcome	Specific outcomes
Work-related outcomes	Increased job performance
	Increased job satisfaction
	Increased organizational commitment
	Increased career development and success
	Reduced job malfunction
	Reduced job burnout and alienation
	Reduced absenteeism
	Reduced turnover intention
Nonwork-related outcomes	Increased life satisfaction
	Increased marital satisfaction
	Increased family performance and satisfaction
	Increased parental satisfaction
	Increased leisure satisfaction
	Reduced health risks
	Reduced cognitive problems
	Reduced conflict with family members
	Reduced psychological distress
	Reduced work-life conflict
	Reduced family-related stress
	Reduced detrimental physiological symptoms

1.2 Nonwork-Related Outcomes

WLB has positive non-work outcomes as well (see Table 1.1). Research has shown that work-life balance of employees increases employees' life satisfaction, marital satisfaction, family performance and satisfaction, parental satisfaction, and leisure satisfaction. Research also found that WLB reduces health risks, cognitive problems, and conflicts with family members (Allen et al., 2000; Anaton, 2013; Carlson et al., 2006; 2010; De Simone et al., 2014; Fisher et al., 2009; Greenhaus & Beutell, 1985; Kossek & Ozeki, 1998; Schaufeli et al., 2002; Schaufeli & Bakker, 2004; Sirgy & Lee, 2018; Westman & Etzion, 2005; Whiston & Cinamon, 2015).

WLB reduces psychological distress. Research has shown that work-life conflict increases psychological distress (i.e., emotional exhaustion, emotional ill-being, anxiety, irritability and hostility, hypertension, and depression) and family-related stress (i.e., affective parental and marital stress), as well as detrimental physiological symptoms (i.e., somatic complaints, high blood pressure and cholesterol, alcohol abuse, and cigarette consumption) (Allen et al., 2000; Anaton, 2013; Blazovich et al., 2014; Carlson et al., 2006; Carlson et al., 2010; De Simone et al., 2014; Fisher et al., 2009; Frone et al., 1992; Frone et al., 1997; Konrad & Yang, 2012; Kossek & Ozeki, 1998; McNall et al., 2010; Sirgy & Lee, 2018; Wayne et al., 2004; Whiston & Cinamon, 2015).

While programs to improve WLB are well-advised in theory, the study findings also indicate that limited attention has been given to understanding the conditions for effective implementation of these programs and policies (Sirgy & Lee, 2018). We need to further understand which programs or policies are effective for whom, why, and under what conditions. That is, there is a scarcity of research based on systematic policy evaluation data to address the question of whether work-life practices are achieving their intended aims of WLB and personal wellbeing (McDonald et al., 2005; Sirgy & Lee, 2018).

As such, this book focuses on the effects of WLB programs on both organizational performance and personal outcomes. We use available research to highlight employee outcomes resulting from organizational strategies of work-life balance, summarize available evidence, and provide answers to three fundamental questions essential to WLB research:

- For whom, are organizational WLB strategies most effective? To whom do organizational WLB strategies need to be directed?
- How do the outcomes of WLB programs manifest? What psychological mechanisms underlie the wellbeing effects of WLB practices?
- When do those consequences occur? Under what individual, organizational, and environmental conditions do WLB practices register their strongest effects?

In answering these questions, we hope to provide the reader with the required building blocks that can help organizational leaders and policy makers better understand the working dynamics of WLB programs and policies.

In sum, the purpose of this book is to answer the following questions: for whom, why, and under what conditions are WLB strategies most effective. In answering these questions, we will first review the literature related to conceptual definitions, theories, antecedents, and consequences of each organizational strategy of work-life balance. Then, we will review the theoretical mechanisms of each strategy's effect on wellbeing. Finally, and most importantly, we identify the moderating conditions (individual, organizational, environmental, and cultural characteristics) that facilitate the efficacy of each strategy. The end goal is to provide recommendations to further develop these policies and programs to increase their effectiveness.

References

Allen, T. D., Herst, D. E., Bruck, C. S., & Sutton, M. (2000). Consequences associated with work-to-family conflict: A review and agenda for future research. *Journal of Occupational Health Psychology, 5*(2), 278–308.

Anaton, L. (2013). A proposed conceptual framework of work-family/family-work facilitation (WFF/FWF) approach in inter-role conflict. *Journal of Global Management, 6*(1), 89–100.

Bidwell, M. J. (2013). What happened to long-term employment? The role of worker power and environmental turbulence in explaining declines in worker tenure. *Organization Science, 24*(4), 1061–1082.

Blazovich, J. L., Smith, K. T., & Smith, L. M. (2014). Employee-friendly companies and work-life balance: Is there an impact on financial performance and risk level? *Journal of Organizational Culture, Communications and Conflict, 18*(1), 1–13.

Boudreau, K. J., & Jeppesen, L. B. (2015). Unpaid crowd complementors: The platform network effect mirage. *Strategic Management Journal, 36*(12), 1761–1777.

Carlson, D. S., Grzywacz, J. G., & Kacmar, K. M. (2010). The relationship of schedule flexibility and outcomes via the work-family interface. *Journal of Managerial Psychology, 25*(4), 330–355.

Carlson, D. S., Kacmar, K. M., Wayne, J. H., & Grzywacz, J. G. (2006). Measuring the positive side of the work-family work/family interface: Development and validation of a work-family enrichment scale. *Journal of Vocational Behavior, 68*(1), 131–164.

De Simone, S., Lampis, J., Lasio, D., Serri, F., Ciotto, G., & Putzu, D. (2014). Influences of work-family interface on job and life satisfaction. *Applied Research in Quality of Life, 9*(4), 831–861.

Fisher, G. G., Bulger, C. A., & Smith, C. S. (2009). Beyond work and family: A measure of work/nonwork interference and enhancement. *Journal of Occupational Health Psychology, 14*(4), 441–456.

Frone, M. R., Russell, M., & Cooper, M. L. (1992). Antecedents and outcomes of work-family conflict: Testing a model of the work-family interface. *Journal of Applied Psychology, 77*(1), 65–78.

Frone, M. R., Yardley, J. K., & Markel, K. S. (1997). Developing and testing an integrative model of the work-family interface. *Journal of Vocational Behavior, 50*(2), 145–167.

Greenhaus, J. H., & Beutell, N. J. (1985). Sources of conflict between work and family roles. *Academy of Management Review, 10*(1), 76–88.

Greenhaus, J. H., Collins, K. M., & Shaw, J. D. (2003). The relation between work-family balance and quality of life. *Journal of Vocational Behavior, 63*, 510–531.

Johnson, S. A., & Ashforth, B. E. (2008). Externalization of employment in a service environment: The role of organizational and customer identification. *Journal of Organizational Behavior: The International Journal of Industrial, Occupational and Organizational Psychology and Behavior, 29*(3), 287–309.

Kalev, A., & Dobbin, F. (2022). The surprising benefits of work/life support. Harvard Business Review (September-October) https://hbr.org/2022/09/the-surprising-benefits-of-work-life-support

Kalleberg, A. L. (2012). Job quality and precarious work: Clarifications, controversies, and challenges. *Work and Occupations, 39*(4), 427–448.

Konrad, A. M., & Yang, Y. (2012). Is using work-life interface benefits a career-limiting move? An examination of women, men, lone parents, and parents with partners. *Journal of Organizational Behavior, 33*(8), 1095–1119.

Kossek, E. E., & Ozeki, C. (1998). Work-family conflict, policies, and the job-life satisfaction relationship: A review and directions for organizational behavior-human resources research. *Journal of Applied Psychology, 83*(2), 139–155.

Manpower Group. (2016). *Millennial careers: 2020 vision: Facts, figures and practical advice from workforce experts*. ManpowerGroup.

McDonald, P., Brown, K., & Bradley, L. (2005). Explanations for the provision-utilization gap in work-life policy. *Women in Management Review, 20*(1), 37–55.

McNall, L. A., Masuda, A. D., & Nicklin, J. M. (2010). Flexible work arrangements and job satisfaction/turnover intentions: The mediating role of work-to-family enrichment. *Journal of Psychology: Interdisciplinary and Applied, 144*(1), 61–81.

Sánchez-Hernández, M. I., González-López, Ó. R., Buenadicha-Mateos, M., & Tato-Jiménez, J. L. (2019). Work-life balance in great companies and pending issues for engaging new generations at work. *International Journal of Environmental Research and Public Health, 16*(24), 5122.

Schaufeli, W. B., & Bakker, A. B. (2004). Job demands, job resources and their relationship with burnout and engagement: A multi-sample study. *Journal of Organizational Behavior, 25*(3), 293–315.

Schaufeli, W. B., Salanova, M., Gonzalez-Roma, V., & Bakker, A. B. (2002). The measurement of engagement and burnout and: A confirmative analytic approach. *Journal of Happiness Studies, 3*(1), 71–92.

Sirgy, M. J., & Lee, D. J. (2018). Work-life balance: An integrative review. *Applied Research in Quality of Life, 13*(1), 229–254.

Sirgy, M. J., & Lee, D. J. (2023). *Work-life balance: Using strategies from behavioral science to enhance wellbeing*. Cambridge University Press.

Wayne, J. H., Musisca, N., & Fleeson, W. (2004). Considering the role of personality in the work-family experience: Relationships of the big five to work-family conflict and facilitation. *Journal of Vocational Behavior, 64*(1), 108–130.

Westman, M., & Etzion, D. (2005). The crossover of work-family conflict from one spouse to the other. *Journal of Applied Social Psychology, 35*(9), 1936–1957.

Whiston, S. C., & Cinamon, R. G. (2015). The work-family interface: Integrating research and career counselling practice. *Career Development Quarterly, 63*(1), 44–56.

Chapter 2
Definitions and Metrics of Work-Life Balance

> *"Striving for excellence motivates you; striving for perfection is demoralizing."—Harriet Braiker (https://teambuilding.com/blog/work-life-balance-quotes)*

Abstract In this chapter we describe to the reader various definitions of work-life balance (WLB). We argue that a good way to appreciate the various definitions is to classify each definition in terms of inputs and outputs (outcomes). With respect to inputs, researchers have conceptualized WLB inputs in three ways: time, engagement, and fit. Similarly, WLB outputs are also classified into three concepts: role effectiveness, role satisfaction, and minimal role conflict. We also make distinctions among time-based, strain-based, and behavior-based conflict. With respect to definitions of WLB in terms of combined dimensions of both inputs and outputs, we discuss two major conceptualizations, one involving the combined effects of work-family balance and work-family fit. The other conceptualization involves the combined effects of time balance, involvement balance, and satisfaction balance.

Before we begin, let's first define work-life balance (WLB), as there are many definitions of the term. We will provide the reader with selected examples that will help set the stage for this book and place the reader in the right frame of mind.

Perhaps a good way to describe the construct of WLB is through a subjective assessment of balance. In other words, WLB is an evaluation of how "balanced" or "imbalanced" a person feels about work and other life domains (e.g., family life, social life, leisure life, community life). Consider the study conducted by Brough et al. (2014). These WLB researchers developed a measure that focuses on items directly asking about "balance" and "facilitation" in contrast to terms such as "conflict" and "interference." Participants rate their responses on a 5-point Likert-type scale: from 1 = strongly disagree to 5 = strongly agree. The survey prompt begins with the following statement: "When I reflect over my work and non-work activities (your regular activities outside of work such as family, friends, sports, study, etc.), over the past 3 months, I conclude that:

D.-J. Lee, M. J. Sirgy, *Organizational Strategies for Work-Life Balance*, Human Well-Being Research and Policy Making,
https://doi.org/10.1007/978-3-031-56314-0_2

- "I currently have a good balance between the time I spend at work and the time I have available for non-work activities."
- "I have difficulty balancing my work and non-work activities." (reverse coded).
- "I feel that the balance between my work demands and non-work activities is currently about right."
- "Overall, I believe that my work and non-work life are balanced."

A similar study conducted by Parkes and Langford (2008) measured WLB using four items. The study assesses the balance between work-life and various other life domains (e.g., work-family balance, work-social balance, and balance between work-life and -other life domains). Responses are captured on a 5-point Likert-type scale: from 1 = strongly disagree and 5 = strongly agree:

- "I maintain a good balance between work and other aspects of my life."
- "I am able to meet my family responsibilities while still doing what is expected of me at work."
- "I have a social life outside of work."
- "I am able to stay involved in non-work interests and activities."

However, we need to recognize that a subjective assessment of WLB is far from complete. WLB has been conceptualized in diverse and complex ways. The reader may be able to better understand these various definitions by organizing them in a systems framework involving inputs and outputs. Input-based WLB definitions refer to the balanced allocation of time and effort across life domains in ways that match resource investment with role demand (e.g., balanced engagement across life domains matching role demand and personal needs). Output-based WLB definitions focus on the consequences of balanced engagement (e.g., successful and satisfying outcomes of role performance with minimal role conflict). Input/output based WLB definitions treat WLB in terms of both input and output (Casper et al., 2018). See Fig. 2.1.

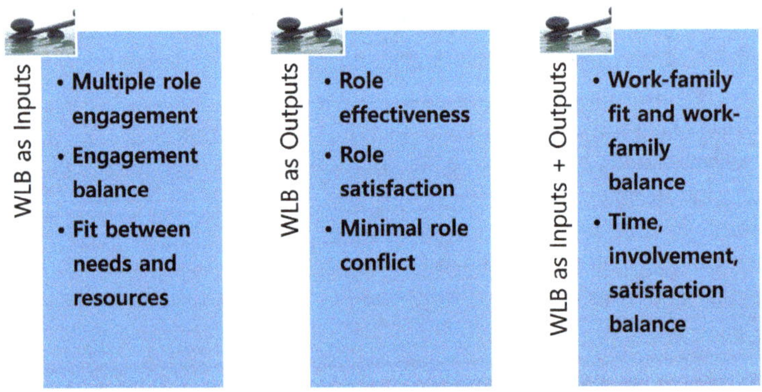

Fig. 2.1 Conceptual definitions of Work-Life Balance (WLB)

2.1 Work-Life Balance As Inputs

In terms of inputs, work-life balance (WLB) researchers have traditionally conceptualized the concept in three ways: (1) work-life balance as multiple roles, (2) work-life balance as engagement balance, and (3) fit between needs and resources.

2.1.1 Work-Life Balance As Multiple Role Engagement

WLB can be defined as the tendency to become fully *engaged* in the performance of every role in one's total role system—to approach every typical role with an attitude of attentiveness and care (Marks & MacDermid, 1996). Put differently, WLB is the practice of evenhanded or equitable awareness, also known as *mindfulness*. In this definition, balance means involvement—a high degree of engagement or involvement in multiple roles. This input-based definition of work-life balance focuses on multiple role engagement.

Below are survey items of a role balance measure developed by Marks and MacDermid (1996) capturing the "input" conceptualization of WLB. Respondents indicate their agreement or disagreement to the following items using a 5-point Likert-type scale:

- "I am pretty good at keeping the different parts of my life in balance; I generally don't let things slide."
- "Some things I do seem very important, but other things I do are a waste of my time" (reverse-scored).
- "Everything I do feels special to me; nothing stands out as more important or more valuable than anything else."
- "I try to put a lot of myself into everything I do."
- "There are some things I like to do so much that I often neglect other things I also care about" (reverse-scored).

2.1.2 Work-Life Balance As Engagement Balance

WLB has also been examined in terms of *time balance (i.e.,* almost equal amounts of time spent in different roles) and *involvement balance (i.e.,* the same level of dedication in fulfilling responsibilities towards work and family)[1] (Greenhaus et al., 2003). That is, the construct refers to an equilibrium between the amount

[1] The involvement balance construct (and its operationalization) is highly akin to the engagement construct described in the preceding section.

of time and effort devoted to work and personal activities to maintain an overall sense of harmony in life (Clarke et al., 2004). This input-based definition of work-life balance focuses engagement balance (i.e., time and involvement balance).

An example of a time balance measure was developed by researchers Sheldon et al. (2010). These researchers presented participants with ten major time categories and asked them to allocate the 24 h of their average day across those categories, the only constraint being that the numbers should sum to 24. The balance measure, called *objective balance*, was operationally defined as the within-subject standard deviation of the actual hour estimates, excluding sleep. The more evenly distributed the 24 h are across the categories (i.e., the lower the standard deviation), the more balanced the person is.

Another measure developed by Ellwart and Konradt (2011) involves the following item in which responses are captured using a 5-point Likert-type scale ([totally disagree (−2) to totally agree (+2)]): "Besides work there is sufficient time for family/private activities."

2.1.3 Work-Life Balance As Fit Between Needs and Resources

WLB has also been examined in terms of the *fit between needs and resources* (Greenhaus & Allen, 2011). Specifically, balance means a match between the demands and resources of a situation—matching the individual's abilities and the demands of the situation or matching the individual's needs and the resources provided by the situation. That is, WLB is a global assessment of whether work and family resources are sufficient to meet work and family demands such that participation is effective in both domains (Voydanoff, 2005a, b). In other words, balance means fit (i.e., a match between role demands and role resources). This input-based definition of work-life balance focuses on fit between role demands and resources.

Consider the measure developed by Ellwart and Konradt (2011). This measure involves the following three items in which responses are captured using a 5-point Likert-type scale ([totally disagree (−2) to totally agree (+2)]):

- I can meet all my work-related demands.
- I can meet all my private/family demands.

Specifically, the measure is essentially a formative conceptualization of work-family balance matching allocation of resources with role demands (i.e., fit).

2.2 Work-Life Balance As Outputs

The output definition of WLB involves three concepts: (1) role effectiveness, (2) role satisfaction, and (3) minimal role conflict.

2.2.1 Work-Life Balance As Role Effectiveness

WLB has been defined as the accomplishment of role-related expectations that are negotiated and shared between an individual and their role-related partners in the work and family domain (Grzywacz & Carlson, 2007; Carlson et al., 2009). In this definition, balance means *role effectiveness*—a high degree of success at balancing multiple roles and/or performing well across various important roles. This output-based definition of work-life balance focuses on role performance or role effectiveness.

Here are measurement items used by Carlson and his colleagues (Carlson et al., 2009) to capture WLB. Responses are captured on a 5-point Likert-type scale: from 1 = strongly disagree to 5 = strongly agree:

- "I am able to negotiate and accomplish what is expected of me at work and in my family."
- "I do a good job of meeting the role expectations of critical people in my work and family life."
- "People who are close to me would say that I do a good job of balancing work and family."
- "I am able to accomplish the expectations that my supervisors and my family have for me."
- "My co-workers and members of my family would say that I am meeting their expectations."
- "It is clear to me, based on feedback from co-workers and family members, that I am accomplishing both my work and family responsibilities."

Haar (2013) also construed WLB as an employee's perception of their overall effectiveness in meeting all their work and life roles. Harr asked individuals to report on WLB by making a global self-evaluation of their ability to adequately manage their roles. Harr used the following measurement item: "I manage to balance the demands of my work and personal/family life well" (responses are captured on a 5-point Likert-type scale: from 1 = strongly disagree to 5 = strongly agree).

2.2.2 Work-Life Balance As Role Satisfaction

WLB is also defined as the overall level of contentment resulting from a positive assessment of one's ability to meet work and family role demands (Valcour, 2007). In this definition, balance means effectiveness (i.e., a high degree of success at meeting demand in multiple roles) and *satisfaction* (i.e., contentment, happiness, or other positive feelings associated with role performance). This output-based definition of work-life balance focuses on satisfaction with role performance.

Consider the following measurement items from the work of Marks and MacDermid (1996), first mentioned in the previous section on role engagement.

Respondents indicate their agreement or disagreement to the following items using a 5-point Likert-type scale:

- "Nowadays, I seem to enjoy every part of my life equally well."
- "There are some parts of my life that I don't care much about, and there are other parts I care deeply about" (reverse-scored).
- "Work time, classes and study time, partner time, friend time, family time, leisure time—I find satisfaction in everything I do."

Haar (2013) argued that WLB involves feelings of satisfaction related to successful role performance. Consider the following measurement items, responses are captured on a 5-point Likert-type scale: from 1 = strongly disagree to 5 = strongly agree):

- "Nowadays, I seem to enjoy every part of my life equally well."
- "I am satisfied with my work–life balance, enjoying both roles."

As previously stated, Valcour (2007) defines WLB as the overall level of satisfaction that stems from positively evaluating one's ability to fulfill the demands of both work and family roles. He developed a measure of WLB that captures an individual's perception of how well they can balance the needs of the job with the needs of family. Respondents are asked how satisfied (using a 5-point scale: from 1 = very dissatisfied to 5 = very satisfied) they are with the following:

- "The way you divide your time between work and personal or family life?"
- "The way you divide your attention between work and home?"
- "How well your work life and your personal or family life fit together?"
- "Your ability to balance the needs of your job with those of your personal or family life?"
- "The opportunity you have to perform your job well and yet be able to perform home-related duties adequately?"

Another variation of a WLB measure based on satisfaction is one developed by Allen and his colleagues (Allen et al., 2010; Allen & Kiburz, 2012). The metric uses the following statement to capture balance satisfaction (responses are captured on a 5-point Likert-type scale: from 1 = strongly disagree to 5 = strongly agree): "I am satisfied with the balance I have achieved between my work life and my family life."

2.2.3 Work-Life Balance As Minimal Role Conflict

WLB has also been defined in terms of *minimum role conflict* (Clark, 2000; Frone, 2003; Wheatley, 2012)—minimal conflict between work and family roles. Work-family conflict is a form of inter-role conflict in which the demands of work and family roles are incompatible in some respect so that participation in one role is made more difficult due to participation in the other role (Greenhaus & Beutell, 1985). This understanding of WLB has been dominant in the research literature and involves work interference with family life. This output-based definition of work-life balance focuses on minimal inter-role conflicts.

Work-to-Family Conflict

Consider the work by Voydanoff (2005a, b), who developed a measure of work-family conflict. Specifically, this measure examines work interference in family life—the demands of work make it difficult to meet family responsibilities. Examples items include (responses are captured on a 5-point frequency scale: from 1 = never to 5 = very often):

- "In the past three months, how often have you not had enough time for your family or other important people in your life because of your job?"
- "How often have you not had the energy to do things with your family or other important people in your life because of your job?"
- "How often has work kept you from doing as good a job at home as you could?"
- "How often has your job kept you from concentrating on important things in your family or personal life?"
- "How often have you not been in as good a mood as you would like to be at home because of your job?"

Work-to-Family Conflict and Family-to-Work Conflict

Frone et al. (1992) made the distinction between two types of work-family conflict: *work-to-family conflict* and *family-to-work conflict*. Work-to-family conflict refers to the extent to which doing work at home interferes with home functioning. Conversely, family-to-work conflict refers to instances in which doing home-related chores at work interferes with work. Here are the measures (responses are captured using a 5-point frequency scale: 1 = almost never; 2 = occasionally; 3 = almost half the time; 4 = frequently; and 5 = almost always.

Items assessing *work-to-family conflict* include:

- "How often does your job or career interfere with your responsibilities at home, such as yard work, cooking, cleaning, repairs, shopping, paying the bills, or childcare?"
- "How often does your job or career keep you from spending the amount of time you would like to spend with your family?"

Items assessing *family-to-work conflict* include:

- "How often does your home life interfere with your responsibilities at work, such as getting to work on time, accomplishing daily tasks, or working overtime?"
- "How often does your home life keep you from spending the amount of time you would like to spend on job or career-related activities?"'

Netemeyer et al. (1996) developed and validated short, self-report scales of work-family conflict and family-work conflict using three samples. Responses are captured using a 7-point scale (1 = strongly disagree to 7 = strongly agree).

Items assessing *work-family conflict* include:

- "The demands of my work interfere with my home and family life."

- "The amount of time my job takes up makes it difficult to fulfill family responsibilities."
- "Things I want to do at home do not get done because of the demands my job puts on me."
- "My job produces strain that makes it difficult to fulfill family duties."
- "Due to work-related duties, I have to make changes to my plans for family activities."

Items assessing *family-work conflict* include:

- "The demands of my family or spouse/partner interfere with work-related activities."
- "I have to put off doing things at work because of demands on my time at home."
- "Things I want to do at work don't get done because of the demands of my family or spouse/partner."
- "My home life interferes with my responsibilities at work such as getting to work on time, accomplishing daily tasks, and working overtime."
- "Family-related strain interferes with my ability to perform job-related duties."

Three Forms and Two Directions of Work-Life Conflict

Carlson et al. (2000) developed a formative measure of work-family conflict involving six dimensions—a combination of three forms of work-family conflict (time, strain, and behavior) and two directions of work-family conflict (work interference with family and family interference with work). Each dimension has three items making up an 18-item measure. Responses to these items are captured on a 5-point Likert-type scale: from 1 = strongly disagree to 5 = strongly agree.

Time-based work interference with family:

- "My work keeps me from my family activities more than I would like."
- "The time I must devote to my job keeps me from participating equally in household responsibilities and activities."
- "I have to miss family activities due to the amount of time I must spend on work responsibilities."

Time-based family interference with work:

- "The time I spend on family responsibilities often interfere with my work responsibilities."
- "The time I spend with my family often causes me not to spend time in activities at work that could be helpful to my career."
- "I have to miss work activities due to the amount of time I must spend on family responsibilities."

Strain-based work interference with family:

- "When I get home from work, I am often too frazzled to participate in family activities/responsibilities."

- "I am often so emotionally drained when I get home from work that it prevents me from contributing to my family."
- "Due to all the pressures at work, sometimes when I come home, I am too stressed to do the things I enjoy."

Strain-based family interference with work:

- "Due to stress at home, I am often preoccupied with family matters at work."
- "Because I am often stressed from family responsibilities, I have a hard time concentrating on my work."
- "Tension and anxiety from my family life often weakens my ability to do my job."

Behavior-based work interference with family:

- "The problem-solving behaviors I use in my job are not effective in resolving problems at home."
- "Behavior that is effective and necessary for me at work would be counterproductive at home."
- "The behaviors I perform that make me effective at work do not help me to be a better parent and spouse."

Behavior-based family interference with work:

- "The behaviors that work for me at home do not seem to be effective at work."
- "Behavior that is effective and necessary for me at home would be counterproductive at work."
- "The problem-solving behavior that work for me at home does not seem to be as useful at work."

Matthews et al. (2010) developed and validated an abbreviated version of Carlson et al. (2000) multidimensional measure of work-family conflict. Responses to the six-item measure are captured using a 5-point Likert-type scale: from 1 = strongly disagree to 5 = strongly agree.

Work-to-family interference:

- "I have to miss family activities due to the amount of time I must spend on work responsibilities." (time-based conflict)
- "I am often so emotionally drained when I get home from work that it prevents me from contributing to my family." (strain-based conflict)
- "The behaviors I perform that make me effective at work do not help me to be a better parent and spouse." (behavior-based conflict)

Family-to-work interference:

- "I have to miss work activities due to the amount of time I must spend on family responsibilities." (time-based conflict)
- "Because I am often stressed from family responsibilities, I have a hard time concentrating on my work." (strain-based conflict)
- "Behavior that is effective and necessary for me at home would be counterproductive at work." (behavior-based conflict)

2.3 Work-Life Balance As Inputs + Outputs

Input + output-based measures of work-life balance (WLB) combine several dimensions of WLB. These include work-family balance, work-family fit, time balance, involvement balance, and satisfaction balance.

2.3.1 Work-Life Balance As Work-Family Fit and Work-Family Balance

Clarke et al. (2004) differentiated work-family fit and work-family balance. They used a single-item measurement that was reflective of the respondents' overall perceptions of balance and fit. Work-family fit describes the relationship between the demands placed on people and their efforts to meet those demands and is based more on the structural aspects of work-family interactions. Whereas work-family balance is based more on psychological factors. As such, WLB in this definition encompasses a combination of work-family fit (work life balance as fit between the needs and the resources; input balance) and work-family balance (work life balance as role effectiveness; output balance).

Specifically, *work-family fit* was measured by a single item, "How easy or difficult is it for you to manage the demands of your work and your family/personal life?" answered on a 4-point "difficulty" scale, with answers ranging from 1 ("very difficult") to 4 ("very easy"). In contrast, *work-family balance* was measured by the question, "All in all, how successful do you feel in balancing your work and personal/family life?" Respondents answered this question on a 7-point "success" scale, with responses ranging from 1 ("extremely unsuccessful") to 7 ("extremely successful").

2.3.2 Work-Life Balance As Time, Involvement, and Satisfaction Balance

Greenhaus et al. (2003) examined WLB by focusing on family balance in terms of three specific components or measures: time balance (equal time between work and family roles; input balance), involvement balance (equal psychological involvement in work and family roles; input balance), and satisfaction balance (equal satisfaction with work and family roles; output balance). WLB in this definition encompasses a combination of time and involvement balance (input balance) and satisfaction balance (output balance).

Time Balance

The measure used to capture time balance involves a comparison between the amount of time spent at work to the amount of time spent on home and family activities. Respondents are first asked how much time they spend on work and family per week (i.e., work hours per week, family hours per week). Responses are then coded as 0 = time balance (equal amount of time devoted to work and family), 1 = work imbalance (more time is devoted to work rather than family), or – 1 = family imbalance (more time is devoted to family rather than work). See Box 2.1 for a company's use of time to capture work-life balance.

Box 2.1 Practical Data-Driven Work-Life Balance Analytics
Here are a few "practical" metrics of work-life balance that you can apply to your organization.

- *After hours meetings*: Count the number of meetings which take place past working hours. Include all employees, irrespective of their seniority level. This should give you an idea how your employee's workday is like.
- *Emails after hours*: Count all the emails sent from your domain during the week and filter out the emails which were sent outside of working hours.
- *Workday length*: Account for the average number of hours between the first and last work activity per day.
- *Time since last balanced week*: Can you measure "a balanced week"? Look at each employee's weekly calendar. Did they work for more than 9 h on any day of the work week (on average)? If so, then your team is suffering from work overload. A balanced week should not exceed 9 h on average.

Source: Adapted from Network Perspective (2023). *Work-life balance analytics.* Accessed at https://www.networkperspective.io/work-life-balance-analytics (retrieved on September 27, 2023).

Involvement Balance

The measure used to capture involvement balance involves a comparison between involvement in work and involvement in family.[2] Like the time-balance measure, respondents are asked about the extent of their involvement at home and with family using the following item: "Most of the important things that happen to me involve

[2] It should be noted that there is a distinction between involvement and time spent. People can have a time balance (equal time devoted to work and family) and yet have an unequal involvement balance. For example, if an individual was physically at home, but often working from home or doing solitary activities that excluded the family, that create a time balance but not an involvement balance.

my family." Responses are captured on a 5-point Likert-type scale: from 1 = strongly disagree to 5 = strongly agree. Following this response, respondents are then presented with the statement, "Most of the important things that happen to me involve my career." Again, responses are captured on a 5-point Likert-type scale: from 1 = strongly disagree to 5 = strongly agree. Based on the responses to the above family and work items, a respondent is then assigned the following code: 0 = involvement balance (equal amount of involvement devoted to work and family), 1 = work imbalance (more involved in work rather than family), or − 1 = family imbalance (more involved in family rather than work).

Satisfaction Balance

Like the preceding measures of time and involvement balance, the measure used to capture satisfaction balance involves a comparison between satisfaction with work to satisfaction with family. Respondents are asked about the extent of their satisfaction at home and with family using the following statement: "I am satisfied with my present family situation." Responses are captured on a 5-point Likert-type scale: from 1 = strongly disagree to 5 = strongly agree. Following this response, respondents are then asked about their work satisfaction using the following statement: "I am satisfied with the success I have achieved in my career." Again, responses are captured on a 5-point Likert-type scale: from 1 = strongly disagree to 5 = strongly agree. Based on the responses to the above family and work items, a respondent is then assigned the following code: 0 = satisfaction balance (equal amount of satisfaction devoted to work and family), 1 = work imbalance (more satisfaction with work rather than family), or − 1 = family imbalance (more satisfaction with family rather than work).

2.3.3 *Other Definitions*

There are many other definitions that combine various input and output dimensions of WLB. For example, Hill et al. (2001) developed a five-item measure of WLB using input and output constructs. Specifically, the measure was designed to capture *balanced involvement in work and family life* (e.g., "How easy or difficult is it for you to balance the demands of your work and your personal and family life"; responses are captured using a 5-point scale ranging from "very easy" to "very difficult"), *time balance* (e.g., "I have sufficient time away from my job at [firm's name] to maintain adequate work and personal/family life balance"; responses are captured on 5-point Likert-type scale varying from "strong disagree" to "strongly agree"), *work disengagement in family life* (e.g., "When I take a vacation, I am able to separate myself from work and enjoy myself"; response are captured on a 5-point Likert-type scale varying from "strongly disagree" to "strongly agree"), *role effectiveness* (e.g., "All in all, how successful do you feel in balancing your work and personal/family life"; responses are captured on a 7-point scale varying from "extremely unsuccessful" to "extremely successful"), and *emotional exhaustion due to work overload* (e.g., How often do you feel drained when you go home from work because of work pressures and problems"; responses are captured using a 5-point scale ranging from "never" to "almost always").

2.4 Summary and Conclusion

In this chapter we exposed the reader to various definitions of work-life balance (WLB). We argued that a good way to appreciate the various definitions is to classify each definition in terms of inputs, outputs, or outcomes. Traditionally, researchers have conceptualized WLB inputs in three ways—time, engagement, and fit. WLB in terms of multiple role engagement means full participation in every role in an individual's system. WLB in terms of time balance means that almost equal amounts of time are spent in different roles. Finally, fit between roles and resources refers to the global assessment that work and family resources are sufficient to meet work and family demands such that participation is effective in both domains. See Table 2.1 for a summary of these concepts.

Similarly, outputs are also traditionally classified into three concepts—role effectiveness, role satisfaction, and minimal role conflict. WLB involves a high degree of success at balancing multiple roles, defined as role effectiveness. This feeds into the second concept, role satisfaction—contentment, happiness, or other positive feelings associated with successful role performance. Lastly, minimal role conflict is another important output of WLB. We differentiated between two types of work-life conflict: work-to-family conflict (i.e., how work demand interferes with family life) and family-to-work conflict (i.e., how family demand interference with work-life). We also made distinctions among time-based, strain-based, and behavior-based conflict.

With respect to definitions of WLB in terms of combined dimensions of both inputs and outputs, we discussed several major conceptualizations. Primarily, WLB involves the combined effects of work-family balance and work-family fit. As well as the combined effects of time balance, involvement balance, and satisfaction balance.

Understanding the complexity of these definitions and conceptualizations of WLB, perhaps the reader may take comfort in a simple definition that reflects the individual's own perception of the balanced life. Examples of survey items capturing this simple and straightforward conceptualization are:

- "I currently have a good balance between the time I spend at work and the time I have available for non-work activities."
- "I have difficulty balancing my work and non-work activities." (reverse coded).
- "I feel that the balance between my work demands, and non-work activities is currently about right."
- "Overall, I believe that my work and non-work life are balanced."

Table 2.1 Summary of definitions and conceptualizations of Work-Life Balance (WLB)

System type	Conceptual dimension	Description
Work-life balance as inputs	Multiple role engagement	WLB in terms of multiple role engagement means full participation in every role in an individual's system
	Engagement balance	WLB in terms of engagement balance means that almost equal amounts of time and efforts are spent in different roles
	Fit between needs and resources	Global assessment that work and family resources are sufficient to meet work and family demands such that participation is effective in both domains
Work-life balance as outputs	Role effectiveness	WLB involves a high degree of success at balancing multiple roles, defined as role effectiveness
	Role satisfaction	WLB as contentment, happiness, or other positive feelings associated with successful role performance
	Minimal role conflict	There are two types of work-life conflict: Work-to-family conflict (i.e., how work demand interferes with family life) and family-to-work conflict (i.e., how family demand interference with work-life). Distinctions were also made among time-based, strain-based, and behavior-based conflict
Work-life balance as inputs + outputs	Work-family fit and work-family balance	WLB involves the combined effects of work-family fit (input) and work-family balance (output)
	Time, involvement, satisfaction balance	WLB involves the combined effects of time and involvement balance (input), and satisfaction balance (output)

In the next chapter, we will discuss a typology of WLB policies and programs, and we outline the most common practices.

References

Allen, T. D., Greenhaus, J. H., & Edwards, J. R. (2010, August). The meaning of work-family balance: An empirical investigation. In *Symposium presented at the annual meeting of Academy of Management, Montreal, Canada*.

Allen, T. D., & Kiburz, K. M. (2012). Trait mindfulness and work-family balance among working parents: The mediating effects of vitality and sleep quality. *Journal of Vocational Behavior, 80*(2), 372–379.

Brough, P., Timms, C., O'Driscoll, M. P., Kalliath, T., Siu, O. L., Sit, C., & Lo, D. (2014). Work-life balance: A longitudinal evaluation of a new measure across Australia and New Zealand workers. *The International Journal of Human Resource Management, 25*(19), 2724–2744.

Carlson, D. S., Grzywacz, J. G., & Zivnuska, S. (2009). Is work-family balance more than conflict and enrichment? *Human Relations, 62*(10), 1459–1486.

Carlson, D. S., Kacmar, K. M., & Williams, L. J. (2000). Construction and initial validation of a multidimensional measure of work-family conflict. *Journal of Vocational Behavior, 56*(2), 249–276.

Casper, W. J., Vaziri, H., Wayne, J. H., DeHauw, S., & Greenhaus, J. (2018). The jingle-jangle of work-nonwork balance: A comprehensive and meta-analytic review of its meaning and measurement. *Journal of Applied Psychology, 103*(2), 182–214.

Clark, S. C. (2000). Work/family border theory: A new theory of work/family balance. *Human Relations, 53*(6), 747–770.

Clarke, M. C., Koch, L. C., & Hill, E. J. (2004). The work-family interface: Differentiating balance and fit. *Family and Consumer Sciences Research Journal, 33*(2), 121–140.

Ellwart, T., & Konradt, U. (2011). Formative versus reflective measurement: An illustration using work-family balance. *The Journal of Psychology, 145*(5), 391–417.

Frone, M. R. (2003). Work-family balance. In J. C. Quick & L. E. Tetrick (Eds.), *Handbook of occupational Health Psychology* (pp. 143–162). American Psychological Association.

Frone, M. R., Russell, M., & Cooper, M. L. (1992). Prevalence of work-family conflict: Are work and family boundaries asymmetrically permeable? *Journal of Organizational Behavior, 13*(7), 723–729.

Greenhaus, J. H., & Allen, T. D. (2011). Work-family balance: A review and extension of the literature. In J. C. Quick & L. E. Tetrick (Eds.), *Handbook of occupational Health Psychology* (pp. 165–183). American Psychological Association.

Greenhaus, J. H., & Beutell, N. J. (1985). Sources of conflict between work and family roles. *Academy of Management Review, 10*(1), 76–88.

Greenhaus, J. H., Collins, K. M., & Shaw, J. D. (2003). The relation between work-family balance and quality of life. *Journal of Vocational Behavior, 63*(3), 510–531.

Grzywacz, J. G., & Carlson, D. S. (2007). Conceptualizing work-family balance: Implications for practice and research. *Advances in Developing Human Resources, 9*(4), 455–471.

Haar, J. M. (2013). Testing a new measure of work-life balance: A study of parent and non-parent employees from New Zealand. *The International Journal of Human Resource Management, 24*(17), 3305–3324.

Hill, E. J., Hawkins, A. J., Ferris, M., & Weitzman, M. (2001). Finding an extra day a week: The positive influence of perceived job flexibility on work and family life balance. *Family Relations, 50*(1), 49–58.

Markes, L. P., & Langford, P. H. (2008). Work-life balance or work-life alignment? A test of the importance of work-life balance for employee engagement and intention to stay in organisations. *Journal of Management & Organization, 14*(3), 267–284.

Marks, S. R., & MacDermid, S. M. (1996). Multiple roles and the self: A theory of role balance. *Journal of Marriage and the Family, 58*(2), 417–432.

Matthews, R. A., Kath, L. M., & Barnes-Farrell, J. L. (2010). A short, valid, predictive measure of work–family conflict: Item selection and scale validation. *Journal of Occupational Health Psychology, 15*(1), 75–90.

Netemeyer, R. G., Boles, J. S., & McMurrian, R. (1996). Development and validation of work-family conflict and family-work conflict scales. *Journal of Applied Psychology, 81*(4), 400–410.

Sheldon, K. M., Cummins, R., & Kamble, S. (2010). Life balance and well-being: Testing a novel conceptual and measurement approach. *Journal of Personality, 78*(4), 1093–1134.

Valcour, M. (2007). Work-based resources as moderators of the relationship between work hours and satisfaction with work-family balance. *Journal of Applied Psychology, 92*(6), 1512–1523.

Voydanoff, P. (2005a). Toward a conceptualization of perceived work-family fit and balance: A demands and resources approach. *Journal of Marriage and Family, 67*(4), 822–836.

Voydanoff, P. (2005b). Social integration, work-family conflict and facilitation, and job and marital quality. *Journal of Marriage and Family, 67*(3), 666–679.

Wheatley, D. (2012). Work-life balance, travel-to-work, and the dual career household. *Personnel Review, 41*(6), 813–831.

Chapter 3
Work-Life Balance Policies and Programs

"We're totally guilty of doing too much at once, all while trying to manage the noise in our heads that says we're not doing enough."—Vanessa Autrey (https://teambuilding.com/blog/work-life-balance-quotes)

Abstract In this chapter we discuss work-life conflict and how it can be reduced through work-life balance (WLB) policies and programs. We describe work-life conflict in terms of three major dimensions, namely: (1) time-based conflict (e.g., time spent on activities in one role impedes the completion of responsibilities in another role), (2) strain-based conflict (e.g., pressure from one role inhibits the fulfillment of obligations in another role), and (3) behavior-based conflict (e.g., behaviors exhibited in one role are incompatible or incongruent with behavior patterns needed in the other role). As such, work-life balance policies and programs in an organization refer to organizational interventions designed to assist employees in reducing work-life conflict. We identify five major groups of WLB practices. These are: (1) work-load management programs, (2) flextime programs, (3) flexplace programs, (4) alternative job arrangements, and (5) family care programs. Work-load management programs are designed to reduce workload (e.g., workhours, time pressure, and role ambiguity).

3.1 Introduction

Failure to achieve work-life balance (WLB) results in work-life conflict. This type of conflict has been defined as a form of inter-role conflict in which the role pressures from the work and life domains are mutually incompatible in some respect (Greenhaus & Beutell, 1985).

D.-J. Lee, M. J. Sirgy, *Organizational Strategies for Work-Life Balance*, Human Well-Being Research and Policy Making,
https://doi.org/10.1007/978-3-031-56314-0_3

But what is *work-life conflict* exactly? Research has identified two distinct though related dimensions of work-life conflict that have independent antecedents and outcomes: work-to-nonwork conflict and nonwork-to-work conflict (Frone et al., 1992). On a facet-specific level, these types of work-life conflict can be further differentiated as: (1) time-based conflict (e.g., time spent on activities in one role impedes the completion of responsibilities in another role), (2) strain-based conflict (e.g., pressure from one role inhibits the fulfillment of obligations in another role), and (3) behavior-based conflict (e.g., behaviors exhibited in one role are incompatible or incongruent with behavior patterns needed in the other role) (Allen et al., 2012; Greenhaus & Beutell, 1985).

Long work hours and heavy workloads are a direct precursor to work-family conflict, as excessive time and effort at work leaves insufficient time and energy for family-related activities. As such, work-family conflict can potentially lead to job dissatisfaction as well as increased turnover intentions (Allen et al., 2000; Mesmer-Magnus & Viswesvaran, 2005).

Thus, it is important for firms to adopt WLB programs to reduce work-life conflict paving the way to WLB. As such, WLB practices and programs within an organization refer to organizational interventions designed to assist employees in reducing work-life conflict (Kossek et al., 2011a; Ryan & Kossek, 2008).

3.2 A Typology of Work-Life Balance Practices

WLB programs can be classified in five major categories: (1) work-load management practices, (2) flextime practices, (3) flexplace practices, (4) alternative job arrangements, and (5) family care practices (e.g., Beauregard & Henry, 2009; Berg et al., 2014; Kossek et al., 2011b; Sánchez-Hernández et al., 2019). See Table 3.1.

Table 3.1 Common work-life balance practices

Program/Policy	Goal	Examples organizational strategies
Work-load management practices	Reduction of job demand	Reduction of workload and time pressure, providing mutual help, working smarter, minimizing work demand during off-work time
Flextime practices	Flexibility in work time	Flextime schedule, compressed workweek schedule, absence autonomy, open-Rota system
Flexplace practices	Flexibility in workplace	Telecommuting, work from home, e-work
Alternative job arrangements	Flexibility in job arrangements	Part time work, job sharing, career breaks, contract work
Family care practices	Support for family care	Childcare/eldercare, family leave, time-off, assistance programs

3.3 Work-Load Management Practices

While job demands are not necessarily negative, problems arise when the demands and stressors associated with the job (perceived workload) outstrip the opportunity to replenish a resource (Bakker et al., 2005). *Job demands* refer to those physical, social, or organizational aspects of the job that require sustained physical or mental effort and are therefore associated with certain physiological and psychological costs. *Job resources* refer to those physical, psychological, social, or organizational aspects of the job that (a) are functional in achieving work goals, (b) reduce job demands and the associated physiological and psychological costs, or (c) stimulate personal growth and development (Bakker et al., 2005). Thus, it is important for organizations to allow employees to replenish their resources through workload management programs and to minimize the negative impact high perceived workloads have on employee wellbeing.

Work-load management practices are designed to reduce workload (e.g., work-hours, time pressure, and role ambiguity) (Kossek & Michel, 2011). These programs seek to reduce qualitative work overload (e.g., very difficult tasks) and quantitative overload (e.g., too many tasks) (Elloy & Smith, 2003).

In Chap. 5, we will discuss specific organizational strategies of work-load management in greater detail. These include reducing workload and time pressure, providing mutual help, working smarter, and minimizing work demand during off-work time. Briefly, *reduction of workload and time pressure* involves a procedure that establishes a standard range for employee performance that is attainable and sustainable with reasonable engagement and effort. *Providing mutual help* involves workload tradeoff, meaning that employees of a similar skill set are trained to increase support for each other and trade-off workload and hours. This enables employees to log more time at work when they estimate having a window of time/energy free (creating credits in the system) and others can request assistance if they feel overloaded. *Working smarter* involves training employees to adopt strategies to work smarter to offset working harder. *Minimizing work demand during off-work time* involves a policy that ensures minimal work demand during off-work time. In other words, managers can reduce work demand by helping their employees to psychologically detach from work when they are off work.

3.4 Flextime Practices

The results of a meta-analysis indicate that flexible work schedules favorably influence productivity, job satisfaction, absenteeism, and satisfaction with work schedule. The implementation of flexible work schedules provides employees with increased job autonomy, reduced absenteeism, and low role states (Baltes et al., 1999). In other words, the data show that the effect of flextime is prominent.

In Chap. 6, we will discuss specific organizational strategies of schedule flexibility. These include flextime or flexible work time, compressed work week, absence autonomy, and open-rota system. Briefly, flextime or flexible work schedule involves the ability to rearrange work hours within certain guidelines offered by the company. *Compressed work schedules* are schedules that that allow employees to work less than 10 days in a biweekly pay period. The standard compressed workweek is 4 days per week, encompassing four 10-h days with either Mondays or Fridays off. *Absence autonomy* allows employees to take time off when needed and make up the time-off on another day. The *open-rota system* means that employees individually schedule their shift preferences and collectively decide and implement a monthly work schedule by adjusting their preferred schedules.

3.5 Flexplace Practices

Chapter 7 will address three types of flexible workplace practices: telecommuting, working from home, and e-working. Briefly, *telecommuting* (also called teleworking) is a form of flexible working that can be done from any location other than the office using technologies such as laptops, tablets, and mobile phones. *Working from home* is a working arrangement where an employee regularly works all, or some of, their time at home. Lastly, *e-working* means online working with locational flexibility—remote work using information and communication technology such as video conferencing.

Commuting is often time consuming and arduous for many employees. Flexplace programs allow employees to work from home—including participating in online meetings and even having virtual office space. Thus, employees can save time otherwise spent commuting and work efficiently from home—allowing them to take care of household duties with fewer interruptions. Through a meta-analysis of 46 studies in natural settings involving 12,883 employees, Gajendran and Harrison (2007) found that telecommuting had small but predominately beneficial effects on short-term WLB outcomes, such as perceived autonomy and reduced work-family conflict. Importantly, telecommuting had no generally detrimental effects on the quality of workplace relationships. Telecommuting also had beneficial effects on long-term outcomes, such as job satisfaction, performance, turnover intent, and role stress.

3.6 Alternative Job Arrangements

When an individual is unable to maintain their full-time schedule due to family demand, instead of leaving the organization, the employee can use alternative job arrangements to achieve work-life balance. Alternative job arrangements refer to job arrangements that diverge from the standard employment model of consistent, full-year, full-time employment (Kalleberg et al., 2000).

In Chap. 8, we will discuss specific organizational strategies of alternative job arrangements. These include part-time work, job sharing, career breaks, and contract work. Specifically, *part-time work* is a job arrangement in which employees work less than 35 h per week on site with a fixed schedule. Individuals may prefer part-time work to accommodate family responsibilities or educational commitments, or to remain mentally engaged while retired. *Job sharing* means that a full-time position is shared by two people, each working part-time hours, which means that both employees also share the single salary and receive benefits. *Career breaks* is a program that permits employees to have sabbatical or leave during their career without losing their job. *Contract work* is a program that limits the terms of employment to a short-term contract (e.g., freelancers, gig work, and short-term contract work through an agency).

3.7 Family Care Practices

Research has demonstrated that the availability and utilization of family care programs decreases family-to-work conflict (e.g., Thomas & Ganster, 1995; Yuile et al., 2012). Consider the following meta-analytic study (Butts et al., 2013). This study demonstrated that the availability of family care policies plays an important role in heightening perceptions that the organization is family supportive. These perceptions, in turn, serve to decrease work-family conflict and increase positive work attitude.

In Chap. 9, we will discuss specific organizational strategies of family care programs. These include childcare programs, family-leave programs, time-off programs, assistance programs, and other similar services. Specifically, *childcare programs* involve affordable, quality dependent care that enables employees to work more quality hours, allowing them to seek advancement more easily and ultimately provide additional income for the household. A common example of this type of program is on-site childcare. Alternatively, family care programs can be manifest as subsidized childcare, referral services, and/or eldercare services.

Family-leave programs encourage employees to utilize leave time when necessary to achieve WLB and signal to workers the importance of maintaining personal health, family support, and psychological wellbeing. A common family-leave program is parental leave during the pregnancy, birth, and early childcare period. Employees can also often take sick leave or leave for dependent care. Many companies have *time-off programs*. These programs include time off for personal and professional development, paid vacations and sabbaticals, and accrued days off. Additionally, some organizations provide information, consultation, and educational services about assistance programs that are offered outside of the organization. *Other assistant programs* include services such as dry-cleaning, employee counselling, postal and mailing services, onsite fitness facilities, healthy food options, and health-related assistance.

3.8 Summary and Conclusion

In this chapter we discuss work-life conflict and how it can be reduced through WLB programs. We described work-life conflict in terms of three major dimensions, namely: (1) time-based conflict (e.g., time spent on activities in one role impedes the completion of responsibilities in another role), (2) strain-based conflict (e.g., pressure from one role inhibits the fulfillment of obligations in another role), and (3) behavior-based conflict (e.g., behaviors exhibited in one role are incompatible or incongruent with behavior patterns needed in the other role). As such, work-life balance programs in an organization refer to organizational interventions designed to assist employees in reducing work-life conflict.

We identified five major groups of WLB programs. These are: (1) work-load management programs, (2) flextime programs, (3) flexplace programs, (4) alternative job arrangements, and (5) family care programs. Work-load management programs are designed to reduce workload (e.g., workhours, time pressure, and role ambiguity). Flextime programs seek to provide employees with scheduling flexibility: flexibility in terms of when work is completed. Flexplace programs seek to provide employees with flexibility in terms of *where* work is completed. Alternative job arrangements refer to work arrangements that diverge from the standard employment model of consistent, full-year, full-time employment. Examples of alternative job arrangements include part-time work (individuals that are contracted to work for anything less than the traditional fulltime hours (40 h per week), part-year, or seasonal work arrangement) and shift work (a work schedule whereby one employee replaces or takes over the same job from another employee within a 24-h period and work with flexible hours). Family care programs often include various benefit programs such as dependent care programs (on-site childcare, referral services, subsidies, eldercare services), leave (maternity, childcare, paternity), vacation, and health care benefits including fitness programs.

See Box 3.1 for an example of work-life balance policies and programs at Google.

Box 3.1 Work-Life Balance Policies and Programs at Google

Google's website at https://www.google.com/about/careers/applications/benefits/ touts the following benefits:

- *Health and wellness*: The company helps their employees achieve work-life balance by providing (1) medical, dental, and vision insurance (for both employees and their dependents); (2) employee assistance programs focused on mental health; (3) workplace accommodations for physical or mental concerns; (4) access to mental health apps;)5) second medical opinion for employees and their families; and (5) medical advocacy program for transgender employees.
- *Financial wellbeing*: The company provides the following benefits: (1) competitive compensation; (2) regular bonus and equity refresh opportunities;

(3) generous 401(k) and regional retirement plans; (4) annual cross-company pay equity analysis and adjustments; (5) student loan reimbursement; and (6) 1-on-1 financial coaching.

- *Flexibility and time-off*: The company offers (1) paid time off, including vacation, bereavement, jury duty, sick leave, parental leave, disability, and holidays; (2) a hybrid model with remote work opportunities; (3) four "work from anywhere" weeks per year; and (4) part-time work and job-sharing opportunities.
- *Family support and care*: Programs include (1) fertility and growing family support; (2) parental leave and baby bonding leave; (3) caregiver leave; (4) elder care and support; (5) backup childcare; and (6) survivor income benefit.
- *Community and personal development*: Programs include (1) educational reimbursement; (2) Googler-to-Googler peer learning and coaching platform; (3) donation matching and time off to volunteer; (4) employee resource groups; and (5) internal Googler community groups and local culture clubs.
- *Googley extras*: Extra perks include (1) inspiring spaces to work, recharge, and collaborate with fellow Googlers; (2) on-site meals and snacks; (3) fitness centers, massage programs, and ergonomic support; (4) on-demand fitness, wellbeing, and cooking classes; and (5) art programs, Talks@Google, legal services, and Dooglers.

In the next chapter, we will discuss why management should consider WLB practices important. Specifically, we will explore research that demonstrates that WLB practices provide significant and positive effects on employees as well as the organization at large.

References

Allen, T. D., Herst, D. E., Bruck, C. S., & Sutton, M. (2000). Consequences associated with work-to-family conflict: A review and agenda for future research. *Journal of Occupational Health Psychology, 5*(2), 278–308.

Allen, T. D., Johnson, R. C., Saboe, K. N., Cho, E., Dumani, S., & Evans, S. (2012). Dispositional variables and work-family conflict: A meta-analysis. *Journal of Vocational Behavior, 80*(1), 17–26.

Bakker, A. B., Demerouti, E., & Euwema, M. C. (2005). Job resources buffer the impact of job demands on burnout. *Journal of Occupational Health Psychology, 10*(2), 170.

Baltes, B. B., Briggs, T. E., Huff, J. W., Wright, J. A., & Neuman, G. A. (1999). Flexible and compressed workweek schedules: A meta-analysis of their effects on work-related criteria. *Journal of Applied Psychology, 84*(4), 496–513.

Beauregard, T. A., & Henry, L. C. (2009). Making the link between work-life balance practices and organizational performance. *Human Resource Management Review, 19*(1), 9–22.

Berg, P., Kossek, E. E., Misra, K., & Belman, D. (2014). Work-life flexibility policies: Do unions affect employee access and use? *ILR Review, 67*(1), 111–137.
Butts, M. M., Casper, W. J., & Yang, T. S. (2013). How important are work-family support policies? A meta-analytic investigation of their effects on employee outcomes. *Journal of Applied Psychology, 98*(1), 1–25.
Elloy, D. F., & Smith, C. R. (2003). Patterns of stress, work-family conflict, role conflict, role ambiguity and overload among dual-career and single-career couple: An Australian study. *Cross Cultural Management, 10*(1), 55–66.
Frone, M. R., Russell, M., & Cooper, M. L. (1992). Antecedents and outcomes of work-family conflict: Testing a model of the work-family interface. *Journal of Applied Psychology, 77*(1), 65–78.
Gajendran, R. S., & Harrison, D. A. (2007). The good, the bad, and the unknown about telecommuting: Meta-analysis of psychological mediators and individual consequences. *Journal of Applied Psychology, 92*(6), 1524–1541.
Greenhaus, J. H., & Beutell, N. J. (1985). Sources of conflict between work and family roles. *Academy of Management Review, 10*(1), 76–88.
Kalleberg, A. L., Reskin, B. F., & Hudson, K. (2000). Bad jobs in America: Standard and nonstandard employment relations and job quality in the United States. *American Sociological Review, 65*(2), 256–278.
Kossek, E. E., & Michel, J. S. (2011). Flexible work schedules. In S. Zedeck (Ed.), *APA handbook of industrial and organizational psychology* (Building and developing the organization) (Vol. 1, pp. 535–572). American Psychological Association.
Kossek, E. E., Baltes, B. B., & Matthews, R. A. (2011a). How work-family research can finally have an impact in organizations. *Industrial and Organizational Psychology, 4*(3), 352–369.
Kossek, E. E., Pichler, S., Bodner, T., & Hammer, L. B. (2011b). Workplace social support and work-family conflict: A meta-analysis clarifying the influence of general and work–family-specific supervisor and organizational support. *Personnel Psychology, 64*(2), 289–313.
Mesmer-Magnus, J. R., & Viswesvaran, C. (2005). Whistleblowing in organizations: An examination of correlates of whistleblowing intentions, actions, and retaliation. *Journal of Business Ethics, 62*(3), 277–297.
Ryan, A. M., & Kossek, E. E. (2008). Work-life policy implementation: Breaking down or creating barriers to inclusiveness? *Human Resource Management, 47*(2), 295–310.
Sánchez-Hernández, M. I., González-López, Ó. R., Buenadicha-Mateos, M., & Tato-Jiménez, J. L. (2019). Work-life balance in great companies and pending issues for engaging new generations at work. *International Journal of Environmental Research and Public Health, 16*(24), 5122.
Thomas, L. T., & Ganster, D. C. (1995). Impact of family-supportive work variables on work-family conflict and strain: A control perspective. *Journal of Applied Psychology, 80*(1), 6–15.
Yuile, C., Chang, A., Gudmundsson, A., & Sawang, S. (2012). The role of life friendly policies on employees' work-life balance. *Journal of Management & Organization, 18*(1), 53–63.

Chapter 4
Impact of Work-Life Balance Policies and Programs

"Never get so busy making a living that you forget to make a life."—Dolly Parton (https://teambuilding.com/blog/work-life-balance-quotes)

Abstract In this chapter we discuss research focused on the effects of work-life balance (WLB) practices on employee and organizational outcomes. With respect to employee outcomes, we describe the evidence demonstrating the impact of WLB policies and programs on work-life conflict, personal health, stress, and family well-being. There is also significant empirical evidence linking WLB practices with positive organizational outcomes such as increased affective commitment, fewer turnover intentions, greater job satisfaction, and less job burnout. We also discuss several theories that explain personal and organizational effects of WLB practices. These theories include conservation of resources, job demand/job control, role conflict, signal, and social exchange.

4.1 Introduction

In this chapter we will discuss research focused on the effect of work-life balance (WLB) policies and programs on employee and organizational outcomes. With respect to employee outcomes, we will describe the evidence demonstrating the impact of WLB policies and programs on work-life conflict, personal health, stress, and family wellbeing. There is also significant empirical evidence linking WLB programs with positive organizational outcomes such as increased affective commitment, fewer turnover intentions, greater job satisfaction, and less job burnout.

This chapter also discusses several theories designed to explain these personal and organizational effects of WLB programs. These theories include conservation of resources, job demand/job control, role conflict, signal, and social exchange.

D.-J. Lee, M. J. Sirgy, *Organizational Strategies for Work-Life Balance*, Human Well-Being Research and Policy Making,
https://doi.org/10.1007/978-3-031-56314-0_4

4.2 Evidence of Impact of Work-Life Balance Practices

There is significant evidence suggesting that WLB practices do positively impact both employees and organizations.

4.2.1 Impact on Employees

Evidence indicates that WLB practices are associated with the following personal consequences. First, WLB practices reduce *work-life conflict*. Through extensive research, WLB scholars have found evidence suggesting that the availability of WLB practices has a negative effect on work-to-life conflict (Frye & Breaugh, 2004; Thompson et al., 1999). Research has also shown that flexible work-life practices have a stronger negative effect on *work interference in family life* than *family interference in work-life* (Shockley & Allen, 2007), and that flextime practices are negatively associated with family interference in work-life, compared to flexplace practices (Allen et al., 2013).

Second, evidence also suggests that WLB practices reduce *role stress*. Research shows that perceived social support from supervisors, an important element of WLB programs and policies, is associated with reduced *work strain, stress, and burnout* (Secret & Sprang, 2001).

Third, research has also demonstrated that WLB practices promote *personal health*. Such practices can contribute to improved health by providing employees more time to engage in *healthy behaviors*, such as exercising or preparing meals (Grzywacz et al., 2007; Moen et al., 2013). Scarcity of time is a key factor that employees commonly attribute to a lack of physical activity, healthy diet, sleep quality, and a host of other health-related behaviors (Grzywacz et al., 2007; Moen et al., 2013). A flexible schedule leaves individuals with more time, energy, and financial security to engage in health-promoting activities, leading to less stress (Shifrin & Michel, 2022).

Fourth, research has also signaled that WLB programs are positively associated with *warmth and responsiveness toward children*, the *quantity and quality of time spent with children* (Estes, 2004), *positive parenting,* and *mother's psychological wellbeing* (Estes, 2004).

4.2.2 Impact on the Organization

Research has established that WLB practices result in increased affective commitment, fewer turnover intentions, greater *job satisfaction*, less *job burnout*, and less *work-to-family conflict* (Saltzstein et al., 2001; Wayne et al., 2013). Let's take a closer look.

First, WLB practices provide organizations with a competitive advantage in terms of recruitment, by enhancing *perceptions of anticipated organizational support among job seekers* (Casper & Buffardi, 2004). Because workplace flexibility programs enable employees to manage work demands in response to non-work demands (both short-term and ongoing), organizations can recruit employees who value these practices as well as retain valuable organizational members who experience life changes that interfere with work-life (Kossek et al., 2014).

Second, evidence suggests that WLB practices tend to enhance *job satisfaction*. The availability of WLB programs and polices seems to increase positive *job-related attitudes* and *work effort* by facilitating positive social exchange between the organization and its employees (Beauregard & Henry, 2009; Brough et al., 2005; Saltzstein et al., 2001). That is, WLB practices tend to assist employees in balancing their work and family demands, which can in turn lead to enhanced *employee productivity* and *job satisfaction* (Beauregard & Henry, 2009).

Third, WLB practices enhance *employee morale and productivity*. Flexible arrangements in WLB practices tend to increase *employee availability for work* by reducing *commuting time* (Golden, 2001; Meyer et al., 2001), and allowing them to *work efficiently* during their highly productive hours (Shepard et al., 1996). In addition, employees with flexible arrangements can *work extra hours* during the organization's peak times in exchange for flexibility at other times (McDonald et al., 2005).

Fourth, there is evidence suggesting that firms with WLB practices reduce *employee absenteeism* and increase *investment attraction*, meaning that employees spend less time off from work (Halpern, 2005). In addition, organizations with such practices have the advantage of attracting more investors by signaling the organization's credibility (Arthur, 2003).

Fifth, work-life balance practices serve to increase *work capacity in periods of increased family demand*. Specifically, Chung and Van der Horst (2018) explored conditions in the United Kingdom, where the right to request flexible working conditions has paved the way to address larger work-life balance issues. Using a large household panel survey (2009–2014), they found that flexible working arrangements help women *stay employed after the birth of their first child*. Data shows that mothers using flextime in conjunction with telework are less likely to reduce their *working hours after childbirth*. Thus, showing that flexible working is not only used as a tool for work-life balance but also to enhance and maintain employees' work capacity during periods of increased family demands (Chung & Van der Horst, 2018).

In sum, the evidence suggests that well managed organizations tend to be not only more productive and more energy efficient, but also typically provide more programs designed to enhance employee wellbeing and WLB (e.g., Bloom et al., 2009). In other words, better managed organizations also have better WLB practices.

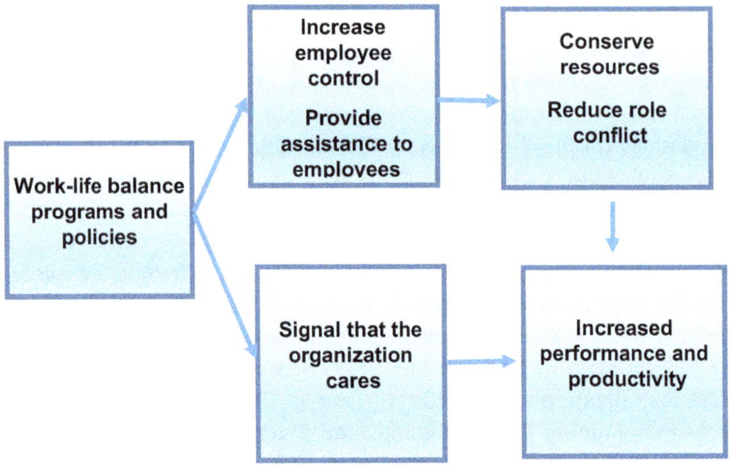

Fig. 4.1 How do work-life balance practices influence employee and organizational outcomes

4.3 The Psychology Behind Work-Life Balance Practices

How do WLB practices impact employees and the organization? WLB practices enable employees to schedule their time to better balance competing demands between work and home, and by helping employees procure third-party assistance with caregiving, thus reducing work-life conflict and augmenting employee performance and organizational effectiveness.

In brief, WLB practices help employees conserve their resources and reduce role conflicts by giving them more options to deal with high job demand and by providing resources to help with home demands. The presence of WLB practices signals that organizations care about their employees, which in turn serves to motivate employees to reciprocate by increasing their performance and productivity (see Fig. 4.1).

The positive consequences of WLB practices are traditionally explained by WLB scholars using the following psychological theories.

4.3.1 Resource Drain Theory

Resource drain theory posits that individuals have a limited number of resources to devote to various roles; thus, if one role requires too many resources, performance in other roles suffers. This theory suggests that high role demand in one domain inhibits meeting role expectations in another domain because individuals must make tradeoffs in allocating time and energy among roles (Edwards & Rothbard, 2000; Greenhaus & Beutell, 1985; Rothbard, 2001). Specifically, resource drain theory suggests that family and work roles are often in conflict because individuals have a limited pool of resources (such as energy and time) that they can allocate between family and work demands.

As such, work-life balance (WLB) practices provide employees with resources that help prevent the drain of resources necessary to meet role expectations in work and family life domains. WLB practices such as family-leave programs, alternative job arrangements, and family care programs are designed to provide employees the certain types of resources that can help them perform successfully in their work and family roles even when demand in one role is high.

Consider the following example. Carol is an assistant professor of psychology at a research university. She has recently completed her doctoral dissertation and received her doctorate from a prestigious university. She has also been married for over 10 years to a man named Joseph—or Joe for short. Joe is also an academic—an associate professor of computer science at another university located in the same city. Both Carol and Joe are in their late thirties and have one child together named Anne, who is 6 years old. Carol and Joe would like to have another child in the near future, and as such they have been trying to conceive. However, Carol feels that the family is in a precarious situation. Being a newly minted faculty at a research university means that she is under enormous pressure, not only to teach (several courses per semester) and serve on several departmental committees, but also to produce published research. The university is a "publish or perish" type of an institution. Carol is aware of several colleagues who recently were denied tenure and promotion because they failed to publish enough, let alone publish in the elite academic journals of their disciplines.

Now let's frame Carol's situation in terms of *resource drain* theory. Carol only has a limited amount of time, effort, and financial resources to do the best she can in her work role as professor and in her family role as a mother and wife. She feels that her resources are stretched to the limit. In other words, she does not have sufficient time, energy, and money to be a good wife and mother as well as perform well enough in her academic job to make tenure and promotion in a few years. *Her resources are drained.* In many instances at home, she finds herself making tough decisions: whether to spend time at night taking care of her daughter, doing house chores, and spending quality time with her husband. And of course, she falls short. In many instances, because of work deadlines, she had to put off house chores and other family demands. And of course, doing so has resulted in work-life conflict. Anne has fallen behind on her schoolwork and has been having behavioral problems at school—her mentor even requested a meeting to discuss it. Her husband has been short-tempered and has been complaining about feeling lonely. In sum, work demand has created a toll on family wellbeing.

On top of this, Carol recently found out that she is pregnant. She met with her department head, Noreen, to give her the news, who is generally very supportive of her faculty. She congratulated Carol and agreed to "stop the tenure clock." This allows Carol to take a year off work—6 months on paid leave (maternity leave) and the other 6 months unpaid. This WLB program was a panacea for Carol and her family. The leave served to *replenish drained resources* and re-allocate desperately needed resources to the family domain. By doing so, Carol was able to take care of her family needs without competition from work. After a while, the maternity leave also served to re-invigorate her research and teaching efforts at the university. A year later when asked by her department head about how she's doing, she expressed her gratitude to Noreen for providing the much-needed family leave. She is now back on track to complete a major research project that is very likely to result in several journal publications in top-tier journals. She gave birth to a boy named Nathan. Anne is very happy to have a baby brother and is more involved in the household chores and has fewer behavioral issues at school. Joe is equally happy. He and Carol can spend quality time together, and he assumed more responsibility with the baby and other family chores. Carol attributes her increased feelings of work and family wellbeing to this WLB program which helped replenish her drained resources.

4.3.2 Conservation of Resources Theory

Conservation of resources theory holds that psychological stress and strain are caused by the loss, or threatened loss, of finite resources. Employees are intrinsically motivated to protect their resources (Hobfoll, 1989). As such, WLB practices help mitigate work-family conflict by enabling employees to allocate time, attention, and energy in more individually efficient ways (Allen et al., 2013).

Specifically, flexibility in WLB programs serves to increase the number of options in decision-making. In other words, flexibility creates additional resource allocation choices that otherwise would not exist (Allen et al., 2013). That is, flexibility provides additional resources to enhance person-environment fit which helps buffer strain (Gajendran et al., 2015).

Overload in work or family life results in work-life conflict as employees fail to meet role demand with available resources— they experience resource drain. WLB practices help employees conserve their resources efficiently to help meet their work and nonwork demands. This is because work-life balance practices allow employees to choose when and where they meet role demand. Flexibility allows them to conserve and use their resources efficiently. By conserving their resources in one domain, employees can use those resources in other domains and avoid resource drain. For example, telecommuting helps conserve resources by allowing employees to complete their daily work assignments while taking care of family responsibilities using the same resources (Allen et al., 2013; Gajendran et al., 2015).

Let's revisit Carol's situation and describe a WLB program she took advantage of to *conserve resources*. As previously mentioned, Carol participated in a WLB program, family leave, which allowed her to take a year off work and recover from resource drain. Returning from family leave, she was worried that her work-life balance would suffer again due to the new demands of an infant. She met with her department head, Noreen, to discuss her situation and explore ways to conserve resources. Currently she teaches two in-person courses per semester, which means that she must go to campus almost every day of the week. Noreen suggested that one way to help her conserve resources would be to make one of her classes an online course. In other words, she can teach one class directly from home and she does not have to go to campus to teach for 2 days of the week. Thus, she can conserve time and energy otherwise spent on commuting and meeting with faculty and students in-person on those days. As such, teaching one class online can be characterized as an example of "flexible workplace"—a WLB program.

4.3.3 *Job Demands-Resources Theory*

The job demands and resources theory proposes that strain occurs when there is an imbalance between the demands placed on an individual and the resources available to meet those demands. The theory categorizes working conditions into two broad categories, job demands and job resources, that are differentially related to specific outcomes. Job demands are primarily related to the exhaustion component of burnout, whereas lack of job resources is primarily related to disengagement (Demerouti et al., 2001). Resources that aid in goal attainment and/or demand reduction can be physical, psychological, and social.

The theory states that while job demands are not necessarily negative, problems arise when the demands and stressors associated with the job (perceived workload) outstrip the opportunity to replenish employee resources. Job strain develops when job demands are high and when job resources are low. That is, job engagement is highest when job resources are high even in the face of high job demand. As such, WLB practices serve as significant resources in mitigating the resource demands of work (Bakker & Demerouti, 2007).

Let's apply the Job Demands-Resources theory to Carol's situation. As described earlier, Carol is struggling in both her work and family roles. Let's say that she did not want to teach one of her classes online, as she likes being in person and is not very tech savvy. Yet she still needs to find a way to balance her work and family demands. She also takes her daughter, Anne, to elementary school every morning, which is a significant commute from home. By the time she arrives on campus to teach, she feels frazzled and not fully prepared. She needs extra time in the morning to settle in her office, review her lecture notes, set up the projection equipment for her PowerPoint slides, and greet her students before they settle down in class.

Noreen suggested another solution: increase Carol's annual working budget by a small margin to allow Carol to hire a work-study student to help with no-work chores.[1] The student would come to Carol's house first thing every morning to take her daughter to her school. Doing so would allow Carol to get to work with enough time to get settled, review her lecture notes, walk to class, prepare the audio-visual equipment, and greet and meet with students before class. The same student could also help with other tasks such as setting up the audio-visual equipment after dropping off Anne at school.

---

[1] Most universities allocate a budget to each faculty member to cover professional expenses.

As such, Carol's situation can be described as *high job demand with low resources* to meet that demand. Noreen's solution can be characterized as WLB solution (a family care program) that serves to help a faculty member meet the high teaching standards of the university by providing that faculty with more resources required to ensure high quality work.

4.3.4 Job Demands-Control Theory

Job Demands-Control theory posits that the more control an individual has over their job demands, the greater their wellbeing. The combination of high job demand and low job control tends to result in employee strain, causing fatigue, physical illness, and job dissatisfaction. That is, the ability to control one's environment (both physical and social) is recognized as an important mechanism in determining one's wellbeing (Ganster & Rosen, 2013). Flexibility, an important feature of WLB practices, serves to heighten control and autonomy over work and life demands (Duxbury & Halinski, 2014; Swanberg et al., 2011). In other words, flexibility is a valued resource that provides employees with the control and autonomy needed to adapt to simultaneous work and family demands (Allen et al., 2013). Employees' sense of control is heightened through WLB practices (e.g., leave, alternative job arrangements) that allow them to have more time to complete their work-related tasks. Their sense of control is further increased through practices that give them more autonomy and flexibility in choosing the time and place to work such as flextime and flexplace programs. In sum, work-life programs enhance employee perception of control in work and nonwork domains, thereby facilitating employee action to meet role demand in work and nonwork domains (Allen et al., 2013).

Let's apply the job-demands/job-control theory to Carol's situation. Carol's job demands are high in relation to teaching, research, and service, in addition to high demand in her family role. As previously seen, Noreen, her department head, is very supportive of her faculty not only in relation to academics but also in relation to family matters. However, Noreen's predecessor firmly believed that faculty should work on campus every day from 9 a.m. to 5 p.m. The former department head was meticulous in accounting for the whereabouts of every member of his faculty during work hours. He expected to reach them at a moment's notice by visiting them in their office and labs. His administrative staff kept a log of all the service committees assigned to his faculty and expected his faculty to participate to assigned committees. He would check attendance logs of committee meetings—who among his faculty were present or absent. Information about committee attendance, physical presence in their offices, labs, and classrooms was integrated into the faculty annual performance reports.

Noreen's management style is very different. She made it very clear to the faculty that their work schedule and place of work is totally under *their control*. Apart from the physical demands of teaching in assigned classrooms at assigned times, the administration refrained from dictating where and when faculty should work.

Allowing faculty to come and go as they please heightened their sense of job control, which in turn enhanced their sense of wellbeing. Letting faculty determine when they work also served to increase their sense of job control. Faculty who have a greater sense of job control are more likely to meet the high demand of their jobs and do better than those with little sense of job control.

In sum, most of the WLB programs are designed to heighten employees' sense of job control, enabling them to meet high job demand. Practices related to schedule flexibility, flexible workplace, alternative job arrangements, and family care practices are all designed to increase employee's sense of job control.

4.3.5 Role Conflict Theory

Role conflict theory posits that the standard work schedule (i.e., 9 a.m. to 5 p.m., Monday through Friday) creates stress for employees who struggle to find an optimal balance between time for work and time for household responsibilities. Workplace flexibility, an example of a WLB program, enables workers to reduce or eliminate several sources of work-family conflict (Allen et al., 2014; Fiksenbaum, 2014; Galovan et al., 2015). Time-based conflict can be reduced through use of workplace and worktime flexibility as workers can restructure the timing, location, or amount of work tasks to facilitate home-related tasks. Utilizing workplace flexibility can help reduce strain-based conflict as it allows employees to leverage workplace resources which in turn helps alleviate stress (Greenhaus & Beutell, 1985).

Specifically, employees experience time-based conflict when time devoted to one role (e.g., work role) makes it difficult to meet the requirements of another role (e.g., family role). WLB programs, such as flexplace and flextime, serve to reduce *time-based conflict* by helping meet family demands, such as childcare and eldercare. Other WLB practices such as leave, shift work, and alternative job arrangements also serve to reduce workload, thereby giving workers more time to allocate to family needs.

Employees experience strain-based conflict when strain produced by one role makes it difficult to meet the demand of another role. WLB practices such as childcare and eldercare programs help employees reduce *strain-based conflict* by providing additional resources to help with family demands. While WLB practices such as alternative job arrangements serve to reduce workload, other practices such as leave programs provide opportunities for recovery. Programs such as telework help reduce strain caused by the daily commute and avoid time-based conflict (Allen et al., 2014; Greenhaus & Beutell, 1985).

Let's apply role conflict theory to Carol's situation. Recall that Carol is experiencing high demand in both her work and family roles. This conflict puts a strain on her relationships, and Carol correctly feels that her husband is somewhat unhappy because she spends her evenings either working or engaging in childcare. As such, Carol experiences a high degree of *role conflict*—conflict between her professional role and her marital role. Previously, we discussed one of Carol's solutions which was to take maternity leave for 1 year, allowing her to recover from resource drain and alleviate role conflict between her work and family role.

4.3.6 Signal Theory

Signal theory posits that work-life balance practices (e.g., flexibility and work-family support programs) influence work attitudes by signaling perceived organizational support (Casper & Harris, 2008). That is, the availability of work-family support programs tends to be interpreted as symbolic of corporate concern (Grover & Crooker, 1995).

In other words, the availability of WLB programs in an organization is often perceived as a sign that the organization cares about its employees. In turn, the perception that the organization cares about its employees serves to increase job satisfaction and organizational commitment from employees.

Again, let's apply signal theory to Carol. Carol is an academic who has a high demand job and significant family responsibilities. Her department head at the university, Noreen, is very supportive and tries to accommodate faculty by helping them meet their family responsibilities. Noreen took it upon herself to publicize the university WLB practices (workload management, schedule flexibility, flexible workplace, alternative job arrangements, and family care policies). This awareness campaign is a standard part of new faculty orientation, which is how Carol first learned about the university's WLB practices. The monthly HR newsletter also regularly contains information about the university's WLB practices and is disseminated across campus. But most importantly Noreen shows advocacy of the university's WLB practices. Noreen makes it a point to bring up these practices at the departmental monthly meetings and encourages faculty to know more about such practices.

In turn, Carol feels very good about the department and the university at large. She believes that university cares about its faculty, their personal lives, and their families. She attributes her positive feelings to the university's benefit programs, particularly the WLB programs. Often, she expresses her positive feelings about the university when discussing administrative issues with other colleagues—other university administrators, and even friends and relatives outside the university. She uses the university's WLB practices as a case in point to justify her favorable opinion of the university.

4.3.7 Social Exchange Theory

Social exchange theory posits that the benefits of the family-friendly programs are perceived by employees as evidence that the organization cares about their wellbeing, and that in response employees will reciprocate through increased loyalty.

Family-friendly programs are perceived as goodwill gestures that can create a positive social exchange between workers and the organization. Returning such favorable treatment (e.g., high performance, commitment to the goals and values, low turnover) is engrained in the norm of reciprocity (Bagger & Li, 2014; Eisenberger et al., 2001). WLB programs allow employees to have high autonomy and flexibility at work, which motivates employees to perform well in return. Reciprocity through high job performance and organizational commitment is seen as a type of social exchange (Allen, 2001; Lambert, 2000; Odle-Dusseau et al., 2012; Tang et al., 2014).

In other words, the presence of WLB programs in an organization is often perceived as a signal that organizations care about their employees. In return for that "favor," employees are motivated to work harder and form a stronger commitment to the organization.

Let's once again apply social exchange theory to Carol's case. Carol is highly motivated to do her best to contribute to the department and the university. This is due to her perception that the university is very generous with its employee benefits, particularly the university's WLB practices. As we have seen, she has taken advantage of the university's WLB programs and policies such as the university's family care programs, its schedule flexibility program, its flexible workplace program, and its career breaks program. As such, she feels that working hard to do her best in teaching, research, and service pays the university back for its generous employee benefits. Her good work for and advocacy of the university (and her department) is simply a *social exchange*. That is, she is merely *reciprocating* by being loyal to the department and the university at large.

4.4 Summary and Conclusion

In this chapter, we analyzed research that documented the effects of WLB programs on employee outcomes as well as organizational outcomes. With respect to employee outcomes, we described the evidence demonstrating the impact of WLB programs on work-life conflict, personal health, stress, and family wellbeing. We also looked at the evidence linking WLB programs with positive organizational outcomes such as increased affective commitment, fewer turnover intentions, greater job satisfaction, and less job burnout.

The theory of conservation of resources asserts that stress and strain result from the loss—or threatened loss—of finite resources, and that individuals are inherently motivated to protect the resources they have as well as build upon existing resources. WLB programs help mitigate work-family conflict in that flexibility enables employees to allocate time, attention, and energy in more individually efficient ways. The theory of Job Demands-Control argues that the more control employees have over their job demand, the better their wellbeing. The combination of high job demand and low job control tends to result in the highest level of strain, causing fatigue, physical illness, and job dissatisfaction. Flexibility provided in WLB programs enhances control/autonomy over work and life demands, reducing

Table 4.1 Theories explaining the impact of Work-Life Balance (WLB) practices

Theories	Explaining the impact of Work-Life Balance practices
Conservation of resources	Stress and strain result from the loss—or threatened loss—of finite resources. WLB programs help mitigate work-family conflict in that flexibility enables employees to allocate time, attention, and energy in more individually efficient ways
Job demands-control	The more control employees have over their job demand, the better their wellbeing. Flexibility provided in WLB programs enhances control/autonomy over work and life demands, reducing work-family conflict
Role conflict	The standard work schedule may create stress for employees who struggle to find an optimal balance between time for work and time for household responsibilities. WLB policies and programs serve to help employees meet demands from work and family roles, and as such mitigate role conflict
Signal	The existence of WLB policies and programs influences work attitudes by signaling perceived organizational support.
Social exchange	Benefits in the family friendly programs are perceived by employees as evidence that the organization cares about their wellbeing motivating them to reciprocate

work-family conflict. Role conflict theory asserts that the standard work schedule may create stress for employees who struggle to find an optimal balance between time for work and time for household responsibilities. WLB policies and programs serve to help employees meet demands from work and family roles, and as such mitigate role conflict. Signal theory posits that the existence of WLB policies and programs influences work attitudes by signaling perceived organizational support. Finally, social exchange theory argues that benefits in the family friendly programs are perceived by employees as evidence that the organization cares about their well-being motivating them to reciprocate. Family-friendly programs are perceived as goodwill gestures that can create a positive social exchange between workers and the organization. Returning such favorable treatment in terms of good job performance and commitment to the goals and values of the organization is essentially guided by the norm of reciprocity—employees are reciprocating to the organization's goodwill efforts. See Table 4.1 for a summary of the theories explaining how WLB policies and programs impact both organizational and employee behavioral outcomes.

References

Allen, T. D. (2001). Family-supportive work environments: The role of organizational perceptions. *Journal of Vocational Behavior, 58*(3), 414–435.

Allen, T. D., Cho, E., & Meier, L. L. (2014). Work-family boundary dynamics. *Annual Review of Organizational Psychology and Organizational Behavior, 1*(1), 99–121.

Allen, T. D., Johnson, R. C., Kiburz, K. M., & Shockley, K. M. (2013). Work-family conflict and flexible work arrangements: Deconstructing flexibility. *Personnel Psychology, 66*(2), 345–376.

Arthur, M. M. (2003). Share price reactions to work-family initiatives: An institutional perspective. *Academy of Management Journal, 46*(4), 497–505.

Bagger, J., & Li, A. (2014). How does supervisory family support influence employees' attitudes and behaviors? A social exchange perspective. *Journal of Management, 40*(4), 1123–1150.

Bakker, A. B., & Demerouti, E. (2007). The job demands-resources model: State of the art. *Journal of Managerial Psychology, 22*(3), 309–328.

Beauregard, T. A., & Henry, L. C. (2009). Making the link between work-life balance practices and organizational performance. *Human Resource Management Review, 19*(1), 9–22.

Bloom, N., Kretschmer, T., & Van Reenen, J. (2009). Work-life balance, management practices and productivity. *International differences in the business practices and productivity of firms*, 15–54.

Brough, P., O'Driscoll, M. P., & Kalliath, T. J. (2005). The ability of 'family friendly' organizational resources to predict work-family conflict and job and family satisfaction. *Stress and Health, 21*(4), 223–234.

Casper, W. J., & Buffardi, L. C. (2004). Work-life benefits and job pursuit intentions: The role of anticipated organizational support. *Journal of Vocational Behavior, 65*(3), 391–410.

Casper, W. J., & Harris, C. M. (2008). Work-life benefits and organizational attachment: Self-interest utility and signaling theory models. *Journal of Vocational Behavior, 72*(1), 95–109.

Chung, H., & Van der Horst, M. (2018). Women's employment patterns after childbirth and the perceived access to and use of flexitime and teleworking. *Human Relations, 71*(1), 47–72.

Demerouti, E., Bakker, A. B., Nachreiner, F., & Schaufeli, W. B. (2001). The job demands-resources model of burnout. *Journal of Applied Psychology, 86*(3), 499–512.

Duxbury, L., & Halinski, M. (2014). When more is less: An examination of the relationship between hours in telework and role overload. *Work, 48*(1), 91–103.

Edwards, J. R., & Rothbard, N. P. (2000). Mechanisms linking work and family: Clarifying the relationship between work and family constructs. *Academy of Management Review, 25*(1), 178–199.

Eisenberger, R., Armeli, S., Rexwinkel, B., Lynch, P. D., & Rhoades, L. (2001). Reciprocation of perceived organizational support. *Journal of Applied Psychology, 86*(1), 42–51.

Estes, S. B. (2004). How are family-responsive workplace arrangements family friendly? Employer accommodations, parenting, and children's socioemotional Well-being. *The Sociological Quarterly, 45*(4), 637–661.

Fiksenbaum, L. M. (2014). Supportive work-family environments: Implications for work–family conflict and Well-being. *The International Journal of Human Resource Management, 25*(5), 653–672.

Frye, N. K., & Breaugh, J. A. (2004). Family-friendly policies, supervisor support, work-family conflict, family-work conflict, and satisfaction: A test of a conceptual model. *Journal of Business and Psychology, 19*(2), 197–220.

Gajendran, R. S., Harrison, D. A., & Delaney-Klinger, K. (2015). Are telecommuters remotely good citizens? Unpacking telecommuting's effects on performance via i-deals and job resources. *Personnel Psychology, 68*(2), 353–393.

Galovan, A. M., Feistman, R. E., Stowe, J. D., & Hill, E. J. (2015). Achieving desired family size in dual-working households: Work and family influences among Singaporean couples. *Journal of Family Issues, 36*(10), 1377–1401.

Ganster, D. C., & Rosen, C. C. (2013). Work stress and employee health: A multidisciplinary review. *Journal of Management, 39*(5), 1085–1122.

Golden, L. (2001). Flexible work schedules: What are we trading off to get them? *Monthly Labor Review, 124*(3), 50–67.

Greenhaus, J. H., & Beutell, N. J. (1985). Sources of conflict between work and family roles. *Academy of Management Review, 10*(1), 76–88.

Grover, S. L., & Crooker, K. J. (1995). Who appreciates family-responsive human resource policies: The impact of family-friendly policies on the organizational attachment of parents and non-parents. *Personnel Psychology, 48*(2), 271–288.

Grzywacz, J. G., Arcury, T. A., Marín, A., Carrillo, L., Burke, B., Coates, M. L., & Quandt, S. A. (2007). Work-family conflict: Experiences and health implications among immigrant Latinos. *Journal of Applied Psychology, 92*(4), 1119–1130.

Halpern, D. F. (2005). How time-flexible work policies can reduce stress, improve health, and save money. *Stress and Health, 21*(3), 157–168.

Hobfoll, S. E. (1989). Conservation of resources: A new attempt at conceptualizing stress. *American Psychologist, 44*(3), 513–524.

Kossek, E. E., Valcour, M., & Lirio, P. (2014). Organizational strategies for promoting work-life balance and wellbeing. In P. Y. Chen & C. L. Cooper (Eds.), *Work and wellbeing* (*Wellbeing: A complete reference guide*) (Vol. 3, pp. 295–319). John Wiley & Sons.

Lambert, S. J. (2000). Added benefits: The link between work-life benefits and organizational citizenship behavior. *Academy of Management Journal, 43*(5), 801–815.

McDonald, P., Guthrie, D., Bradley, L., & Shakespeare-Finch, J. (2005). Investigating work-family policy aims and employee experiences. *Employee Relations., 27*(5), 478–494.

Meyer, C. S., Mukerjee, S., & Sestero, A. (2001). Work-family benefits: Which ones maximize profits? *Journal of Managerial Issues, 13*(1), 28–44.

Moen, P., Lam, J., Ammons, S., & Kelly, E. L. (2013). Time work by overworked professionals: Strategies in response to the stress of higher status. *Work and Occupations, 40*(2), 79–114.

Odle-Dusseau, H. N., Britt, T. W., & Greene-Shortridge, T. M. (2012). Organizational work-family resources as predictors of job performance and attitudes: The process of work-family conflict and enrichment. *Journal of Occupational Health Psychology, 17*(1), 28–40.

Rothbard, N. P. (2001). Enriching or depleting? The dynamics of engagement in work and family roles. *Administrative Science Quarterly, 46*(4), 655–684.

Saltzstein, A. L., Ting, Y., & Saltzstein, G. H. (2001). Work-family balance and job satisfaction: The impact of family-friendly policies on attitudes of federal government employees. *Public Administration Review, 61*(4), 452–467.

Secret, M., & Sprang, G. (2001). The effects of family-friendly workplace environments on work-family stress of employed parents. *Journal of Social Service Research, 28*(2), 21–45.

Shepard, E. M., Clifton, T. J., & Kruse, D. (1996). Flexible work hours and productivity: Some evidence from the pharmaceutical industry. *Industrial Relations, 35*(1), 123–139.

Shifrin, N. V., & Michel, J. S. (2022). Flexible work arrangements and employee health: A meta-analytic review. *Work & Stress, 36*(1), 60–85.

Shockley, K. M., & Allen, T. D. (2007). When flexibility helps: Another look at the availability of flexible work arrangements and work-family conflict. *Journal of Vocational Behavior, 71*(3), 479–493.

Swanberg, J. E., McKechnie, S. P., Ojha, M. U., & James, J. B. (2011). Schedule control, supervisor support and work engagement: A winning combination for workers in hourly jobs. *Journal of Vocational Behavior, 79*(3), 613–624.

Tang, S. W., Siu, O. L., & Cheung, F. (2014). A study of work-family enrichment among Chinese employees: The mediating role between work support and job satisfaction. *Applied Psychology, 63*(1), 130–150.

Thompson, C. A., Beauvais, L. L., & Lyness, K. S. (1999). When work-family benefits are not enough: The influence of work-family culture on benefit utilization, organizational attachment, and work-family conflict. *Journal of Vocational Behavior, 54*(3), 392–415.

Wayne, J. H., Casper, W. J., Matthews, R. A., & Allen, T. D. (2013). Family-supportive organization perceptions and organizational commitment: The mediating role of work-family conflict and enrichment and partner attitudes. *Journal of Applied Psychology, 98*(4), 606–622.

Part II
Specific Work-Life Balance Policies and Programs

In Part II of this book, we will examine in depth five established work-life balance (WLB) practices. Specifically, we will describe each practice in detail, including the research related to the link between the program/policy and employee WLB as well as the various conditions that make the program/policy more effective. See Fig. 1.

Fig. 1 Organizational strategies for work-life balance

Chapter 5
Workload Management

"I wish I had treasured the doing a little more and the getting it done a little less."—Anna Quindlen (https://teambuilding.com/blog/work-life-balance-quotes)

Abstract In this chapter we describe much of the research literature focusing on workload management programs that organizations institutionalize to achieve higher levels of employee work-life balance. We also discuss how workload management programs are customarily implemented. We then discuss program implementation through four objectives, namely reducing workload and time pressure, providing mutual help, working smarter, and minimizing work demand during off-work time. We then describe conditions under which workload management programs are more effective: personal, organizational, and environmental moderators.

5.1 Introduction

Research has shown that work-life balance (WLB) can be achieved through the management of workload. Work-life imbalance is caused, at least partly, by work overload. As such, the purpose of workload management programs is to mitigate work overload to achieve work-life balance.

This chapter covers much of the research literature focusing on workload management programs that organizations can institutionalize to achieve higher levels of employee work-life balance. Specifically, we make the point that the driving force or impetus behind workload management programs is *work overload*. Work overload produces significant adverse effects for employees as well as the organization. As such, workload management programs are essentially designed to reduce work overload. We explain the negative consequences associated with work overload through four well-established theories, namely resource drain, conservation of resources, job demands and resources, and job demands/job control.

D.-J. Lee, M. J. Sirgy, *Organizational Strategies for Work-Life Balance*, Human Well-Being Research and Policy Making,
https://doi.org/10.1007/978-3-031-56314-0_5

We also discuss how workload management programs are customarily implemented. We discuss program implementation through four objectives, namely reducing workload and time pressure, providing mutual help, working smarter, and minimizing work demand during off-work time.

We then explain the conditions under which workload management programs are more effective. As such, we describe the research dealing with personal moderators (e.g., low job control, high value on family time, high income, job dissatisfaction, heavy family responsibilities, female employees, young adults, and low familial support), organizational moderators (e.g., high organizational support, lack of employee autonomy and control, and high role ambiguity), and environmental moderators (e.g., individualistic cultures, developed countries, and countries with high levels of connectivity).

5.2 Work Overload

Increased workplace demand for higher focus and engagement usually stems from several factors, namely time pressure (i.e., tightening of deadlines), increased pace of work (i.e., speeding up the rate at which work is performed), and/or work overload (trying to accomplish more work in same amount of time) (Kossek et al., 2014).

What is *work overload* exactly? Work overload is the perception of having too many work-role tasks and not enough time or other resources necessary to accomplish them (Michel et al., 2011).

Much research has documented the negative consequences of work overload. Specifically, work overload takes a huge toll on both psychological and physical wellbeing. Evidence links high levels of work overload with strain, depression, distress, fatigue, emotional exhaustion, depersonalization, and physical malaise (Bowling et al., 2015).

In a meta-analysis on correlates of workload, Bowling et al. (2015) found that workload is positively associated with role ambiguity, role conflict, and work-family conflict and that workload is negatively associated with social support. Their study findings indicate that work overload is negatively associated with several indices of psychological and physical wellbeing, as well as affective organizational commitment. Work overload is also positively associated with turnover intention and absenteeism. In addition, high levels of role overload are likely to lead to elevated levels of physical or psychological fatigue, which may then undermine an individual's ability to fulfill or adequately complete their role-related responsibilities (Frone et al., 1997).

Furthermore, work overload increases work-life conflict (Lembrechts et al., 2015). Evidence suggests that a high level of workload strips resources, which in turn contributes to work-life conflict and decreases satisfaction with WLB (Holland et al., 2019). Perceived work overload was shown to have a stronger influence on work-life conflict than the number of work hours (Byron, 2005). Work overload increases work-family conflict because it causes physical fatigue, pain, and insecurity in the work environment (Voydanoff, 2004). In a large-scale survey of nursing professionals ($n = 2984$), Holland et al. (2019) found that high workload increases work-life conflict driving nurses to consider leaving the field. High workload negatively affected the nurse's wellbeing and satisfaction with work-life.

Moreover, work overload has a negative impact on job attitude (e.g., satisfaction and organizational commitment). High job demand and work overload causes employees to experience negative feelings about their job (Holland et al., 2019), which in turn increases turnover intentions and absenteeism (Bowling et al., 2015).

As such, workload management programs are designed to mitigate work overload (Kossek et al., 2014; Michel et al., 2011). An organization's effective management of workload serves to reduce work-life imbalance (Thompson et al., 1999) by fostering increased engagement in both work and non-work life domains (Bulger & Fisher, 2012; Greenhaus & Beutell, 1985; Kopelman et al., 1983; Whiston & Cinamon, 2015).

In sum, research has established that work overload is directly correlated with work-life conflict and stems from various forms of job demand. First, work overload stems from time-based demand and strain-based demand. *Time-based demand* is related to work-family conflict through the process of resource drain in which the time or involvement required for participation in one domain limits the time or involvement available for participation in another domain. For example, Carol, the assistant professor at the aforementioned research university experiences work-family conflict because she spends most of her time in the evenings working on her research projects, meaning that she has little time left to spend with her children or her husband, all of whom feel neglected. Thus, the time-based demand in family life cause quite a bit of strife (i.e., work-family conflict).

Strain-based demand is linked to work-family conflict through a process of psychological spillover in which the strain associated with participating in one domain is carried over to another domain such that it creates strain in the second domain, thereby hindering role performance in that domain (Michel et al., 2011). Applying this to Carol, the time-demand in family life is causing strain in her role as mother and wife. This strain in family life spills over to work-life, thus amplifying feelings of conflict between work-life and family life. See Fig. 5.1.

Second, work overload comes from the physical job demand as well as the psychological job demand. *Physical job demand* may originate from the excessive

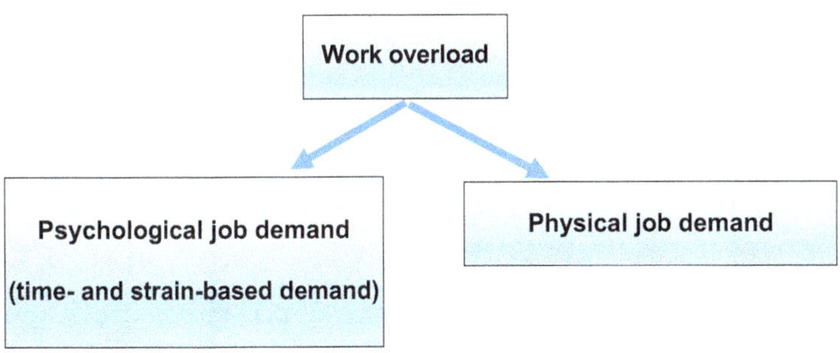

Fig. 5.1 What is work overload?

workload and atypical schedules that include shift work, weekends, and nights (Garrett & McDaniel, 2001; Greenglass et al., 2001). Going back to Carol, physical job demand may translate into staying up at night way past her normal bedtime to attend to urgent issues related to her research projects. Staying up late is causing sleep deprivation that leads to negative physical health consequences (e.g., physical fatigue the next day, overeating, drinking beverages with caffeine which causes a certain degree of hypertension, feeling anxious and short-tempered, etc.).

Psychological job demand refers to those factors related to time pressure, mental load, and coordination responsibilities. Psychological job demand is usually assessed in conjunction with the physical demands of the job. Specifically, this type of assessment allows management to determine whether any aspect of the job might be a hazard to the worker's health and wellbeing (Nordenmark et al., 2012). In the case of Carol, staying up late at night to work on her research projects is not only causing problems with her physical health but also mental health, manifesting as anxiety and depression.

5.3 How Does Work Overload Produce These Negative Consequences?

The negative personal wellbeing consequences of work overload can be explained using the following theoretical models that have an established footing in WLB literature: (1) resource drain theory, (2) conservation of resources, (3) the job demand and resource model, and (4) the job demand and control model. The psychological dynamics can be captured through Fig. 5.2.

5.3.1 Resource Drain Theory

Work overload negatively impacts the physical and psychological wellbeing of employees as it drains their available resources. Resource drain theory treats resources such as time, attention, and energy (physical and psychological) as finite (Edwards & Rothbard, 2000) and role stressors that occur in each domain subtract from the finite resources available to the individual. That is, when role pressures are

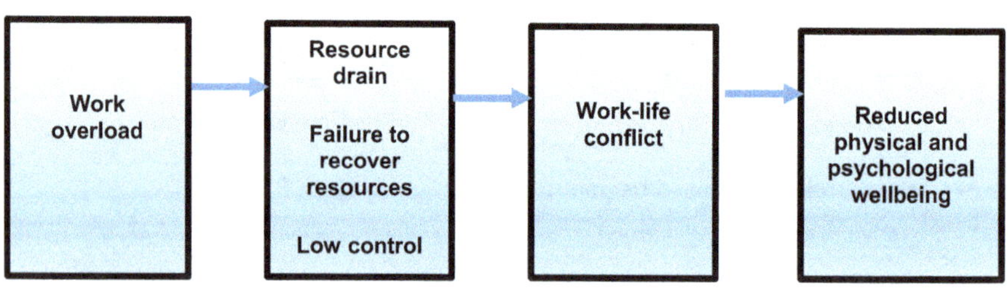

Fig. 5.2 How does work overload influence employee wellbeing

encountered (conflict, ambiguity, overload, and time demands), resource drain occurs.

The focus of this theory is the notion that too much job demand results in resource drain. When limited resources (e.g., time and energy) are transferred from one domain to another, available resources in the original domain decrease (Edwards & Rothbard, 2000). For example, long commuting time reduces the individual's available time to engage in other health- and social-related activities such as sleep, exercise, time spent with family and friends, participation in social groups, and leisure trips (Besser et al., 2008; Mattisson et al., 2015), all of which are important components of subjective wellbeing.

5.3.2 *Conservation of Resources*

Conservation of resources theory is composed of four main principles, namely the primacy of loss, resource investment, gain paradox, and desperation (Hobfoll et al., 2018). The *primacy of loss* principle refers to the tendency for people to experience resource loss as disproportionately more salient than resource gain. The *resource investment* principle asserts that people must invest resources in order to protect against resource loss, recover from losses, and gain resources. The *gain paradox* principle posits that resource gain increases in salience in the context of resource loss. In other words, when resource loss is perceived as high, resource gains are perceived to be more important. Finally, the *desperation* principle argues that when people's resources are overstretched or exhausted, they enter a defensive mode to preserve the self which is often defensive, aggressive, and may become irrational. As such, conservation of resources theory posits that stress occurs under three conditions (a) when central or key resources are threatened with loss, (b) when central or key resources are lost, or (c) when there is a failure to gain central or key resources following significant effort.

Work overload has a negative impact on physical and psychological wellbeing because it leads to loss of resources while also preventing conservation of resources. Conservation of resources theory posits that people experience work stress when they are confronted with losses of resources (actual or anticipated). Resource losses produced by excessive workload in turn result in negative effects on psychological and physical wellbeing (Hobfoll, 1989). To conserve resources, people seek to reduce the impact of stress through investment of resources (Halbesleben et al., 2014; Hobfoll, 2002).

5.3.3 *Job Demands-Resources Model*

Work overload has a negative impact on physical and psychological wellbeing because it represents excessive and prolonged job demand compared to resources available. The Job Demands-Resources model posits that employees experience work stress when they experience work overload. The result is resource drain which outstrips the opportunity to replenish and conserve resources (Schaufeli & Bakker, 2004). The focus of this theory is on the comparison between job demand and resources. High job demand forces the individual to allocate greater effort and energy into job-related tasks to achieve job-related goals, which in a positive sense can also create opportunities for personal growth and development (e.g., workload, time pressure, emotionally and cognitively challenging interactions with others, high responsibility, new projects, and challenging demands) (Van den Broeck et al., 2010). However, excessive or prolonged job demand results in physical and psychological costs that lead, via energy depletion, to impaired health and exhaustion (Bakker & Demerouti, 2007). In contrast, job resources are all those physical, psychological, social, or organizational characteristics of the work that serve to help workers achieve goals and reduce the psychological costs associated with job demand (e.g., work autonomy, feedback relating to performance, social support, supervision, coaching, and time control) (Van den Broeck et al., 2010). As such, job resources promote motivation and engagement, and reduce work-related stress by offsetting the costs associated with psychological demand (Bakker & Demerouti, 2007). In other words, job resources, rather than job demand, are key predictors of positive work attitudes.

5.3.4 *Job Demands-Control Model*

Work overload has a negative impact on physical and psychological wellbeing because work overload represents excessive and prolonged job demand that employees do not have control over. Karasek (1979) Job Demands-Control model, also known as the "decision latitude model" (Karasek, 1979; Karasek & Theorell, 1990), has been highly influential in occupational stress research. The model assumes that strain is produced by high job demand in conjunction with low job control. That is, the stressors have their greatest negative impact when job control is low and job demand is high, whereas an increase in job control serves to attenuate the negative effects of job demand on strain. Job control has a moderating effect on the relationship between job demand and job strain (interaction effect). As such, employees experience work stress when they perceive a lack of control over their heavy workload. Yet, high work demand does not lead to negative outcomes when employees have higher control over their workload. The high-strain situation (high demand/low control) is associated with a high risk of poor health, active (high demand/high control) and passive (low demands/low control) work is associated with an average risk of poor health, and low-strain (low demands/high control) work is associated with better-than-average health (Holman & Wall, 2002; Jonge et al., 1996).

5.4 Implementing a Workload Management Program

Now that we understand the concept of work overload and its negative consequences, the next question is: How do organizations implement an effective workload management program? Workload management programs can be classified into four categories: (1) reduction of workload and time pressure, (2) provision of mutual help, (3) work smarter, and (4) minimization of workload during off-time. Examples of activities for each workload management program are as follows.

First, examples of activities to reduce workload and time pressure include (a) setting realistic deadlines and planning work activities accordingly, (b) establishing a standard range for employee performance that is attainable and sustainable with reasonable engagement and effort, and (c) reducing overtime (Kossek et al., 2014; Voydanoff, 2005).

Second, examples of activities to provide mutual help include (a) design work to foster high levels of social support, (b) cross-train employees to be able to share workload, (c) reward helping behavior, and (d) train leaders to care about workers and encourage workers to care about each other (Kossek et al., 2011).

Third, examples of activities that enable employees to work smarter include (a) valuing quality over quantity or speed and allowing employees to perform to the best of their abilities, (b) allowing for a measure of job control or discretion over employees work and performance, and (c) evaluation based on results, not appearances (Kossek et al., 2014).

Fourth, examples of activities to minimize workload during off-time include (a) creating and fostering a culture of healthy work practices (e.g., no job demand or no job-related communications during off-time), and (b) leave control for time off work (Kossek et al., 2014). We will discuss all of these strategies in further detail below.

See Table 5.1 for a handy list of Do and Don't to help manage workload.

Table 5.1 A handy list of Do and Don't for managers to help manage work overload

Do	Don't
Devote time in your schedule for thinking through your strategy for delegating	Be overly rigid about your workload delegation strategy; when projects crop up and priorities shift, you need to be flexible
Make a list of all the work that needs to get done and then assign tasks according to your team members' specific function, position, and strengths	Burn out your top performer. Before you lean on her more, identify the projects that can go on the backburner
Create a culture that values productivity over hours worked by openly praising strong performance	Beat around the bush with an employee who's not pulling his weight. Be direct about your expectations

Source: Adapted from Knight (2016)

5.4.1 Reduce Workload and Time Pressure

Organizations can reduce workload and time pressure by establishing a standard range for employee performance that is attainable and sustainable with reasonable engagement and effort. The organization could provide adequate manpower to do the job with reasonable expectations for time allotment and effort. Organizations can also reduce chronic overtime work through careful manpower planning (Allan et al., 2007; Frone et al., 1997; Skinner & Pocock, 2008).

Organizations could also set realistic deadlines for work assignments and should avoid speeding up the work pace to achieve organizational efficiency and reduce costs. The organization should allow their employees enough latitude to exert job control or discretion over their own work (Bulger & Fisher, 2012; Kossek et al., 2014; Michel et al., 2011; Valcour, 2007).

There are several significant dimensions to work demand, such as time pressure (i.e., tight deadlines), high speed of work, and the quantity of work (Frone et al., 1997; Skinner & Pocock, 2008). Research has shown that quantity of work (or work overload) is the strongest predictor of full-time employees' work-life conflict. As such, reducing employee workload and time pressure can go a long way towards achieving work-life balance.

A good example of high workload and time pressure can be seen in the sales industry. Salespeople frequently contend with escalating customer expectations, more competition arising from globalization, rapidly changing technology, continuous marketplace change, the increasing prevalence of Internet usage by customers, and less differentiation in products and services (Jones et al., 2000). And as in any industry, salespeople often have significant responsibilities in the family domain. As a result, work-role conflict arises when time and effort demanded by multiple roles become incompatible with each other and overwhelming—that is, participation in one role makes it more difficult to participate in another. These factors combined can overwhelm workers in fast-paced and high-pressure positions—such as salespeople. Employees perceive that role overload occurs when the job demand exceeds the employee's capabilities (intensity of job assignment) and there is high expectation that the job should be performed within a short time (time pressure).

To recap, it is important for organizations to manage work overload (trying to accomplish more work in the same amount of time), time pressure (e.g., tightening of deadlines), and/or increased pace (speeding up the rate at which work is performed). To manage work overload, management should evaluate workload and provide adequate manpower for the job. Management should assign tasks that can be handled within the employee's capabilities and resources. It is also important for management to provide employees with enough control or discretion over the pace of work by setting realistic deadlines and planning activities accordingly.

Let's apply some of these strategies to Carol in her academic position at her research university. Can Noreen, her department head, reduce Carol's workload and time pressure? This can be done by reducing her service commitments. As is the norm at most research universities, senior and junior faculty are assigned to various committees to fulfill their service commitments. But as a junior faculty member (e.g., assistant professor) Carol only has around 6 years to demonstrate her research competency through scholarship and publication. As such, Noreen can reduce the workload of junior faculty like Carol by minimizing their time spent on committees and thus reducing their service commitments.

5.4.2 *Provide Mutual Help*

Programs that provide mutual assistance through workload tradeoff are another effective type of workload management. That is, employees of a similar skill set could be allowed to trade off both workload and hours, thereby increasing social support. Employees could log in more time at work when they have time/energy free (creating credits in the system) and others can request assistance if they feel overloaded. Those that return the favor of sharing are rewarded by organizational recognition as role models (Kossek et al., 2014).

Management can design work to foster social support and cross-train employees to share workload. For example, a firm can mandate that two sales representatives work together on each prospect or assignment. When one of the sales representatives is on leave or engaging in other duties, the other can step in and act as the primary contact for customers.

Additionally, management should foster the development of a work climate that values employees going beyond the call of duty (i.e., mutual help, organizational citizenship behaviors). In doing so, management should select and reward employees who engage in organizational citizenship behaviors.

In a university setting, it is common to assign a mentor to junior faculty (e.g., assistant professors). In Carol's case, Noreen, her department head, can assign a senior faculty in the department to mentor Carol. This mentor can help in many ways. The mentor can look over her course syllabi and attend lectures, after which the mentor can make suggestions on how to improve Carol's teaching methods. Carol would consult her mentor about her research projects to ascertain the potential of being able to publish the study findings in reputable academic journals that are acceptable for promotion and tenure. The mentor can advise Carol on specific protocols related to serving on committees—answering whatever questions Carol might have about administrative procedures. And so on.

See Box 5.1 for a case study on how to create a culture where team members help each other and collaborate.

Box 5.1 Creating a Collaborative Culture to Help Reduce Work Overload

Michelle Garvey, Director of HR Transformation at Ford Motor Company, has established a reputation for being effective in managing work overload. The catch is to create an environment where team members assist each other during peak times. Michelle oversaw the implementation of a global HR technology platform, called "Genesis." The platform was designed to improve workforce planning and analytics for Ford's 150,000 employees across 42 countries. The Genesis team involved 12 HR professionals in the US, Mexico, China, and Germany in addition to other employees from IT, finance, the office of the general counsel, and purchasing. The problem, of course, was the fact that Genesis" project was afflicted by work overload issues. This is the way that Michelle handled the problem of work overload.

First, Michelle developed a plan to distribute the workload by matching her team members' roles with the various tasks. Next, she set clear expectations for each team member. She communicated her expectations through one-on-one conversations and in team meetings and made it clear that their jobs were to support the overall team objectives. The goal was to instill a strong sense of purpose. Third, she used project management tools (e.g., work plans and milestone charts) to make sure the project was on track and to address workload issues on an ongoing basis. To make sure that everyone was pulling his weight and no task was left incomplete, she held regular forums. The goal here was to ask her team members questions such as "'What are we missing? What is keeping you up at night? What help do you need?"

Source: Adapted from Knight (2016).

5.4.3 Work Smarter

Management could also develop strategies that enable employees to work smarter to offset working harder. Doing so should reduce the workload. That is, the organization should seek synergies in the work process by streamlining necessary procedural steps (i.e., working smarter) (Kossek et al., 2014).

Management can foster a work climate that values quality over quantity of work. As such, employees can be evaluated by their work performance and quality of output, not by work hours or appearances. Management could then share methods and approaches of working smarter with other employees within the organization using tools such as social media. Which would allow them to identify ways to eliminate low-value and unnecessary work such as meetings that are time-consuming and poorly run.

Can these ideas help Carol in her academic position? Here are some examples of working smarter that apply to Carol. At their core, universities are just managed committees. There is a committee for every administrative task imaginable. There are committees to approve new courses, committees related to the honors court (to adjudicate cases related to student misconduct), committees that approve research protocols, committees related to promotion and tenure, multicultural diversity committees (to ensure minority faculty, staff, students, and other candidates are not discriminated against due to their ethnicity, religion, sex, national origin, etc.), a commencement committee, faculty ethics committee, a computer committee, etc. Faculty are expected to serve on a variety of committees to help manage their department, their college, their university, their professional association, and other stakeholder groups important to the university (e.g., local community, region, state).

How can the workload related to service committees be managed to reduce work overload? Her department head, Noreen, can assign Carol to fewer committees. Carol can also be assigned to committees that have fewer time and energy demands. For example, curriculum committees can be laborious and time consuming. Noreen can avoid assigning her those type of committees until Carol has more time and energy to spare. Noreen can also help reduce Carol's workload by assigning her fewer classes to teach to help her concentrate on research and scholarship. Noreen can help reduce Carol's research workload by assigning her one or more graduate research students to assist with research-related tasks. And so on.

5.4.4 Minimize Work Demand During Off-Work Time

Lastly, organizations should try to minimize work demand during off-work time. That is, managers can reduce work demand by helping their employees to psychologically detach from work when they are off work (Kossek et al., 2014).

Managers can do so by examining the prevalence of their employees' work-related communications or activities outside of regular business hours. They can take measures to ensure that their employees have opportunities to "switch off" from work demands during off-work time. The rising trend in which employees receive a stipend to buy a laptop or smartphone of their choice for both work and personal purposes may increase expectations for employees to work at home during off-work hours (Madkour, 2008). Of course, management should make it clear that employees are not expected to take their work home. In other words, management should foster an organizational culture that values personal life and make a concerted effort not to interrupt personal time—ensuring that personal time is freed up to handle personal life demands.

In the case of Carol, her department head may instruct her staff not to contact any of the faculty members at home during off-hours. Specific guidelines can be established regarding certain emergencies that would justify a breach of protocol. For example, if Carol is involved in a lab doing animal research, there are urgent situations that may necessitate immediate action. A power outage in the lab may jeopardize the health and safety of the animals—feeding problems, temperature control, plumbing problems, fire hazards, etc. However, barring an emergency, Carol is not expected to answer any emails or calls during her off-hours.

Table 5.2 Factors moderating the effectiveness of workload management policies and programs

Type of moderator	Specific conditions
Personal moderators	Low job control High value on family time High income Job dissatisfaction Heavy family responsibilities Female employees Young adults Low familial support
Organizational moderators	High organizational support Lack of employee autonomy and control High role ambiguity
Environmental moderators	Individualistic cultures Developed countries Countries with high levels of connectivity

5.5 Under What Conditions Is a Workload Management Program Most Effective

First, workload reduction programs are effective in reducing work stress when employees have a high perceived workload. Employees are likely to perceive their workload as being high when they are expected to be always online and available (Currie & Eveline, 2011). With the rise of telework and flexible scheduling, communication outside of traditional work hours is becoming more and more common (Mazmanian et al., 2013). Perception of high workload also occurs when employees perceive unfairness in workload among organizational members, and when there is role ambiguity (Michel et al., 2011).

In the sections below we will examine a set of moderators that govern the effectiveness of workload management policies and programs. Specifically, we will discuss research related to personal moderators, organizational moderators, and environmental moderators. See Table 5.2 for a summary of these factors.

5.5.1 *Personal Moderators*

Research has shown that workload management programs tend to be most effective given the following personal moderators: (1) low job control, (2) high value on family time, (3) high income, (4) job dissatisfaction, (5) heavy family responsibilities, (6) female employees, (7) young adults, and (8) low familial support.

Workload reduction programs are most effective in reducing work stress not only when employees experience high job demand but also a *low degree of job control*. High job demand combined with low job control is likely to result in a high level of work stress. High work demand does not lead to negative outcomes when employees have more control over their work (Holman & Wall, 2002; Jonge et al., 1996). This is because job control enables employees to effectively deal with job demand by using strategies such as delegating work tasks (Kirkcaldy & Furnham, 1999), prioritizing goals and tasks (Adams & Jex, 1999), and taking breaks that allow workers to recover (Sonnentag, 2001). The job-demands-and-control model posits that employees experience work stress when they perceive lack of control over their heavy workload (Holman & Wall, 2002; Jonge et al., 1996). Yet, high work demand does not lead to negative outcomes when employees have a reasonable control over their workload. Workload reduction programs are effective in reducing work stress when employees experience high job demand and a *low degree of job control* because workload reduction programs provide employees with certain degree of control over the work demand.

Workload reduction programs are effective for those employees who *value family time*. Those who strongly value personal/family time will be more satisfied and committed to occupations that allow them to better balance work and personal demands through workload reduction (Young et al., 2022). WLB is achieved when there is a high degree of fit between role demands and resources (Greenhaus & Allen, 2011). Specifically, those who value family time need more family time to achieve work-life balance. Thus, workload reduction should substantially help them achieve a match between their family role commitment and resources. In sum, workload reduction programs are effective for those employees who *value family time* because the workload programs serve to reduce their work-family conflicts.

Workload reduction programs are more effective for those who do not have to regularly work overtime and instead have a salaried position. Specifically, workload reduction is effective for the wellbeing of *middle/upper income employees* because they tend to have shorter work hours and do not typically have to worry about a reduction in income due to reduced hours from taking advantage of programs such as family leave (Jacobs & Gerson, 2001). In contrast, workload reduction programs may not produce positive outcomes for those employees who are classified as low income. Employees in lower-income jobs may need to work long hours to support their income needs (Jacobs & Gerson, 2001). As such, WLB programs should consider the combined paid work of family members (e.g., family income) as well as individual work time and schedules. In sum, workload reduction programs may be less effective for those who need to work overtime for financial reasons and/or are considered low-income households.

Workload reduction programs effectively reduce work-family conflict for those who are *not satisfied with their job*. For employees with satisfying jobs, even high demands at work may not result in depletion, and so they may not experience a negative impact on their WLB (Hewlett & Luce, 2006; Van Steenbergen et al., 2011). *Role expansion theory* (Marks, 1977) asserts that heavy workload does not necessarily deplete an individual and can even create energy for use in work and nonwork roles under the right conditions (Hewlett & Luce, 2006; Marks, 1977). Van Steenbergen et al. (2011) have argued that the association between workload and trajectories of marital satisfaction depend on circumstances that may constrain or facilitate partners' ability to negotiate their multiple roles. Specifically, they hypothesized that the covariance between changes in workload and marital satisfaction over time should be moderated by the extent to which spouses like their work and their parental status. Analyses drawing upon eight waves of data on workload, work satisfaction, and marital satisfaction from 169 newlywed couples assessed over 4 years confirmed these predictions. Specifically, the study found that the negative impact of workload on marital satisfaction is higher for those who are less satisfied with their job. Thus, management should make a concerted effort to reduce workload especially for those who are less satisfied with their job compared to those who are satisfied.

Workload reduction programs tend to be more effective for those employees with *heavy family responsibilities*. A heavy workload for parents—especially those with a dependent age 5 years or younger—results in high work-life conflict. Work hour reduction programs are effective for those employees with young children (Hill et al., 2010). When there are no children in the household, working hard can be energizing and can complement one's role as a spouse, translating into higher marital satisfaction. For parents with young children, however, more time and energy devoted to work significantly increases work-life conflicts, resulting in declines in marital satisfaction (Van Steenbergen et al., 2011). Van Steenbergen et al. (2011) study on workload and marital satisfaction of newlywed couples also indicate that increases in husbands' workload covaried with declines in marital satisfaction for parent couples with family responsibilities. Workload reduction programs tend to be especially effective for those employees with *heavy family responsibilities* because workload reduction programs help reduce work-family conflict.

Workload reduction programs will be more effective for *female than for male employees*. This is because most women employed outside of the home continue to assume a greater share of household and family care responsibilities (including child and elder care) than men, and that employed mothers seem to worry more about the adequacy of their child-care arrangements than working fathers (MacDonald et al., 2005; Rosenfield, 1989; Schieman et al., 2009). Using Canadian social survey data, MacDonald et al. (2005) examined the time spent by women and men aged 25 to 54 on paid work, childcare, eldercare, household work, volunteering, and education, and then assessed its impact on stress and work-life balance. They found that women's greater hours of unpaid work contributed to women experiencing more stress than men, and of that work, hours spent on eldercare and housework are more stressful than those spent on childcare. For women, all types of unpaid work also increase time stress, but eldercare and housework hours are more likely to increase time stress than childcare hours, showing that not all work is equal in terms of stress. For men, unpaid work rarely has any association with time stress. Thus, workload reduction programs tend to be more effective for WLB of *female than male employees* because women experience a higher degree of time stress than men.

Workload reduction programs are more effective for early adults or young adults (Huffman et al., 2013). Compared to older individuals, *young adults* tend to face higher demands at work (e.g., acquiring new skills and knowledge, choosing career paths) and family life (e.g., starting a family, raising young children), while having fewer resources (e.g., lack of experience, lower job status, lack of job autonomy) to help them cope with work-family conflicts (Demerouti et al., 2012; Huffman et al., 2013; Reichl et al., 2014). Thus, workload reduction programs are more effective for young adult employees. For example, Huffman et al. (2013) examined work-family conflict for individuals aged 18–70, focusing on explanations for why age is differentially related to work-family conflict at different points in one's life. Their survey results indicate a curvilinear relationship, with the youngest and oldest workers experiencing the fewest conflicting demands between work and home. Whereas young adult workers beginning their career (in the establishment career stage, aged 25–49) appear to experience the greatest work-family conflict compared to workers of other ages. During this stage in life, factors at work and home are the most taxing on resources. Further, the results demonstrated that family satisfaction and the age of the youngest child (older children are less-taxing on resources) help explain why the youngest and oldest workers are less likely to experience family interference with work. Workload reduction programs are more effective for early adults because they tend to experience a higher degree of demand both in work and family life than other ages.

Work reduction programs are more effective for *those who do not have family support* for their heavy role demands. This is because those without family support are likely to experience greater work-life conflict (Seiger & Wiese, 2009). In contrast, the availability of familial support serves as a resource for coping with stresses at work and in nonwork domains (Cohen & Wills, 1985; Seiger & Wiese, 2009; van Daalen et al., 2006). Through survey questionnaires and standardized diaries of working mothers, Seiger and Wiese (2009) found that social support from supervisors, co-workers, life partners, and family members directly reduces work-family conflict. In addition, social support may alter the impact of stressors and strain on work-family conflict in such a way that employees who feel strongly supported by their environment are less affected by stressors and strain and, in turn, experience less work-family conflict. As such, one can assert that work reduction programs are more effective for *those who do not have family support* for their heavy role demands compared to those who do have the support.

5.5.2 Organizational Moderators

Research has shown that workload reduction programs are most effective for WLB given the following organizational conditions: (1) high organizational support, (2) lack of employee autonomy and control, and (3) high role ambiguity.

Evidence shows that workload reduction programs are effective in reducing work-life conflict when the programs are accompanied by high *organizational support*. Organizational support from supervisors and co-workers serves to reduce actual and perceived workload (Bowling et al., 2015). In addition, emotional support helps employees cope with work-related stress (Bowling et al., 2015). Perceived organizational support serves to reduce aversive psychological and psychosomatic reactions (i.e., strains) to stressors by signaling the availability of material aid and emotional support when needed to cope with high job demand (Rhoades & Eisenberger, 2002). Bowling et al. (2015) meta-analytic study found that support provided by both one's supervisor and support provided by one's co-workers yielded negative relationships with workload (i.e., reduction of perceived workload). Receiving social support serves to reduce one's perceived workload because those providing support shoulder part of the burden of the job demand. In other words, the support recipient's workload is lessened because some of their work responsibilities are distributed across one or more supporters. Similarly, the receipt of informational or emotional support may make it easier for the support recipient to meet their job demand, thus resulting in a reduction in actual or perceived workload and resulting work-life conflict.

Furthermore, research indicates that workload reduction programs are effective in reducing work-life conflict when employees have no or low *autonomy and control* in the way they carry out their job-related tasks (Bal et al., 2017; Brauner et al., 2019; Grönlund, 2007; Hobfoll, 2002; Valcour, 2007; Van der Doef & Maes, 1999). Specifically, autonomy at work provides employees with the necessary control to decide how they complete tasks and to adjust working conditions). When employees experience low autonomy and do not have control over job demand, they are likely to experience a high level of work-life conflict and are unlikely to cope well with high job demand. Studies found that a reduction in work hours contributes significantly to the WLB of employees who do not have control over their work time. For employees with high levels of control over work time, by contrast, there was no significant relationship between work hours and satisfaction with work-life balance. With a representative sample of full-time employees in Germany, Brauner et al. (2019) classified distinct types of work schedules based on working time demands and working time control and examined their associations with health and work-life balance. Their study found that subjective health was highest for work schedules comprising high working time control and autonomy (e.g., control over the beginning and end of workday) and that employees with high working time demands and low control represent risk groups prone to dissatisfaction. Thus, we can safely conclude that workload reduction programs are effective in reducing work-life conflict when employees do not have control in their work.

Finally, there is also evidence suggesting that workload reduction programs are more effective when the programs are accompanied by job task clarification. Lack of clarity in job-related tasks (i.e., *role ambiguity*) makes it difficult to cope with high workload (Bowling et al., 2015; Michel et al., 2011; Spector & Jex, 1998). Role ambiguity refers to a lack of necessary information (specificity and predictability) about duties, objectives, and responsibilities needed for a particular work-role or the lack of work-role clarity. In a meta-analysis on workload, Bowling et al. (2015) found that role ambiguity ($\rho = 0.28$) and role conflict ($\rho = 0.44$) are positively associated with workload. As such, management can reduce employee work-family conflict by ensuring job duties and responsibilities are clear, compatible, and consistent.

5.5.3 Environmental Moderators

Research has demonstrated that workload reduction programs are most effective under the following environmental conditions: (1) individualistic cultures, (2) developed countries, and (3) countries with high levels of connectivity.

Workload reduction programs are more effective in *individualistic cultures* than in collectivistic cultures. Employees in an individualistic country customarily view job demand as naturally competing with family demand (e.g., demand from work interferes with family life), whereas employees in a collectivistic country will not (e.g., they work hard for the benefit of the family) (Lu et al., 2006; Reichl et al., 2014; Spector et al., 2007). In addition, employees in an individualistic country tend to have nuclear families (e.g., spouses and children); as such, they are less likely to receive assistance from extended relatives. The lower levels of familial support in individualist cultures mean they are more likely to experience higher levels of work-life conflict and burnout. In contrast, employees in collectivistic countries tend to cohabitate with extended family; as such, they are likely to receive assistance and support from extended-family members. For example, Lu et al. (2006) conducted a survey to examine the relationship between work-family demands and work-life conflict in both individualistic (United Kingdom) and collectivistic (Taiwan) societies. They found that for a country with an individualistic culture (United Kingdom), there was a stronger positive relationship between workload and work-family conflict, as well as a stronger positive relationship between sharing household chores and family-work conflict, compared to a country with a collectivistic culture (Taiwan). Workload reduction programs are more effective in *individualistic cultures* than in *collectivistic cultures* because employees in the individualistic culture tend to experience higher work-family conflict with limited familial support. Thus, it can be asserted that workload reduction is likely to be more effective in reducing work-family conflicts in individualistic cultures than in collectivistic cultures.

Furthermore, evidence suggests that workload reduction programs are more effective in *developed (rather than developing) countries*. This is due in part to the fact that workhour reduction—an important aspect of workload reduction—is typically less effective for employees in less-developed countries who need to work extended hours to make ends meet. Employees in developing countries tend to view work as a means of supporting the family and maintaining familial financial security (Yang et al., 2000). Thus, workload reduction programs should only be implemented after considering the target country's level of economic development. Specifically, Yang et al. (2000) conducted a comparative analysis of work and family demands among employees in the United States and China, and the effects of these demands on work-family conflict. They found that family demand had a greater impact on work-family conflict in the developed country (United States), whereas work demand had a greater impact on work-family conflict in the developing country (China). The differences primarily stem from the relative values placed on family and work time between the developed and developing countries. The authors contended that for employees in the developing country (China), sacrificing family time for work is viewed as self-sacrifice for the benefit of the family or as a short-term cost incurred to gain long-term benefits (e.g., financial security of the family), but that in the economically developed country (United States), sacrificing family time for work is often perceived as a failure to be a good caregiver and partner. As extra work after official hours means a self-sacrifice made for the financial security of the family, employees in developing countries may not experience high work-family conflict from workload, and thus they may not wish to participate in workload reduction programs that incorporate strategies such as workhour reduction which correlates to reduced income. In sum, workload reduction programs with reduced work hours may be less effective in economically developing countries. In contrast, workhour reduction is effective for employees in developed countries who do not have to work extended hours for extra income.

Finally, research has shown that workload reduction programs are more effective in countries with *increased connectivity*, compared to countries with less connectivity. Increased connectivity allows for more flexible WLB programs and policies such as telework and flextime/flexplace. However, this often also means increased pressure to be constantly available, increased workload, and greater difficulty disconnecting from work after office hours (Mazmanian et al., 2013), which in turn increases work-life conflict. In a survey and interview with academics in Australia, Currie and Eveline (2011) found that while increased connectivity allows work to be done anywhere and anytime, it also intensifies workload making it difficult to separate work and family life. That is, they found that increased connectivity deteriorates working conditions for Australian academics whose work has intensified and extended into their private lives with longer working hours and a faster work pace. Thus, workload reduction programs are more effective in countries with increased connectivity and work overload, compared to countries with less connectivity where employees often have stronger boundaries separating work and family life.

5.6 Summary and Conclusion

This chapter focused on various workload management programs and policies. Evidence suggests that WLB can be achieved through the effective management of workload. Work-life imbalance is caused, at least partly, by work overload. Hence, the goal of workload management programs is to mitigate work overload.

We explained the negative consequences associated with work overload through four well-established theories, namely resource drain, conservation of resources, job demands and resources, and job demands and control. Resource drain theory treats resources such as time, attention, and energy as finite, and role stressors that occur in each domain subtract from these finite resources. The theory of conservation of resources argues that people experience work stress when they are confronted with the loss of resources, which is often the result of excessive workload. To conserve resources, people seek to reduce the impact of stress through the investment of resources. Job Demands-Resources theory asserts that employees experience work stress when they experience work overload. The result is resource drain which outstrips the opportunity to replenish and conserve resources. High job demand forces the individual to allocate greater effort and energy into job-related tasks to achieve job-related goals, which in a positive sense, can also create opportunities for personal growth and development. However, excessive or prolonged job demand results in higher physical and psychological costs that lead, via energy depletion, to impaired health and exhaustion. Finally, the Job Demands-Control model posits that employees experience work stress when they perceive lack of control over their heavy workload. Yet, high work demand does not lead to negative outcomes when employees have control over the workload.

We then discussed how workload management programs are customarily implemented by developing policies that can reduce workload and time pressure, provide mutual help, allow employees to work smarter, and minimize work demand during off-work time.

Lastly, we explained the conditions under which workload management programs are more effective. As such, we described the research dealing with personal moderators (e.g., low job control, high value on family time, high income, job dissatisfaction, heavy family responsibilities, female employees, young adults, and low familial support), organizational moderators (e.g., high organizational support, lack of employee autonomy and control, and high role ambiguity), and environmental moderators (e.g., individualistic cultures, developed countries, and countries with high levels of connectivity).

See Box 5.2 for "practical recommendations" from practitioners.

Box 5.2 Practical Recommendations From Industry Practitioners About Workload Management

To effectively manage work overload, management should regularly review employees' workload. Employees with huge workloads and limited time to complete the required tasks are likely to suffer from physical and mental stress. To address the stress issue, managers should be heavily engaged in planning workloads, prioritizing work, delegating tasks, and saying no to projects. Specifically, managers should regularly review the allocation of duties among employees to ensure achievable workloads.

How to manage work overload? The answer is not only to reduce employees' workloads but also develop cross-training programs. Cross-training employees should help distribute the workload to different departments and ensure the smooth running of operations.

Furthermore, when there are urgent tasks to be completed within deadlines, managers should bring in more employees from other departments (or perhaps hire new part-time employees) to help reduce the workload.

Another course of action involves training employees to manage their time more wisely. In-house seminars by managers or health experts and career coaches can help employees better understand the importance of time management and the techniques that can be implemented.

Another approach is to be less rigid about lunch break hours. For some employees, lunch break is their way to run errands, attend to family matters, or just take some time for themselves. Managers could emphasize that their team members should take a "reasonable" amount of time for their lunch break. More importantly, the less rigid lunch schedule is often perceived as a sign that management trusts and cares about them. Employees are likely to reciprocate through increased productivity and organizational commitment.

Source: Adapted from https://www.timedoctor.com/blog/employee-work-life-balance/, https://www.timedoctor.com/blog/employee-work-life-balance/, and https://www.frontstream.com/blog/work-life-balance-strategies

References

Adams, G. A., & Jex, S. M. (1999). Relationships between time management, control, work–family conflict, and strain. *Journal of Occupational Health Psychology, 4*(1), 72–77.

Allan, C., Loudoun, R., & Peetz, D. (2007). Influences on work/non-work conflict. *Journal of Sociology, 43*(3), 219–239.

Bakker, A. B., & Demerouti, E. (2007). The job demands-resources model: State of the art. *Journal of Managerial Psychology, 22*(3), 309–328.

Bal, P. M., Hofmans, J., & Polat, T. (2017). Breaking psychological contracts with the burden of workload: A weekly study of job resources as moderators. *Applied Psychology, 66*(1), 143–167.

Besser, L. M., Marcus, M., & Frumkin, H. (2008). Commute time and social capital in the US. *American Journal of Preventive Medicine, 34*(3), 207–211.

Bowling, N. A., Alarcon, G. M., Bragg, C. B., & Hartman, M. J. (2015). A meta-analytic examination of the potential correlates and consequences of workload. *Work & Stress, 29*(2), 95–113.

Brauner, C., Wöhrmann, A. M., Frank, K., & Michel, A. (2019). Health and work-life balance across types of work schedules: A latent class analysis. *Applied Ergonomics, 81*, 102906.

Bulger, C. A., & Fisher, G. G. (2012). Ethical imperatives of work/life balance. In N. P. Reilly, M. J. Sirgy, & C. A. Gorman (Eds.), *Work and quality of life* (pp. 181–202). Springer.

Byron, K. (2005). A meta-analytic review of work-family conflict and its antecedents. *Journal of Vocational Behavior, 67*(2), 169–198.

Cohen, S., & Wills, T. A. (1985). Stress, social support, and the buffering hypothesis. *Psychological Bulletin, 98*(2), 310–357.

Currie, J., & Eveline, J. (2011). E-technology and work/life balance for academics with young children. *Higher Education, 62*(4), 533–550.

Demerouti, E., Bakker, A. B., Sonnentag, S., & Fullagar, C. J. (2012). Work-related flow and energy at work and at home: A study on the role of daily recovery. *Journal of Organizational Behavior, 33*(2), 276–295.

Edwards, J. R., & Rothbard, N. P. (2000). Mechanisms linking work and family: Clarifying the relationship between work and family constructs. *Academy of Management Review, 25*(1), 178–199.

Frone, M. R., Yardley, J. K., & Markel, K. S. (1997). Developing and testing an integrative model of the work-family interface. *Journal of Vocational Behavior, 50*(2), 145–167.

Garrett, D. K., & McDaniel, A. M. (2001). A new look at nurse burnout: The effects of environmental uncertainty and social climate. *JONA: The Journal of Nursing Administration, 31*(2), 91–96.

Greenglass, E. R., Burke, R. J., & Fiksenbaum, L. (2001). Workload and burnout in nurses. *Journal of Community & Applied Social Psychology, 11*(3), 211–215.

Greenhaus, J. H., & Allen, T. D. (2011). Work-family balance: A review and extension of the literature. In J. C. Quick & L. E. Tetrick (Eds.), *Handbook of occupational health psychology* (pp. 165–183). American Psychological Association.

Greenhaus, J. H., & Beutell, N. J. (1985). Sources of conflict between work and family roles. *Academy of Management Review, 10*(1), 76–88.

Grönlund, A. (2007). More control, less conflict? Job demand-control, gender and work-family conflict. *Gender, Work and Organization, 14*(5), 476–497.

Halbesleben, J. R., Neveu, J. P., Paustian-Underdahl, S. C., & Westman, M. (2014). Getting to the "COR" understanding the role of resources in conservation of resources theory. *Journal of Management, 40*(5), 1334–1364.

Hewlett, S. A., & Luce, C. B. (2006). Extreme jobs: The dangerous allure of the 70-hour workweek. *Harvard Business Review, 84*(12), 49–59.

Hill, E. J., Erickson, J. J., Holmes, E. K., & Ferris, M. (2010). Workplace flexibility, work hours, and work-life conflict: Finding an extra day or two. *Journal of Family Psychology, 24*(3), 349–358.

Hobfoll, S. E. (1989). Conservation of resources: A new attempt at conceptualizing stress. *American Psychologist, 44*(3), 513–524.

Hobfoll, S. E. (2002). Social and psychological resources and adaptation. *Review of General Psychology, 6*(4), 307–324.

Hobfoll, S. E., Halbesleben, J., Neveu, J. P., & Westman, M. (2018). Conservation of resources in the organizational context: The reality of resources and their consequences. *Annual Review of Organizational Psychology and Organizational Behavior, 5*, 103–128.

Holland, P., Tham, T. L., Sheehan, C., & Cooper, B. (2019). The impact of perceived workload on nurse satisfaction with work-life balance and intention to leave the occupation. *Applied Nursing Research, 49*(October), 70–76.

Holman, D. J., & Wall, T. D. (2002). Work characteristics, learning-related outcomes, and strain: A test of competing direct effects, mediated, and moderated models. *Journal of Occupational Health Psychology, 7*(4), 283–301.

Huffman, A., Culbertson, S. S., Henning, J. B., & Goh, A. (2013). Work-family conflict across the lifespan. *Journal of Managerial Psychology, 28*(7/8), 761–780.

Jacobs, J. A., & Gerson, K. (2001). Overworked individuals or overworked families? Explaining trends in work, leisure, and family time. *Work and Occupations, 28*(1), 40–63.

Jones, E., Roberts, J. A., & Chonko, L. B. (2000). Motivating sales entrepreneurs to change: A conceptual framework of factors leading to successful change management initiatives in sales organizations. *Journal of Marketing Theory and Practice, 8*(2), 37–49.

Jonge, J. D., Janseen, P. P., & Van Breukelen, G. J. (1996). Testing the demand-control-support model among health-care professionals: A structural equation model. *Work & Stress, 10*(3), 209–224.

Karasek, R. (1979). Job demands, job decision latitude and mental strain: Implications for job redesign. *Administrative Science Quarterly, 24*(2), 285–308.

Karasek, R., & Theorell, T. (1990). *Healthy work: Stress, productivity, and the reconstruction of working life*. Basic Books.

Kirkcaldy, B., & Furnham, A. (1999). Stress coping styles among German managers. *Journal of Workplace Learning, 11*(1), 22–26.

Knight, R. (2016). Make sure your team's workload is divided fairly. *Harvard Business Review*. Retrieved on September 28, 2023 from https://hbr.org/2016/11/make-sure-your-teams-workload-is-divided-fairly

Kopelman, R. E., Greenhaus, J. H., & Connolly, T. F. (1983). A model of work, family, and interrole conflict: A construct validation study. *Organizational Behavior and Human Performance, 32*(2), 198–215.

Kossek, E. E., Pichler, S., Bodner, T., & Hammer, L. B. (2011). Workplace social support and work-family conflict: A meta-analysis clarifying the influence of general and work-family-specific supervisor and organizational support. *Personnel Psychology, 64*(2), 289–313.

Kossek, E. E., Valcour, M., & Lirio, P. (2014). Organizational strategies for promoting work-life balance and wellbeing. In P. Y. Chen & C. L. Cooper (Eds.), *Work and wellbeing* (*Wellbeing: A complete reference guide*) (Vol. 3, pp. 295–319). John Wiley & Sons.

Lembrechts, L., Dekocker, V., Zanoni, P., & Pulignano, V. (2015). A study of the determinants of work-to-family conflict among hospital nurses in Belgium. *Journal of Nursing Management, 23*(7), 898–909.

Lu, L., Gilmour, R., Kao, S., & Huang, M. (2006). A cross-cultural study of work/family demands, work/family conflict and wellbeing: The Taiwanese vs British. *Career Development International, 11*(1), 9–27.

MacDonald, M., Phipps, S., & Lethbridge, L. (2005). Taking its toll: The influence of paid and unpaid work on women's Well-being. *Feminist Economics, 11*(1), 63–94.

Madkour, R. (2008, September 25). BYOC: bring your own computer — to work. Associated Press. http://www.msnbc.msn.com/id/26889537/

Marks, S. P. (1977). Multiple roles and role strain: Some notes on human energy, time and commitment. *American Sociological Review, 42*(6), 921–936.

Mattisson, K., Håkansson, C., & Jakobsson, K. (2015). Relationships between commuting and social capital among men and women in southern Sweden. *Environment and Behavior, 47*(7), 734–753.

Mazmanian, M., Orlikowski, W. J., & Yates, J. (2013). The autonomy paradox: The implications of mobile email devices for knowledge professionals. *Organization Science, 24*(5), 1337–1357.

Michel, J. S., Kotrba, L. M., Mitchelson, J. K., Clark, M. A., & Baltes, B. B. (2011). Antecedents of work-family conflict: A meta-analytic review. *Journal of Organizational Behavior, 32*(5), 689–725.

Nordenmark, M., Vinberg, S., & Strandh, M. (2012). Job control and demands, work-life balance and wellbeing among self-employed men and women in Europe. *Vulnerable Groups & Inclusion, 3*(1), 188–196.

Reichl, C., Leiter, M. P., & Spinath, F. M. (2014). Work-nonwork conflict and burnout: A meta-analysis. *Human Relations, 67*(8), 979–1005.

Rhoades, L., & Eisenberger, R. (2002). Perceived organizational support: A review of the literature. *Journal of Applied Psychology, 87*(4), 698–714.

Rosenfield, S. (1989). The effects of women's employment: Personal control and sex differences in mental health. *Journal of Health and Social Behavior, 30*(1), 77–91.

Schaufeli, W. B., & Bakker, A. B. (2004). Job demands, job resources, and their relationship with burnout and engagement: A multi-sample study. *Journal of Organizational Behavior, 25*(3), 293–315.

Schieman, S., Glavin, P., & Milkie, M. A. (2009). When work interferes with life: Work-nonwork interference and the influence of work-related demands and resources. *American Sociological Review, 74*(6), 966–988.

Seiger, C. P., & Wiese, B. S. (2009). Social support from work and family domains as an antecedent or moderator of work-family conflicts? *Journal of Vocational Behavior, 75*(1), 26–37.

Skinner, N., & Pocock, B. (2008). Work-life conflict: Is work time or work overload more important? *Asia Pacific Journal of Human Resources, 46*(3), 303–315.

Sonnentag, S. (2001). Work, recovery activities, and individual Well-being: A diary study. *Journal of Occupational Health Psychology, 6*(3), 196–210.

Spector, P. E., & Jex, S. M. (1998). Development of four self-report measures of job stressors and strain: Interpersonal conflict at work scale, organizational constraints scale, quantitative workload inventory, and physical symptoms inventory. *Journal of Occupational Health Psychology, 3*(4), 356–267.

Spector, P. E., Allen, T. D., Poelmans, S. A., Lapierre, L. M., Cooper, C. L., Michael, O. D., & Widerszal-Bazyl, M. (2007). Cross-national differences in relationships of work demands, job satisfaction, and turnover intentions with work-family conflict. *Personnel Psychology, 60*(4), 805–835.

Thompson, C. A., Beauvais, L. L., & Lyness, K. S. (1999). When work-family benefits are not enough: The influence of work-family culture on benefit utilization, organizational attachment, and work-family conflict. *Journal of Vocational Behavior, 54*(3), 392–415.

Valcour, M. (2007). Work-based resources as moderators of the relationship between work hours and satisfaction with work-family balance. *Journal of Applied Psychology, 92*(6), 1512–1523.

van Daalen, G., Willemsen, T. M., & Sanders, K. (2006). Reducing work-family conflict through different sources of social support. *Journal of Vocational Behavior, 69*(3), 462–476.

Van den Broeck, A., Vansteenkiste, M., De Witte, H., Soenens, B., & Lens, W. (2010). Capturing autonomy, competence, and relatedness at work: Construction and initial validation of the work-related basic need satisfaction scale. *Journal of Occupational and Organizational Psychology, 83*(4), 981–1002.

Van der Doef, M., & Maes, S. (1999). The job demand-control (−support) model and psychological Well-being: A review of 20 years of empirical research. *Work & Stress, 13*(2), 87–114.

Van Steenbergen, E. F., Kluwer, E. S., & Karney, B. R. (2011). Workload and the trajectory of marital satisfaction in newlyweds: Job satisfaction, gender, and parental status as moderators. *Journal of Family Psychology, 25*(3), 345–355.

Voydanoff, P. (2004). The effects of work demands and resources on work-to-family conflict and facilitation. *Journal of Marriage and Family, 66*(2), 398–412.

Voydanoff, P. (2005). Toward a conceptualization of perceived work-family fit and balance: A demands and resources approach. *Journal of Marriage and Family, 67*(4), 822–836.

Whiston, S. C., & Cinamon, R. G. (2015). The work-family interface: Integrating research and career counseling practice. *The Career Development Quarterly, 63*(1), 44–56.

Yang, N., Chen, C. C., Choi, J., & Zou, Y. (2000). Sources of work-family conflict: A Sino-US comparison of the effects of work and family demands. *Academy of Management Journal, 43*(1), 113–123.

Young, D. K., McLeod, A. J., & Carpenter, D. (2022). Examining the influence of occupational characteristics, gender and work-life balance on IT professionals' occupational satisfaction and occupational commitment. *Information Technology & People*, (ahead-of-print): https://www.emerald.com/insight/0959-3845.htm

Chapter 6
Schedule Flexibility

> *"Thinking about work as a day job has made a big difference in the way I approach what I do. It also helped me not to confuse who I am with what I do."—Bob Goff (https://teambuilding.com/blog/work-life-balance-quotes)*

Abstract In this chapter, we define flexible work schedule policies and program. We describe the positive and negative consequences related to these practices—outcomes related to both employee and organizational wellbeing. We explain these effects in terms of theories related to perception of control, person-job fit, and reciprocity. We then describe a variety of different types of flexible scheduling practices, namely flexible work time, compressed work week, absence autonomy, and open rota. We then discuss factors that moderate the effectiveness of schedule flexibility in terms of personal, program, and environmental factors.

6.1 Introduction

A flexible work schedule refers to an employee's ability to control their own work hours and work outside of the traditional work week—negotiated and agreed upon with their employer. Research has shown that schedule flexibility decreases work-to-family conflict (Anderson et al., 2002; Thomas & Ganster, 1995). Specifically, schedule flexibility minimizes work-family conflict, promotes work-family enrichment, and improves functioning and performance at both work and home (Carlson et al., 2010). As such, the purpose of a schedule flexibility program is to provide employees with a sense of control over their work schedule. This allows them to have more control over their work-life, which significantly contributes to work-life balance.

Two common examples of schedule flexibility programs include flextime (a flexible work schedule) and a compressed work week. Flextime refers to a flexible work

D.-J. Lee, M. J. Sirgy, *Organizational Strategies for Work-Life Balance*, Human Well-Being Research and Policy Making,
https://doi.org/10.1007/978-3-031-56314-0_6

schedule that varies from the traditional Monday to Friday, 9 a.m. to 5 p.m. workweek in which the employee chooses their start and end times while still working full-time hours. Whereas a compressed work week allows employees to work fewer days per week while still maintaining a standard 38-40 h working week. This is done by compressing the workweek into fewer than 5 days (often 4) and working more hours to compensate on the remaining workdays (Baltes et al., 1999; Lewis & Cooper, 2005).

Box 6.1 Inflexible Scheduling

Research has shown that 80% of employees have little say about their schedules, 70% face last-minute shifts, and 50% have back-to-back shifts. How can an employee be a good parent under these conditions? Rigid working hours are particularly problematic for professionals in finance and consulting. They are frequently expected to be at work not only during regular business hours but also off-hours including weekends. It is a culture of inflated expectations. The problem is not limited to only professionals; low-wage workers in manufacturing and healthcare suffer too. In manufacturing, finding a skilled worker willing to staff a 12-h position is nearly impossible. Such rigid scheduling policies are tough on parents on the production line. Workers are penalized by demerits every time they miss a shift—even if they call in sick. After a few demerits they get fired. The same holds true for healthcare workers. One line-manager confided about the hardship saying, "I don't know how they do it. It is very much: Clock in at 7:00, clock out 3:30, with no exceptions."

Before the pandemic some eight in 10 companies offered flextime. Paradoxically, employees rarely took advantage of flextime even when it is offered. This may be because managers keep it under wraps. An HR manager at an advertising agency admitted that he doesn't publicize flexibility options for fear that "within minutes the line would be out the door and down the hall." The fact is that employee surveys show that most workers reported that they needed more flexibility. This was right before the pandemic.

Even when companies offer flexible scheduling, employees don't ask for it, fearing they'll be penalized if they do. The fear is when employees ask for flexible scheduling their managers tag them as unreliable and irresponsible. Managers view employees who take advantage of flexible scheduling as lacking commitment. Those employees end up with poor performance ratings, meager raises, and less-frequent promotions. Even after the pandemic, many managers continue to send the message that people who use this option of work-life balance will pay a price.

Source: Adapted from Kalev and Dobbin (2022).

6.2 Consequences of Schedule Flexibility

Not all consequences of schedule flexibility are positive—some are negative. As such, we will break down this discussion in terms of first positive and then negative consequences.

6.2.1 Positive Consequences

Under a flextime schedule, employees can decide what time they will arrive at and leave from work. When allowing flextime, employers commonly designate a specific time during which each employee must be present (Baltes et al., 1999).

Research has demonstrated that flexible schedule programs lead to several positive personal consequences. First, empirical studies found that flexible work schedules are associated with low work-to-life conflict (Anderson et al., 2002; Hill et al., 2001). This effect may be because flexible schedule programs provide employees with a sense of control over their workload and helps them easily respond to situations involving work-life conflict. If employees have the option to work on a flextime work schedule, they can make work demands and family demands more compatible; the result is less stress. For example, women are more likely to assume a larger share of the household chores and caretaker responsibilities, such as taking a child to the doctor's office. These responsibilities contribute to women's higher rates of absenteeism in the workplace. With a flextime schedule, it is possible to schedule family activities and doctor's appointments on the employees' flex day or make up the hours by working later, thereby reducing the need to take time off work to accommodate family responsibilities.

Anderson et al. (2002) conducted a survey of employees that examined the effects of work-family practices (e.g., work schedule flexibility) on work-family conflict. Respondents were asked if they are allowed to choose their starting and quitting times within some range of hours or change the starting and quitting times on a daily basis. The study found that schedule flexibility was negatively associated with work-family conflict; as such, it promotes work-life balance. Byron (2005) meta-analytic study involving eight studies found that schedule flexibility was significantly associated with less work-family conflict. The weighted average correlation was −0.30 for the relationship between schedule flexibility and work interference with family and −0.17 for the relationship between schedule flexibility and family interference with work.

Second, flexible schedule programs serve to reduce employee absenteeism. For example, employees can schedule personal appointments during normal business hours but make up for the missed work time later in the day (Kossek & Michel, 2011). Additionally, research has documented a link between participation in flexible schedule programs and employee stress (Grzywacz et al., 2008). Decreased employee stress associated with flexible schedule programs has been found to be associated with decreased absenteeism (Parker & Kulik, 1995). In a large-scale survey across industries, Grzywacz et al. (2008) examined the relationships among employee participation in formal flexible work arrangements, perceived flexibility, stress, and burnout. The results indicated that employees engaged in each type of formal flexible arrangement reported lower levels of stress and burnout compared to workers not engaged in these arrangements.

Third, evidence suggests that flexible schedule programs increase job satisfaction and organizational commitment among employees. Specifically, research demonstrates that the use of flexible work schedules increases job satisfaction (Allen, 2001; Baltes et al., 1999), increases organizational commitment, and reduces turnover intentions (Aryee et al., 1998; Batt & Valcour, 2003; Halpern, 2005; Houston & Waumsley, 2003; McNall et al., 2010). Consider the following study by McNall et al. (2010) which examined the relationship between the availability of flexible work arrangements (i.e., flextime and compressed workweek) and work-to-family enrichment and, in turn, the mediating role of work-to-family enrichment in the relationship between job satisfaction and turnover intentions. The survey, conducted among employed working adults, indicated that work-to-family enrichment mediated the relationship between flexible work arrangements and both job satisfaction and turnover intentions—after controlling for gender, age, marital status, education, number of children, and hours worked. In other words, schedule flexibility helps employees experience greater enrichment from work to home, which, in turn, is associated with higher job satisfaction and lower turnover intentions.

See Box 6.2 for how a company (The Gap) implemented a flexible scheduling program and reaped benefits.

Box 6.2 Flexible Scheduling at the Gap

In 2015, The Gap ran an experiment to figure out how much it would cost to make employees' schedules more predictable and flexible. The company ended their practice of "on-call shifts" and began providing work schedules 2 weeks in advance. The goal here is to increase predictability. To increase flexibility, the company offered "electronic shift-swapping"— managers were instructed to schedule consistent start and finish times whenever possible, add hours for part-timers who wanted them, and increase peak-hours staffing. The results were encouraging. After 9 months the company employees reported increased work-life balance— they were better able to deal with family demand. The newly instituted program improved employee morale and productivity. Notably, instead of costing the company money, the program was credited for a 7% increase in sales and 5% in labor productivity.

Source: Adapted from Kalev and Dobbin (2022).

6.2.2 Negative Consequences

Research has also uncovered the several negative personal consequences of flexible scheduling. First, flexible schedule programs may result in increased physical fatigue. Employees using the compressed workweek program must work longer hours, which may result in reduced alertness and burnout. Employees participating in a flexible work schedule are more likely to stay in connected via electronic communication during nonwork hours, even when it is outside of their flexible work hours, resulting in increased stress from always being "on" and work-to-nonwork conflict (Barley et al., 2011). Evidence also suggests that time spent on electronic communication is positively related to anger, which in turn adds to work-family conflict.

Second, employees participating in a compressed work schedule may find it difficult to meet non-work demands due to mental fatigue (Golden, 2010). In a compressed work schedule (4/40), employees usually work 10–12 h a day to have an extra day off per week. Mental fatigue may be one of the biggest downsides to a compressed workweek. In one company, those who worked 10–12 h in a single day experienced lower level of alertness, as one might expect (Bird, 2010).

Third, employees participating in a compressed work schedule may find it difficult to meet unexpected nonwork demand. Employees participating in flexible schedule programs may experience difficulties coordinating with increased work demand because of schedule unpredictability (McCrate, 2012). For some workers, *variable* hours may do far more to disrupt their ability to plan for activities such as childcare, family time, second jobs, school, and leisure. For example, a food service employee who is told at the beginning of each week what her hours will be for the next 5 days cannot plan very far in advance for her unscheduled hours. A nurse who must frequently be on call at the hospital faces a similar predicament. Precisely because flexible scheduling makes planning for time off very difficult, it may be even less desirable than a rigid but more routine schedule.

6.3 How Does Schedule Flexibility Produce Positive Outcomes

In this section, we will examine why flexible schedule programs result in positive personal consequences, which illustrates in what context flexible scheduling programs are likely to be most successful.

6.3.1 Perception of Control

Research indicates that flexible schedule programs provide employees with a greater sense of control over job demand and help them cope with non-work demands during regular work hours (Kossek & Ozeki, 1999). As such, we can assert that flexible work hours are likely to heighten employee perception of control over time and workload, which in turn may increase organizational commitment.

Specifically, employees often have other obligations outside of their organizational roles, and thus are sensitive to the compatibility among different life roles. Flexible work schedules can increase this compatibility because they allow employees to (a) more easily switch between day and evening shifts, (b) change the numbers of hours worked, and (c) configure the work schedule in ways to accommodate extra-organizational obligations. Therefore, flexible work schedules are likely to increase the perception of control and serve to reduce role conflict (Baltes et al., 1999; Krausz et al., 2000).

6.3.2 Person-Job Fit

Furthermore, research shows that flexible schedule programs increase employee productivity because they allow employees to work during their peak hours in terms of personal productivity (Shepard et al., 1996). Additionally, flexible schedule programs allow individuals to make more efficient use of their own circadian rhythms, the normal 24-h physiological sleep-wake cycle (Pierce & Newstrom, 1980).

In sum, flexible schedules reduce work-life conflict and stress by allowing employees to better meet their work and family needs. The programs promote increased work efficiency by allowing employees to work according to their individual circadian rhythms, increasing alertness. Flexible working hours also take advantage of the cyclical nature of individual productivity by allowing employees to work when during the time of day that they are usually most productive (Baltes et al., 1999; Pierce & Newstrom, 1980).

6.3.3 Reciprocity

Evidence suggests that flexible working arrangements signal that an organization cares about its employees. Flexible schedule programs may invoke the principle of reciprocity, wherein employees work extra hours during peak times in exchange for the ability to tailor their hours to suit their own personal needs at other times (McDonald et al., 2005. As a result, flexible working arrangements contribute to increased employee attitude and higher work performance (Allen, 2001; Baltes et al., 1999).

That is, work schedule flexibility is perceived by employees as a sign of organizational care, which then plays an important role in employees' perceptions of a quality relational exchange with employers. This positive exchange then elicits employee reciprocity that translates into increased organizational commitment.

6.4 Implementing a Schedule Flexibility Program

How can an organization's effectively implement a schedule flexibility program? There are many different variations of flexible scheduling, including flexible work time, compressed work week, absence autonomy, and an open rota system. We will discuss these in further detail below.

6.4.1 Flexible Work Time

Flexible work time allows employees to choose arrival and departure times that best fit their needs within the workday. Management can provide some parameters by setting a range of times that employees must stay within. Employees can select different starting and finishing times for each day (working from 10:30 a.m. to 7 p.m. instead of 8:30 a.m. to 5 p.m.) (Byron, 2005; Lewis & Cooper, 2005; Voydanoff, 2005; Wadsworth & Facer, 2016). This program is a divergence from the standard 40-h, 9 a.m. to 5 p.m. workweek, but still requires employees to work 38–40 h per week.

In contrast to non-traditional schedules established to meet business objectives (e.g., shift work), flexible schedules are work-family policies that are voluntary options available to employees. In this chapter, we discuss three different aspects of flexibility. The first two, fixed and variable flexible work schedules, are arrangements that reflect a schedule agreement between employees and supervisors. A *fixed* flexible schedule is one where start and end times are nontraditional, but they remain the same from week to week. For example, an employee might come to work at 7:00 a.m. and leave at 3:00 p.m. to be home in the afternoon to supervise school-age children. A *variable* flexible schedule allows employees to change their arrival and departure times from day-to-day or week-to-week (presumably the total number of hours per week remains constant). A third type of flexibility is the *occasional adjustment* made to a particular workday. Occasional adjustments might enable the employee to take care of personal or family responsibilities (e.g., taking an elderly relative to the doctor). This last type of flexibility is more periodic by nature and may or may not entail an explicit agreement between employee and their supervisor (Swanberg et al., 2005).

Employees in flexible schedule programs are often required to work during preset core hours, but they can select their own work hours outside of this. For example, a company has core hours between 9 a.m. and 3 p.m. The employees then have the choice to start anytime between 6:30 a.m. and 9 a.m., and the choice to leave anytime between 3:30 p.m. and 6 p.m., if they work 8 h. They also have a lunch break that lasts between 30 min to 1 h. Another variation requires employees to arrive between 7 a.m. and 9 a.m., have a minimum 30-min lunch break between 11 a.m. and 1 p.m., and finish between 3:30 p.m. and 6:30 p.m.—again provided 8 h are worked (Hicks & Klimoski, 1981).

The idea of allowing employees some choice in starting and quitting times was first introduced as a means of relieving transit and commuting problems. Flexible work time is a low-cost employee benefit that raises employee morale while enabling organizations to improve coverage and extend service hours. Flexible work time not only contributes to a reduction of paid absences and idle time on the job, but also serves to decrease the costs of utilities, maintenance, and security (Schmidt & Duenas, 2002).

Let's put this in perspective using Carol, who is an assistant professor at a research university and who has been struggling with work-life conflict in our previous examples. Carol's university— as is true for most research-type universities— has a flexible scheduling policy. In other words, faculty attend their scheduled classes and their scheduled committee meetings, yes; but they also have total autonomy in scheduling work related to their research projects and office hours—if they meet a certain number of required hours. For each.

6.4.2 Compressed Work Week

Another variation of flexible scheduling, compressed work week involves changes to the duration of shifts and shift patterns. That is, management can allow employees to compress their workweek into fewer than 5 days (Baltes et al., 1999; Lewis & Cooper, 2005). A compressed workweek schedule involves working longer shifts for fewer days of the week, rather than the traditional 8-h workday, 5 days per week. An employee can have every Friday off by working 10 h per day for 4 days (e.g., 4/10 schedule) or have every other Friday off by working 9 h per day over two weeks (e.g., 9/80 schedule).

In a 4/10 schedule, employees can work four 10-h days during a workweek and have Friday off (10 h *4 days = 40 h per week). Alternatively, employees can work 9 h from Monday to Thursday and work only 4 h on Friday (9 hours * 4 days + 4 h* 1 day = 40 h per week).

In a 9/80 schedule, employees work 9 h Monday to Thursday and one 8-h Friday (9 h * 4 days +8 h * 1 day = 44 h in the first week), and the employee has every other Friday off work over the 2 week period (9 h * 4 days = 36 h in the second week). In total, the employee works 40 hours over the period of 9 working days in 2 weeks.

In sum, the compressed work system allows employees to take an extra day off by working longer hours per day and employees can take care of personal matters during the additional day off.

Going back to Carol's case, the reader should note that most universities, especially research-type universities, not only have flexible scheduling but also compressed work week scheduling. The most common compressed work week configuration is a 4/10 schedule, working Monday through Thursday with Friday off. That is, classes are predominately scheduled on Mondays and Wednesdays and/

or Tuesdays and Thursdays. Classes are rarely scheduled on Fridays. This compressed week allows teaching faculty to use Fridays for either work or non-work-related tasks.

See Box 6.3 for a current look at the news concerning the compressed work week.

Box 6.3 How a 4-Day Workweek Actually Works

Compressed work week does not only mean compressing a 40-h workweek into 4 days but also reducing the number of work hours (i.e., 32 h of work a week). The 4-day, 32-h workweek is gaining ground. Consider the following. The United Auto Workers is currently negotiating with management to implement this program with Detroit automakers. Lawmakers in California and Massachusetts and other states in the U.S. are introducing bills to encourage businesses to adopt a 4-day work schedule.

Businesses that have adopted the shortened work week program report that their employees are happier and healthier. They also report less turnover, increased employee recruitment, with no loss in productivity. Given this trend, let's examine the nitty-gritty aspects of the program to see how it works.

Employees at *ThredUp*, an Oakland, Calif.-based online clothing reseller, say that the four-day workweek (Monday-to-Thursday week) is worth it. It gives them more time to recharge. The company implemented this program to its nearly 300 salaried employees. Doing so entailed culling meetings, focusing on the most important work, and curtailing lengthy email exchanges.

At Qwick, a company in the hospitality industry located in Phoenix Arizona, the results of implementing a shortened workweek program were also positive. However, management had to roll out a seven-day customer-support schedule and automate more processes. It also had to cancel many meetings and streamline others.

With this said, many companies that adopted the shortened workweek program are struggling "to put the theory into practice in a way that is productive." This is the case for ActivTrak, a maker of workforce analytics software with 158,000 employees at 1900 companies. A handful of large companies such as Unilever and Samsung have experimented with a shorter week on a limited basis, but most firms that adopted the program with successful results are much smaller.

It seems that the program has its good and bad. For example, Collective Campus, a corporate innovation and startup accelerator in Australia, tested the effectiveness of this program. The results based on a survey administered to employees indicate that the program served to increase employee emotional wellbeing. This is the "good" that came out of the program. In contrast, the "bad" is the fact that productivity, measured by revenue, marketing leads and other metrics, dropped 20%.

Source: Adapted from Fuhrmans (2023)

6.4.3 Absence Autonomy

What is "absence autonomy"? This concept refers to allowing employees to take time off when needed and make up that time on another day (Galinsky et al., 1993; Lewis & Cooper, 2005). For example, employees can take a break during the work week to attend a school function or doctor's appointment and make up the time lost later in the week—without using a day of annual or sick leave.

In some companies, employees have the flexibility to come and go as they please if they are digitally connected to the office. This type of autonomy allows employees to meet their family needs more effectively.

Going back to Carol, the academic, one should note that absence autonomy is part of the culture in higher-education institutions, if Carol is completing her research, teaching at an acceptable level, holding regular office hours, and attending required committee meetings, she is not required to physically be in her office on campus for 40 h per week.

6.4.4 Open-Rota System

The open-rota system is another type of flexible work program that is specifically formatted for shift work (Kilpatrick & Lavoie-Tremblay, 2006; Pryce et al., 2006; Voydanoff, 2005). The open-rota system is a self-scheduling shift program that provides shift employees with some degree of ownership and choice over their work-rest schedules. That is, employees select their preferred shifts, and substantial effort is made to accommodate those preferences. In an open-rota system, employees schedule their shift preferences and collectively decide and implement a monthly work schedule by adjusting their preferred schedules to make a cohesive master schedule. The ability to choose their own work schedule gives employees a feeling of control and autonomy over their work schedule, which in turn boosts work-life balance.

Consider the following study by Pryce et al. (2006) which surveyed nurses to examine the benefits of the open-rota system. Within this system, employees were asked to input their shift preferences into an open rota, or roster. When doing so, they were further asked to do so responsibly and fairly by considering the needs and preferences of others. One or two employees were responsible for fine-tuning the plan, and this responsibility was rotated each week between the staff. Nurses who used the open-rota system reported that they were more satisfied with their work hours, less likely to swap their shift when working within the open-rota system, and reported significant increases in work-life balance, job satisfaction, social support, and community spirit when compared with nurses in the control group.

Table 6.1 Factors moderating the effectiveness of schedule flexibility policies and programs

Type of moderator	Specific conditions
Personal moderators	Employees with family responsibilities Female employees Employees experiencing high levels of work-family conflict Lower-level employees with limited autonomy and flexibility
Program/organizational moderators	Program availability Conjoint effects of flexible schedule and flexible place No reduction in employee income
Environmental moderators	Individualistic cultures

6.5 Under What Conditions Is a Schedule Flexibility Program Most Effective

In this section we will discuss several factors that moderate the effectiveness of schedule flexibility on work-life balance (WLB). These factors are categorized as personal moderators, program/organizational moderators, and environmental moderators. See Table 6.1 for a summary of these factors.

6.5.1 *Personal Moderators*

Research has shown that flexible schedule programs are more effective in contributing to WLB in the presence of one or all of the following conditions: (1) employees with family responsibilities, (2) female employees, (3) employees experiencing high levels of work-family conflict, and (4) lower-level employees with limited autonomy and flexibility.

Flexible schedule programs are effective for those employees *with family responsibilities*. Research has shown that availability of flexible schedule policies is associated with employee loyalty for those employees with family responsibilities (Roehling et al., 2001). Research has also demonstrated that the existence of a flexible work hour program is associated with increased job satisfaction and organizational commitment for all employees with family responsibilities, regardless of whether flexible scheduling is being utilized (Nelson et al., 1990; Scandura & Lankau, 1997). Flexible scheduling serves to reduce work-family conflict by facilitating one's ability to attend to family matters without breaching work obligations (Shockley & Allen, 2007). Daytime family-related activities (e.g., doctor's appointments, teacher conferences, extracurricular events) that are made difficult by standard work arrangements are facilitated by flexible schedule programs. For this reason, those with a great deal of family responsibility stand to gain from flexible scheduling. Shockley and Allen (2007) surveyed a group of working women and found that flexible schedule programs lower work-family conflicts for *those with a high family responsibility*. For those employees with lower family responsibility, however, the study found no relationship between flexible schedule programs and work-life conflict. This may be because employees with low family responsibility experience little or no work-family conflict.

Evidence also suggests that flextime reduces work-family conflict (Casper & Harris, 2008) and enhances both organizational commitment and job satisfaction (Scandura & Lankau, 1997), much more so for *women* than for *men*. In other words, research shows that schedule flexibility is more strongly associated with decreased stress (Jang et al., 2012) and reduced work-family conflict (Carlson et al., 2010) for female workers than for male workers. Using a sample of 607 full-time employees who participated in either schedule flexibility or traditional working arrangements, Carlson et al. (2010) tested whether gender moderates the effect of schedule flexibility on work-family conflicts. They hypothesized that the negative effect of schedule flexibility on work-family conflict would be greater for women than for men. The results indicated that gender did moderate the effect of schedule flexibility on work-family conflict such that women benefited more from flexible working arrangements than men. This can be explained by the fact that women more often have greater household responsibilities than men and women with young children experience a high degree work-family conflict and stress (cf. Hill et al., 2008).

As we have explored, flexible schedule programs are effective for *those experiencing work-family conflict*. Flexible schedule programs provide employees with resources to better cope with family conflict. Flexible work scheduling allows employees experiencing work-family conflict to conserve or accrue more useful resources to better cope with family conflict (Lambert, 2000). Increased flexibility of temporal boundaries eases transitioning between roles. Another individual wants to fulfill their parental role by coaching their child's little league games at 4 p.m. and would be unable to do so if working a traditional workday. However, the temporal flexibility afforded by flexible work scheduling, they can arrive at work early and leave early to make this role transition (Rau & Hyland, 2002). As such, individuals with high levels of work-family conflict tend to prefer flexible work schedule programs (Rau & Hyland, 2002).

Studies have documented the effectiveness of flexible scheduling with *employees with limited autonomy and flexibility* (e.g., lower-level employees). Providing employee control over scheduling variation (flextime) may benefit lower-level workers the most (Kossek & Lautsch, 2018). In other words, the positive effect of flextime on WLB is greater for those with limited autonomy in their job. For example, managers and professionals may be less affected by schedule interventions than entry-level employees (i.e., blue-collar, administrative support, service employees, etc.), particularly if they already possess a large amount of autonomy regarding their work schedules before the introduction of a flexible schedule. The results of a meta-analysis by Baltes et al. (1999) indicate that flextime work schedules demonstrated positive effects on work-related outcomes for general employees, whereas they had no effect on high-level professionals and managers. Likely because flexible work schedules are unlikely to benefit those who already have a high degree of work autonomy and perceived control. It is important to allow employees to participate in the development of flexible work programs and allow them to choose schedules that best fit their family needs.

6.5.2 Program/Organizational Moderators

Research suggests that flexible scheduling in an organization is more effective when the program has the following characteristics: (1) program availability, (2) conjoint effects of flexible schedule and flexible place, (3) no reduction in employee income.

Research indicates that availability of a flexible schedule program in an organization has a stronger positive effect on WLB than actual use of the program. The simple presence of the program provides employees with a sense of control over job and family demand. Consider the study by Hill et al. (2010). Through a large-scale survey of IBM workers administered in 75 countries ($n = 24{,}436$), these researchers found that paid-work hours contribute to work-life conflict (beta =0.35, $p < 0.05$), but both schedule flexibility and workplace flexibility significantly reduce work-life conflict. They also found that perceived work schedule flexibility (beta = –0.268, $p < 0.05$) was a stronger predictor of work-life conflict than workplace flexibility (beta = −0.172, $p < 0.05$). Similarly, another study by Shockley and Allen (2007) found that flextime is more effective in reducing work-life-conflict than flexplace. Specifically, using a sample of employed women, these researchers found that schedule flexibility relates more highly to work interference with family than to family interference with work. They also found that flexible work schedule has a stronger negative relationship with work-family conflict than flexible workplace.

Research also indicates that a compressed workweek is effective only when the *program does not decrease total number of work hours and resulting income* (Lazar et al., 2010). As such, a compressed work week arrangement may be particularly useful for employees who wish to reduce the number of days per week spent at work but cannot financially afford to decrease their working hours. Specifically, a compressed workweek can be beneficial for employees in terms of additional days off work (e.g., longer weekends allowing more breaks) and reduced commuting time. Such an arrangement also benefits employers by allowing them to extend their daily operating hours with less need to resort to overtime.

6.5.3 Environmental Moderators

Research suggests that flexible schedule programs are more effective in countries with an *individualistic culture*. Flextime availability is positively associated with job satisfaction in individualistic countries but not in collectivistic countries. Consider the following study by Masuda et al. (2012). These researchers examined the effect of flexible work arrangements on outcome variables (e.g., job satisfaction, turnover intentions, and reduced work-to-family conflict) across individualist countries (Anglo counties) and collectivist countries (Asian and Latin American countries). The results indicate that managers in individualistic (i.e., Anglo) countries were generally more likely to report working in companies that offer flextime and compressed working week compared with managers in collectivistic (i.e., Asian and Latin American) countries. These results stress the importance of examining the impact of culture on adoption of flexible schedule programs. Employees in an individualistic culture tend to value their privacy and independence in meeting role demand. The results also indicate that flextime had significant favorable relationships with the outcome variables for Anglo managers. Yet, flextime was unrelated to time-based work-family conflict for collectivist countries. This can be explained by the fact that employees in an individualistic culture are more likely to experience high levels of work-life conflict, partly because they usually fail to receive (or simply do not seek) assistance from close relatives such as grandparents and siblings (Spector et al., 2007). As such, flexible schedule programs are more effective for employees in individualistic countries than employees in collectivistic cultures.

6.6 Summary and Conclusion

What is a flexible work schedule program or policy? We defined it as an organizational initiative that enables employees to set their own working hours, negotiated between the employee and employer.

Research has shown that there are numerous benefits to flexible scheduling, as well as some negative outcomes. With respect to the positive consequences, evidence suggests that a flexible work schedule is associated with low work-to-life conflict. This effect is attributed to the possibility that such a program provides employees with a sense of control over their workload; as such, the program helps them easily respond to work-life conflict. There is also evidence suggesting that scheduling flexibility serves to reduce employee absenteeism, reduce employee stress, increase job satisfaction, and increase organizational commitment.

With respect to the program's negative consequences, research has shown that flexible schedules may result in physical fatigue due to working longer hours. Physical fatigue can lead to reduced alertness, burnout, increased stress, and work-to-nonwork conflict. Moreover, flexible scheduling could backfire in the sense that employees may find it more difficult to meet non-work demand due to the less predictable nature of flexible scheduling. Additionally, organizations implementing flexible schedule programs may experience coordination difficulties with increased cost.

Flexible schedule programs also result in positive personal consequences because such programs serve to enhance employee perception of control, allow employees to choose to work during their peak hours of personal productivity, make more efficient use of their circadian rhythms, and signal that the organization cares about its employees.

There are a variety of different types of flexible scheduling. Flexible schedule programs can be implemented through flexible work time (e.g., employees can select different start and end times for each day), a compressed work week (i.e., employees can compress the workweek into fewer than 5 days while still maintaining a 40 h week), absence autonomy (i.e., allowing employees to take time off when needed and make up the time later), and an open rota system (i.e., employees designing their own work-rest schedule, choice of the length, and timing of lunch breaks).

We then discussed factors that moderate the effectiveness of schedule flexibility on WLB in terms of personal, program, and environmental moderators. With respect to personal moderators, research has found that schedule flexibility programs are more suited for employees with family responsibilities, female employees, those experiencing high levels of work-family conflict, and lower-level employees with limited autonomy and flexibility.

With respect to program/organizational moderators, the effectiveness of schedule flexibility programs can be enhanced when a given program is perceived to be available to all employees within the organization, when a flextime program is conjoined with a flexplace program, and when the program is configured in ways to prevent income loss for the participants.

With respect to environmental moderators, research suggests that flexible schedule programs are more effective in countries with an individualistic culture compared to a collectivist one. This is attributed to the possibility that employees in an individualistic culture are likely to experience high levels of work-life conflict and low levels of familial support because they usually fail to receive (or simply do not seek) assistance from close relatives such as grandparents and siblings.

See Box 6.4 for "practical recommendations" from practitioners.

Box 6.4 Practical Recommendations from Industry Practitioners About Schedule Flexibility

Many employers are replacing the 9-to-5 model and a model allowing employees to choose their own hours. Employers are recognizing that the workday is no longer one-size-fits-all. Employees are likely to be more productive early in the morning or later in the day. Flexible work hours allow employees to choose arrival and departure times that best fit their needs. Management can provide some parameters by setting a range of times that employees must stay within. This flexibility can be an invaluable strategy for employees to achieve work-life balance.

For effective implementation of flextime practices, managers should communicate to their team members that they don't have a daily punch clock. But of course, managers should expect their staff to get their work done. Also, managers should communicate to their employees that it's their responsibility to finish their tasks within the allotted time. Managers might also consider implementing "summer hours" where employees could work half-days on certain Fridays, especially during the holiday seasons.

In sum, employees are highly motivated to work harder and better when they're allowed to dictate their own hours.

Source: Adapted from https://www.frontstream.com/blog/work-life-balance-strategies

In the next chapter, we will analyze research related to flexible workplace programs. Specifically, we will discuss the positive and negative consequences associated with this WLB practice. We will also describe how this practice helps employees achieve WLB followed by a discussion on how organizations commonly implement this practice. Finally, we will discuss those conditions that influence the overall effectiveness of this WLB practice.

References

Allen, T. D. (2001). Family-supportive work environments: The role of organizational perceptions. *Journal of Vocational Behavior, 58*(3), 414–435.

Anderson, S. E., Coffey, B. S., & Byerly, R. T. (2002). Formal organizational initiatives and informal workplace practices: Links to work-family conflict and job-related outcomes. *Journal of Management, 28*(6), 787–810.

Aryee, S., Luk, V., & Stone, R. (1998). Family-responsive variables and retention-relevant outcomes among employed parents. *Human Relations, 51*(1), 73–87.

Baltes, B. B., Briggs, T. E., Huff, J. W., Wright, J. A., & Neuman, G. A. (1999). Flexible and compressed workweek schedules: A meta-analysis of their effects on work-related criteria. *Journal of Applied Psychology, 84*(4), 496–513.

Barley, S. R., Meyerson, D. E., & Grodal, S. (2011). E-mail as a source and symbol of stress. *Organization Science, 22*(4), 887–906.

Batt, R., & Valcour, P. M. (2003). Human resources practices as predictors of work-family outcomes and employee turnover. *Industrial Relations, 42*(2), 189–220.

Bird, R. C. (2010). The four-day work week: Old lessons, new questions. *Connecticut Law Review, 42*(4), 1059–1080.

Byron, K. (2005). A meta-analytic review of work-family conflict and its antecedents. *Journal of Vocational Behavior, 67*(2), 169–198.

Carlson, D. S., Grzywacz, J. G., & Kacmar, K. M. (2010). The relationship of schedule flexibility and outcomes via the work-family interface. *Journal of Managerial Psychology, 25*(4), 330–355.

Casper, W. J., & Harris, C. M. (2008). Work-life benefits and organizational attachment: Self-interest utility and signaling theory models. *Journal of Vocational Behavior, 72*(1), 95–109.

Fuhrmans, V. (2023). How a four-day workweek actually works, from the companies pulling it off: Few meetings, busier days and other ways to fit a week's work into 32 hours. *The Wall Street Journal*, September 25, 2023 Retrieved from September 28, 2023 https://www.wsj.com/lifestyle/careers/how-a-4-day-workweek-actually-works-from-the-companies-pulling-it-off-1a5c0e2a

Galinsky, E., Bond, J. T., & Friedman, D. E. (1993). *The changing workforce: Highlights of the national study*. Diane Publishing.

Golden, L. (2010). A purpose for every time? The timing and length of the work week and implications for worker well-being. *Connecticut Law Review, 42*(4), 53–74.

Grzywacz, J. G., Carlson, D. S., & Shulkin, S. (2008). Schedule flexibility and stress: Linking formal flexible arrangements and perceived flexibility to employee health. *Community, Work and Family, 11*(2), 199–214.

Halpern, D. F. (2005). How time-flexible work policies can reduce stress, improve health, and save money. *Stress and Health, 21*(3), 157–168.

Hicks, W. D., & Klimoski, R. J. (1981). The impact of flexitime on employee attitudes. *Academy of Management Journal, 24*(2), 333–341.

Hill, E. J., Erickson, J. J., Holmes, E. K., & Ferris, M. (2010). Workplace flexibility, work hours, and work-life conflict: Finding an extra day or two. *Journal of Family Psychology, 24*(3), 349–358.

Hill, E. J., Hawkins, A. J., Ferris, M., & Weitzman, M. (2001). Finding an extra day a week: The positive influence of perceived job flexibility on work and family life balance. *Family Relations, 50*(1), 49–58.

Hill, E. J., Jacob, J. I., Shannon, L. L., Brennan, R. T., Blanchard, V. L., & Martinengo, G. (2008). Exploring the relationship of workplace flexibility, gender, and life stage to family-to-work conflict, and stress and burnout. *Community, Work and Family, 11*(2), 165–181.

Houston, D. M., & Waumsley, J. A. (2003). *Attitudes to flexible working and family life*. Policy Press.

Jang, S., Zippay, A., & Park, R. (2012). Family roles as moderators of the relationship between schedule flexibility and stress. *Journal of Marriage and Family, 74*(4), 897–912.

Kalev, A., & Dobbin, F. (2022). The surprising benefits of work/life support. *Harvard Business Review* (September-October). https://hbr.org/2022/09/the-surprising-benefits-of-work-life-support

Kilpatrick, K., & Lavoie-Tremblay, M. (2006). Shiftwork: What health care managers need to know. *The Health Care Manager, 25*(2), 160–166.

Kossek, E. E., & Lautsch, B. A. (2018). Work-life flexibility for whom? Occupational status and work-life inequality in upper, middle, and lower-level jobs. *Academy of Management Annals, 12*(1), 5–36.

Kossek, E. E., & Michel, J. S. (2011). Flexible work schedules. In S. Zedeck (Ed.), *APA handbook of industrial and organizational psychology* (*Building and developing the organization*) (Vol. 1, pp. 535–572). American Psychological Association.

Kossek, E. E., & Ozeki, C. (1999). Bridging the work-family policy and productivity gap: A literature review. *Community, Work & Family, 2*(1), 7–32.

Krausz, M., Sagie, A., & Bidermann, Y. (2000). Actual and preferred work schedules and scheduling control as determinants of job-related attitudes. *Journal of Vocational Behavior, 56*(1), 1–11.

Lambert, S. J. (2000). Added benefits: The link between work-life benefits and organizational citizenship behavior. *Academy of Management Journal, 43*(5), 801–815.

Lazar, I., Osoian, C., & Ratiu, P. (2010). The role of WLB practices in order to improve organizational performance. *European Research Studies Journal, 13*(1), 201–214.

Lewis, S., & Cooper, C. (2005). *Work-life integration: Case studies of organisational change*. John Wiley & Sons.

Masuda, A. D., Poelmans, S. A., Allen, T. D., Spector, P. E., Lapierre, L. M., Cooper, C. L., et al. (2012). Flexible work arrangements availability and their relationship with work-to-family conflict, job satisfaction, and turnover intentions: A comparison of three country clusters. *Applied Psychology, 61*(1), 1–29.

McCrate, E. (2012). Flexibility for whom? Control over work schedule variability in the US. *Feminist Economics, 18*(1), 39–72.

McDonald, P., Guthrie, D., Bradley, L., & Shakespeare-Finch, J. (2005). Investigating work-family policy aims and employee experiences. *Employee Relations, 27*(5), 478–494.

McNall, L. A., Nicklin, J. M., & Masuda, A. D. (2010). A meta-analytic review of the consequences associated with work-family enrichment. *Journal of Business and Psychology, 25*(3), 381–396.

Nelson, D. L., Quick, J. C., Hitt, M. A., & Moesel, D. (1990). Politics, lack of career progress, and work/home conflict: Stress and strain for working women. *Sex Roles, 23*(3), 169–185.

Parker, P. A., & Kulik, J. A. (1995). Burnout, self-and supervisor-rated job performance, and absenteeism among nurses. *Journal of Behavioral Medicine, 18*(6), 581–599.

Pierce, J. L., & Newstrom, J. W. (1980). Toward a conceptual clarification of employee responses to flexible working hours: A work adjustment approach. *Journal of Management, 6*(2), 117–134.

Pryce, J., Albertsen, K., & Nielsen, K. (2006). Evaluation of an open-Rota system in a Danish psychiatric hospital: A mechanism for improving job satisfaction and work-life balance. *Journal of Nursing Management, 14*(4), 282–288.

Rau, B. L., & Hyland, M. A. M. (2002). Role conflict and flexible work arrangements: The effects on applicant attraction. *Personnel Psychology, 55*(1), 111–136.

Roehling, P. V., Roehling, M. V., & Moen, P. (2001). The relationship between work-life policies and practices and employee loyalty: A life course perspective. *Journal of Family and Economic Issues, 22*(2), 141–170.

Scandura, T. A., & Lankau, M. J. (1997). Relationships of gender, family responsibility and flexible work hours to organizational commitment and job satisfaction. *Journal of Organizational Behavior, 18*(4), 377–391.

Schmidt, D. E., & Duenas, G. (2002). Incentives to encourage worker-friendly organizations. *Public Personnel Management, 31*(3), 293–308.

Shepard, E. M., Clifton, T. J., & Kruse, D. (1996). Flexible work hours and productivity: Some evidence from the pharmaceutical industry. *Industrial Relations, 35*(1), 123–139.

Shockley, K. M., & Allen, T. D. (2007). When flexibility helps: Another look at the availability of flexible work arrangements and work-family conflict. *Journal of Vocational Behavior, 71*(3), 479–493.

Spector, P. E., Allen, T. D., Poelmans, S. A., Lapierre, L. M., Cooper, C. L., Michael, O. D., et al. (2007). Cross-national differences in relationships of work demands, job satisfaction, and turnover intentions with work-family conflict. *Personnel Psychology, 60*(4), 805–835.

Swanberg, J. E., Pitt-Catsouphes, M., & Drescher-Burke, K. (2005). A question of justice: Disparities in employees' access to flexible schedule arrangements. *Journal of Family Issues, 26*(6), 866–895.

Thomas, L. T., & Ganster, D. C. (1995). Impact of family-supportive work variables on work-family conflict and strain: A control perspective. *Journal of Applied Psychology, 80*(1), 6–15.

Voydanoff, P. (2005). Consequences of boundary-spanning demands and resources for work-to-family conflict and perceived stress. *Journal of Occupational Health Psychology, 10*(4), 491–503.

Wadsworth, L. L., & Facer, R. L. (2016). Work-family balance and alternative work schedules: Exploring the impact of 4-day workweeks on state employees. *Public Personnel Management, 45*(4), 382–404.

Chapter 7
Flexible Workplace

"No is a complete sentence."—Anne Lamont (https://teambuilding.com/blog/work-life-balance-quotes)

Abstract In this chapter we describe the research related to flexible workplace policies and programs. Specifically, we discuss the positive and negative consequences associated with work-life balance (WLB) practices: employee and organizational wellbeing outcomes. We also explain how this WLB practices contribute to employee and organizational wellbeing in terms of reduced employee cost of working, time savings, perceived autonomy, boundary flexibility, signaling management trust and support for employees, and comfort and ambiance of the new workplace. We then describe how this WLB strategy is commonly implemented through telecommuting, working from home, and e-working. Finally, we discuss those conditions (personal, organizational, and environmental conditions) that influence the overall effectiveness of this WLB practice.

7.1 Introduction

This chapter focuses on the concept of flexible workplace and its effects on work-life balance (WLB). Specifically, we will define flexible workplace practices and evaluate both the positive and negative consequences of this practice. We will also explain how flexible workplace programs impact WLB and those conditions that make such programs more effective—personal, program, organizational, and environmental conditions.

Before we begin, we must define flexible workplace programs. Flexible workplace refers to any form of work conducted during normal business hours but performed outside of the physical workplace. Flexible workplace arrangements include telecommuting, home working, and e-working (e.g., Kossek et al., 2006; McCarthy et al., 2010). That is, flexible workplace arrangements involve working from a

D.-J. Lee, M. J. Sirgy, *Organizational Strategies for Work-Life Balance*, Human Well-Being Research and Policy Making,
https://doi.org/10.1007/978-3-031-56314-0_7

variety of alternative locations outside of a physical office including full-time work from home, remote work, virtual work, among others (Allen et al., 2015).

7.2 Consequences of Flexible Workplace Programs

As we saw when we examined schedule flexibility programs, not all consequences of flexible workplace are positive—though some are. As such, we will break down this discussion in terms of positive and negative consequences.

7.2.1 *Positive Consequences*

Research shows that flexible workplace programs (e.g., telecommuting) produce the following positive personal consequences:

Flexible workplace programs (e.g., telecommuting) have been proven to increase *job performance* (Allen et al., 2003; Gajendran & Harrison, 2007; Kossek et al., 2006; Martin & MacDonnell, 2012). For example, Martin and MacDonnell (2012) meta-analysis of 32 correlations across empirical studies found a small but positive relationship between telework and organizational outcomes. Telework appears to increase employee productivity, secure employee retention, strengthen organizational commitment, and improve job performance.

Evidence also demonstrates that flexible workplace programs (e.g., telecommuting) increases *employee productivity* (Allen et al., 2003; Gajendran & Harrison, 2007; Hill et al., 1998; Martin & MacDonnell, 2012). Increased employee productivity is regularly reported as a perceived benefit of telework. Reasons cited include working at peak efficiency hours, fewer distractions and interruptions, being in an environment conducive to increased concentration, and reducing incidental absence.

Flexible workplace programs also increase *organizational commitment* and *employee retention* (Allen et al., 2003; Gajendran & Harrison, 2007; Kossek et al., 2006; Martin & MacDonnell, 2012). The positive association between flexible workplace programs and organizational commitment may be attributed to the reciprocal relationship between employees who perceive that management cares about them by offering workplace flexibility programs. For example, Martin and MacDonnell (2012) meta-analysis found that flexible work programs (e.g., telework) is positively correlated with organizational commitment ($r = 0.10$, 95% CI = [0.03, 0.18]).

Evidence also suggests that flexible workplace programs increase *employee morale* and *job satisfaction* (Allen et al., 2003; Gajendran & Harrison, 2007; Hill et al., 2010; Kossek et al., 2006; Raghuram & Wiesenfeld, 2004). For example, Gajendran and Harrison (2007) meta-analysis analyzing different 19 studies found that telecommuting was positively related to job satisfaction. This beneficial relationship appeared to be at least partially mediated by perceived autonomy. It should also be noted that the relationship between the extent of telecommuting and job satisfaction may be curvilinear—meaning that satisfaction and amount of telecommuting are positively related at lower levels of telecommuting, but satisfaction plateaus at higher levels of telecommuting (around 15.1 h per week). The explanation for this curvilinear effect may lie in the social and professional isolation that telecommuters face when telecommuting frequently (Allen et al., 2015).

More evidence suggests that flexible workplace programs decrease *work-life conflict* (Allen et al., 2003; Gajendran & Harrison, 2007; Hill et al., 2010; Kossek et al., 2006; Martin & MacDonnell, 2012). For example, Gajendran and Harrison (2007) meta-analysis of 19 studies found telecommuting was related to less work-family conflict with an effect size of 0.13. In addition, telecommuting is reported to also be associated with lower *work-role stress* ($r = -0.11$, 95% CI = [−0.15, −0.07]) (Gajendran & Harrison, 2007). Kossek et al. (2006) found that remote e-workers who had strong boundaries between work and family as well as control over where and when they teleworked, reported positive *individual wellbeing*.

7.2.2 *Negative Consequences*

There are also several negative personal consequences of flexible work programs (e.g., telecommuting, working from home).

Research has shown that although flexible workplace programs are designed to decrease *work-life conflict*, they may backfire by leading to high work-family conflict due to increased work hours and blurred boundaries between work and family roles (e.g., Allen et al., 2013, 2015; Golden et al., 2006; Schieman & Young, 2010). Working from home may actually increase family demands on the remote worker, thereby increasing opportunities for family-work conflict. For example, the telecommuter may be expected to deal with home-repair workers, daytime appointments, errands, and so on due to their presence at home. Thus, to realize the benefits of flexible workplace programs, it is important for individuals who work from home to establish clear boundaries and expectations with family and friends (Allen et al., 2015).

There is also evidence that flexible workplace programs can cause *social isolation*. Flexible workplace programs can weaken social bonds with coworkers or supervisors, which may result in career stagnation (Baruch & Nicholson, 1997; Golden, 2006; Nardi & Whittaker, 2002). Gajendran and Harrison (2007) meta-analysis found that telecommuting does not affect coworker relationship quality under low-intensity telecommuting arrangements ($r = 0.03$, 95% CI = [0.01, 0.07]), but it has a negative effect under high-intensity arrangements ($r = -0.19$, 95% CI = [−0.30, −0.08]). In addition, Golden (2007) found that a higher prevalence of teleworkers in an organization is associated with less satisfaction between teleworkers and employees not engaged in any flexible workplace programs.

Despite arguments that flexible workplace arrangements can save commuting time, save energy, and contribute to work-life balance, they can also increase *workload* and work hours (Noonan & Glass, 2012). Flexible workplace arrangements are only possible due to the extensive use of technology, which often causes work time to intrude into home time. Digital connectivity increases pressure to work more hours and to be available outside of normal working hours. For example, working-at-home arrangements can have disadvantageous side effects because they blur the boundaries between family and work, thus increasing work-family conflict (Desrochers et al., 2005; Peters & Van der Lippe, 2007). E-working is often associated with overworking due to communication overload (Grant et al., 2019). For example, based on data from the nationally representative National Longitudinal Survey of Youth and special supplements from the U.S. Census Current Population Survey, Noonan and Glass (2012) reported that the probability of working overtime is higher for telecommuters than for non-telecommuters. This is attributed to the increased prevalence of technology causing the penetration of work into home life.

There are negative organizational consequences associated with flexible workspaces as well. As previously stated, flexible workplace programs tend to result in limited *interactions with co-workers and managemen*t. Changing one's workplace from a conventional office to a home or an alternate location is likely to reduce the frequency and quality of knowledge sharing that one typically experiences in an office (Gajendran & Harrison, 2007; Golden & Raghuram, 2010). As such, these flexible workplaces may reduce *citizenship behaviors*. That is, employees taking advantage of a flexible work program may be less available to provide the discretionary help and support critical for dealing with the many spontaneous workplace demands that cannot be anticipated or incorporated into formal job descriptions (Elsbach et al., 2010). Furthermore, flexible workplace programs can reduce *organizational commitment*. The physical isolation that can come from working remotely is correlated with feeling less respected by the organization, which weakens *organizational identification and commitment* (Bartel et al., 2012). Specifically, the increased physical isolation stemming from flexible workplace programs reduces *opportunities to observe prototypical members* (i.e., employees who are socially attractive and competent) in the organization. As such, employees taking advantage of flexible workplace policies are unlikely to gain the respect and friendship of coworkers, which in turn reduces *organizational identification*. Through two field studies using survey methods, Bartel et al. (2012) found that physical isolation is negatively associated with respect for other organization members, which in turn reduces organizational identification and commitment.

To reduce possible negative consequences of flexible workplace programs, it is important for those employees in flexible places to establish clear boundaries and make a diligent effort to reduce family-to-work interference (Allen et al., 2015). It is also important for employees in flexible workplaces to frequently interact with other members of the organization to prevent social isolation. Managers should provide opportunities for employees in flexible workplace programs to socially interact with one another virtually and strengthen shared organizational values.

Table 7.1 Theories explaining the work-life balance impact of flexible workplace

Theories of flexible workplace	Brief description
Reduced employee cost of working	Flexible workplace programs serve to reduce the cost of working to the employee through cost savings (e.g., transportation costs). They also serve to increase temporal resources (i.e., time) to meet family demands
Time savings	Flexible workplace programs increase job performance and productivity through increased work hours made possible by time saved from not commuting. In addition, flexible workplace programs can increase extra-role behaviors
Perceived autonomy	Flexible workplace programs serve to enhance actual and perceived job autonomy. They do so by providing employees with a choice over the location and means of work
Boundary flexibility	Flexible workplace programs enhance employee's boundary flexibility—the degree to which the location of work is under the employee's control. Increased boundary flexibility helps employees regulate and synchronize demands between work and family and, potentially, reduce work-family conflict
Signaling management trust and support for employees	By providing employees with the flexibility to work from home, management sends a positive signal, visibly demonstrating trust and support for employee wellbeing
Comfort and ambiance of the new workplace	Working from home is comfortable because it has all the amenities of home and possibly the aesthetic qualities of the home

7.3 How Does Flexible Workplace Help with Work-Life Balance

There are also a variety of ways in which flexible workplace programs play an important role in creating work-life balance, which include: (1) reduced employee cost of working, (2) time savings, (3) perceived autonomy, (4) boundary flexibility, (5) signaling management trust and support for employees, and (6) comfort and ambiance of the new workplace. See Table 7.1 for a summary of these theories.

7.3.1 Reduced Employee Cost of Working

Flexible workplace programs serve to reduce the cost of working to the employee. They do so via cost savings (e.g., transportation costs) (Gajendran & Harrison, 2007). Flexible workplace programs also serve to increase temporal resources (i.e., time) that are used to meet family demand (Greenhouse & Buetel, 1985).

Specifically, benefits to employees in flexible workplace programs include decreased *transportation costs*, decreased *commuting time*, decreased cost of formal wear, increased control over work environments, and increased flexibility. Flexible workplaces allow workers to do the work when they are the most productive. That is, flexible workplace programs enable individuals to manage resources, such as time, more effectively and allocate them in a way that enhances performance outcomes (Golden, 2006).

7.3.2 Time Savings

Evidence suggests that flexible workplace programs increase *job performance* and *productivity* (Allen et al., 2003; Gajendran & Harrison, 2007; Kossek et al., 2006; Martin & MacDonnell, 2012). Flexible workplace programs increase job performance and productivity through increased work hours made possible by time saved from not commuting. In addition, flexible workplace programs (e.g., virtual work) can increase extra-role behaviors (Gajendran et al., 2015; Gajendran & Harrison, 2007).

Specifically, a meta-analysis by Gajendran and Harrison (2007) has suggested that telecommuting is positively associated with supervisor-rated or objectively measured job performance ($r = 0.18$, $p < 0.05$). In addition, research showed that supervisor-rated task and contextual performance were evaluated as higher for telecommuters than for non-telecommuters (Gajendran et al., 2015). However the reader should note that the correlation between telecommuting and self-rated job performance is not significant (Gajendran & Harrison, 2007). The authors explained that this may be because telecommuting—although it has certain benefits (autonomy, time savings, and efficiency)—it also leads to social isolation and limits on information sharing.

7.3.3 Perceived Autonomy

Flexible workplace programs tend to enhance actual and perceived job autonomy. They do so by providing employees with a choice over the location and means of work (DuBrin, 1991; Standen et al., 1999). Employees taking advantage of flexible workplace programs are also likely to experience increased feelings of freedom and discretion because they are spatially and psychologically removed from direct, face-to-face supervision (DuBrin, 1991).

Research has demonstrated that telecommuters report a higher level of perceived autonomy than non-telecommuters (Gajendran et al., 2015; Gajendran & Harrison, 2007). In their meta-analytic study, Gajendran and Harrison (2007) found that autonomy fully mediated the relationship between telecommuting and job satisfaction, and partially mediated the relationships between telecommuting and supervisor-rated performance, turnover intent, and role stress. They conclude that flexible workplace programs tend to enhance actual and perceived job autonomy.

7.3.4 Boundary Flexibility

Flexible workplace programs enhance employee's boundary flexibility—the degree to which the location of work is under the employee's control (Ashforth et al., 2000). Increased boundary flexibility helps employees regulate and synchronize demands between work and family and, potentially, reduce work-family conflict (Kirchmeyer, 1995).

Evidence suggests that teleworking often increases the permeability of the boundary between work and family domains (Crosbie & Moore, 2004). As such, increased boundary flexibility allows employees to schedule work optimally to minimize interference from family. In sum, flexible workplace programs can enhance employee's boundary flexibility.

7.3.5 Signaling Management Trust and Support for Employees

Evidence suggests that flexible workplace programs increase organizational commitment and retention (Allen et al., 2003; Gajendran & Harrison, 2007; Kossek et al., 2006; Martin & MacDonnell, 2012). By providing employees with the flexibility to work from home, management sends a positive signal, visibly demonstrating trust and support for employee wellbeing. This signal, in turn, contributes to increased psychological commitment and a decreased tendency to quit (Rhoades & Eisenberger, 2002).

Through a meta-analysis of more than 70 studies on perceived organizational support, Rhoades and Eisenberger (2002) found that beneficial treatment received by employees (e.g., supervisor support, good work conditions, benefit programs) were associated with perceived organizational support, which in turn facilitates job satisfaction, organizational commitment, and job performance. In other words, flexible workplace programs tend to increase organizational commitment and retention because they signal a caring attitude toward employees—signaling strong organizational support to help meet employees' daily demands.

7.3.6 Comfort and Ambiance of the New Workplace

As previously discussed, studies have demonstrated a link between flexible workplace programs and job satisfaction (Allen et al., 2003; Gajendran & Harrison, 2007; Hill et al., 2010; Kossek et al., 2006; Raghuram & Wiesenfeld, 2004). That is, flexible workplace programs may serve to enhance job satisfaction. This finding may be attributed to the increased comfort and ambiance of the workplace when teleworking. The flexible workplace (e.g., working from home) is comfortable because it has all the amenities of home (e.g., food from the home kitchen, the comfort of the home bathroom facilities, the relaxation offered by the home living room) and possibly the aesthetic qualities of the home (e.g., located in a nice neighborhood, plentiful of natural light) (Virick et al., 2010).

7.4 Implementing a Flexible Workplace Program

Flexible workplace programs can take several forms including: (1) telecommuting, (2) working from home, (3) e-working. Let us now describe each of these forms.

7.4.1 Telecommuting

Telecommuting involves having employees perform all or part of their work at any location outside of employer's premises (Dutcher, 2012; Kossek et al., 2006; Noonan & Glass, 2012). It could be any place: a coffee shop, a hotel, home, a satellite office located in a more convenient place, etc.

Data from The Society for Human Resources Management's (SHRM) large-scale survey of randomly selected human resource professionals ($n = 275{,}000$) indicate that in 2014, 59% of U.S. employers allowed for some form of telecommuting. More specifically, 54% of respondents indicated that their organizations offered telecommuting on an ad hoc basis (i.e., intermittently throughout the year or as a one-time event), 29% on a part-time basis, and 20% on a full-time basis (Society for Human Resource Management, 2014).

7.4.2 Working from Home

Working from home (or homeworking) is more restrictive in terms of location. The work is conducted specifically from home (Noonan & Glass, 2012; Peters & Van der Lippe, 2007). Homeworking is defined as any paid work that is conducted primarily from home for at least 20 h per week (Crosbie & Moore, 2004; Felstead & Jewson, 2000). Homeworking increases boundary flexibility and helps employees manage home and work duties with little work-family conflict.

However, it should be noted that homeworking can often increase the permeability of the boundary between work and family domains, which in some cases makes balancing work and family schedules more difficult (Crosbie & Moore, 2004).

See Box 7.1 for an interesting exposé about Google and working from home.

Box 7.1 Google and Working from Home

It is reported that many business executives believe that remote work is bad for employee well-being. Consequently, these executives support policies that force workers to work at the office. They claim that remote and hybrid work lead to a sense of social isolation, meaninglessness, and lack of work-life boundaries. That's the rationale executives at Google use to justify office work—work at the office serves to strengthen social bonds among employees, contributing to trust, which in turn contributes to productivity. This perception is reinforced by studies related to social isolation and loneliness. Celebrity authors such as Arthur Brooks has long asserted that "the aggravation from commuting is no match for the misery of loneliness, which can lead to depression, substance abuse, sedentary behavior, and relationship damage, among other ills." Another celebrity author, Malcolm Gladwell, has also advocated return to the office after the pandemic by claiming that "we want you to have a feeling of belonging and to feel necessary… I know it's a hassle to come into the office, but if you're just sitting in your pajamas in your bedroom, is that the work life you want to live?"

However, a survey of over 1000 Google employees indicates that two-thirds feel unhappy about being forced to work in the office 3 days per week.

The author of this article, Gleb Tsipursky, rebuts by saying "These arguments may sound logical to some, but they fly in the face of my own experience as a behavioral scientist and as a consultant to Fortune 500 companies. In these roles, I have seen the pitfalls of in-person work, which can be just as problematic, if not more so. Remote work is not without its own challenges, but I have helped 21 companies implement a series of simple steps to address them."

Source: Adapted from Tsipursky (2022).

7.4.3 E-Working

E-working means online working with locational flexibility—remote working using information and communication technology such as videoconferencing (McCarthy et al., 2010; Niles, 2007). That is, e-working reflects the ability to work flexibly using remote technology to communicate with the workplace.

It should be noted that although e-working practices have been found to alleviate work stressors by avoiding meetings and interruptions, e-working can also lead to over-work as boundaries are more permeable (Fonner & Roloff, 2010; Grant et al., 2013; Kelliher & Anderson, 2010).

Read Box 7.2 about an interesting study that focused on e-working in relation to work-life balance.

Box 7.2 Measuring Remote e-Working: The E-Work Life Scale
The authors, Christine Anne Grant and her co-authors (Louise M. Wallace, Peter C. Spurgeon, Carlo Tramontano, and Maria Charalampous) developed a measure capturing the effects of e-work on work-life balance. The measure is called the E-Work Life (EWL) scale. It is designed to capture e-working experience related to job effectiveness, relationship with the organization, well-being, and work-life balance. The author validated the measure using a sample of 260 e-workers (65 per cent female, age range 25–74). The study revealed significant correlations between EWL scores and general health scores. Additionally, significant correlations were reported with other measures of mental health and vitality.

Source: Adapted from Grant et al. (2019).

7.5 Under What Conditions Is a Flexible Workplace Program Most Effective

In this section we will discuss the research on flexible workplace programs dealing with conditions under which these programs were found to be more effective. As such we will describe three sets of moderators: (1) personal moderators, (2) organizational moderators, and (3) environmental moderators. See Table 7.2 for a summary.

Table 7.2 Factors moderating the effectiveness of workplace flexibility policies and programs

Type of moderators	Specific conditions
Personal moderators	Creative personnel Managers and high-level professionals Low family responsibilities Low family-to-work interference High family responsibilities Female employees Prior experience using workplace flexibility programs
Organizational moderators	Voluntarily initiated by employees Work can be performed cooperatively and independently Close relationship and trust with supervisors Supervisor empowering their workers Only used selectively and intermittently Used conjointly with a flexible schedule program
Environmental moderators	Individualistic cultures

7.5.1 Personal Moderators

Workplace flexibility programs tend to be more effective given the following personal moderators: (1) creative personnel, (2) managers and high-level professionals, (2) low family responsibilities, (3) low family-to-work interference, (4) high family responsibilities, (5) female employees, and (6) prior experience using workplace flexibility programs.

First, workplace flexibility programs tend to achieve better WLB results when *employees are engaged in creative tasks*, not repetitive work (Dutcher, 2012). More flexibility in the workplace may be the key to the increase in productivity for creative tasks. Less-structured environments are currently used by many companies, such as Google, which rely heavily on employee creativity. Consider the following study. Dutcher (2012) examined the effect of telecommuting on worker productivity through an experiment. The results indicate that telecommuting has a negative impact on productivity of dull tasks, while telecommuting has a positive impact on productivity of creative tasks. This is because a high level of flexibility is important for creative tasks; thus, workplace flexibility is more effective when employees are engaged in creative tasks.

Second, workplace flexibility programs work better when employees have a high level of autonomy and control over their work schedule, as in the case of *managerial and high-level professionals* (Noonan & Glass, 2012). Evidence suggests that workplace flexibility programs are effective for those who can control and self-regulate task complexity. These programs benefit managers and high-level professionals who can control separation from work and self-regulate complexity. In contrast, the same programs do not provide significant benefits and are rarely available for lower-level jobs (Kossek & Lautsch, 2018). That is, workplace flexibility programs are suitable for tasks that can be done independently with discretion (i.e., managerial and knowledge tasks). The ability to work from home is tied to authority and status in that managerial and high-level professional workers are more likely than others to engage in the types of tasks that can be performed remotely. For example, workplace flexibility programs are suitable for non-routine digital-based tasks with large amounts of task variety and uncertainty. In contrast, workplace flexibility programs may be less suitable for tasks that need to be implemented interdependently and simultaneously (i.e., line production).

Third, workplace flexibility programs may work better when there is *less family-to-work interference* (ten Brummellian & Van der Lippe, 2010). Workplace flexibility programs may result in increased penetration of work into home time because of blurred boundaries between life domains. Specifically, a study by ten Brummellian and Van der Lippe (2010) compared the effects of telecommuting on work performance between single employees and employees with children. They found that the positive relationship between telecommuting and work outcomes is moderated by family structure. Specifically, workplace flexibility programs work better for *single employees* than for employees with children because single employees have fewer interfering family tasks. As we will discuss next, workplace flexibility programs may also work best for those with high family responsibilities, and their efficacy is highly situationally dependent.

Fourth, workplace flexibility programs may also be most effective for those with *high family responsibilities*. When family responsibilities are great (e.g., childcare, eldercare), workplace flexibility programs become particularly beneficial because they serve to reduce work-family conflict (Edwards & Rothbard, 2000; Hill et al., 2010; Shockley & Allen, 2007). For example, work-at-home and schedule flexibility are particularly beneficial to parents of small children or with elders at home. Shockley and Allen (2012) also reported that individuals with greater family responsibilities were more likely to endorse life management practices (e.g., workplace programs) than were individuals with less family responsibilities. Hill et al. (2010) meta-analysis found that having a dependent child aged 5 years or younger and working more hours were associated with increased family responsibilities and work-life conflict. The study also found that workplace flexibility significantly reduces work-life conflict. This may result from an increased capacity for parents to overlap work time effectively with unexpected child-care situations. Yet, it should be noted that workplace flexibility programs often exacerbate family-to-work conflict (Shockley & Allen, 2007). As we discussed in the previous moderator, workplace flexibility programs were also shown to be more effective where there are lower family responsibilities, as workplace flexibility often increases work penetration into family life. Thus, the efficacy of workplace flexibility programs when moderated by family responsibility can be highly situational.

Fifth, workplace flexibility programs tend to be more effective for women than for men. Women often bear a significantly disproportionate and considerably larger burden of care responsibilities compared to men, meaning that they benefit the most from flexible workplace programs designed to help workers with caregiving obligations (Bureau of Labor Statistics, 2010). These programs provide employees with control over the workplace, and *women* benefit more through increased control over work and family domains, compared to men (Gajendran & Harrison, 2007). Thus, women in workplace flexibility programs experience greater benefits (e.g., improved performance and perceived career prospects) because the programs reduce work-life conflict and role stress. Gajendran and Harrison (2007) conducted a meta-analysis of 46 studies in natural settings involving 12,883 employees. As expected, telecommuting had small but mainly beneficial effects on proximal outcomes, such as perceived autonomy and lower work-family conflict. Importantly, telecommuting had no generally detrimental effects on the quality of workplace relationships. Telecommuting also had beneficial effects on more distal outcomes, such as job satisfaction, performance, turnover intent, and role stress. These beneficial consequences appeared to be at least partially mediated by perceived autonomy. Also, high-intensity telecommuting (more than 2.5 days per week) accentuated telecommuting's beneficial effects on work-family conflict but harmed relationships with coworkers. Considering the benefit of workplace flexibility especially in reducing work-family conflicts and the role-stress by women at home, it can be said that workplace flexibility programs will be more effective for women than for men.

Finally, workplace flexibility programs are effective for those with *experience in using workplace flexibility programs*. Research has shown that experience with telecommuting strengthens the beneficial impact of telecommuting on work-family conflict and role stress (Gajendran & Harrison, 2007). Specifically, Gajendran and Harrison's study revealed that telecommuting was associated with a more beneficial relationship with work-family conflict among employees who had been telecommuting for over a year ($r = -0.22$, 95% CI = [−0.17, −0.27]) relative to those with less than a year's experience ($r = -0.12$, 95% CI = [−0.21, −0.03]), suggesting that greater experience enables individuals to better capitalize on telecommuting.

7.5.2 Organizational Moderators

Research shows that flexible workplace programs are most effective under the following organizational characteristics: (1) voluntarily initiated by employees, (2) work can be performed cooperatively and independently, (3) close relationship and trust with supervisors, (4) supervisor empowering their workers, (5) only used selectively and intermittently, and (6) used conjointly with a flexible schedule program.

First, evidence suggests that a flexible workplace program (e.g., telework) results in higher levels of positive outcomes when the programs are *voluntarily initiated by employees* rather than imposed by the organization (Beauregard & Henry, 2009). That is, the data suggests that employee initiated, or mutually initiated, rather than supervisor-initiated telework programs generate higher levels of productivity. Due to varying preferences among workers regarding the integration versus segmentation of work and family roles, work-life programs may be ineffective in reducing inter-role conflict if they fail to align with a worker's specific values, needs, or preferences in managing multiple roles (Ashforth et al., 2000). Thus, it can be said that flexible workplace programs (e.g., telework) result are more successful when the programs are *voluntarily initiated by employees.*

Second, flexible workplace programs can produce more positive job performance results when the *work can be performed both cooperatively and independently* (Gajendran & Harrison, 2007). In case studies of teleworking during new product development projects, Coenen and Kok (2014) found that telework has a positive effect on new product development performance because flexible workplace programs such as telework facilitated knowledge sharing and functional cooperation among members, even though face-to-face contact was not completely replaced by virtual contact. Additionally, Golden and Veiga (2005) investigated task interdependence as a moderator between telecommuting and job satisfaction. They found that telecommuters with interdependent tasks reported lower job satisfaction than those telecommuters with independent tasks.

Third, evidence shows that flexible workplace programs lead to positive outcomes when there is a *close relationship and high trust with supervisors* (Lautsch et al., 2009). Specifically, flexible workplace programs often result in more negative than positive outcomes when the relationship between employee and supervisor is tenuous and lacking in trust. In contrast, telework employees experience less work conflict, register better job performance, and exhibit more citizenship behavior when they have supervisors who engage in regular communication while avoiding constantly monitoring job performance. High quality supervisor relationships (a) create physical, cognitive, social, and psychological resources; (b) nurture reciprocity; and (c) help satisfy the basic need to belong (Bono & Yoon, 2012). Drawing on surveys and interviews with 90 days of supervisors and subordinates, Lautsch et al., 2009) found that telecommuting results in high performance when supervisors stay in close contact with telecommuters for the purpose of information sharing rather than to closely monitor work schedules and performance. That is, telecommuters supervised with an information-sharing approach were more likely to report lower work-family conflict, increased performance, and were more likely to help co-workers. Thus, it can be said that flexible workplace programs lead to positive outcomes when there is a *close relationship and trust with supervisors.*

Fourth, flexible workplace programs lead to positive outcomes when *supervisors empower their workers* (Mello, 2007; Solís, 2017). Specifically, flexible work programs such as telework do better when the supervisor feels comfortable delegating responsibilities and allowing discretion in the way their workers complete work assignments. Effective telework depends on whether supervisors feel comfortable delegating responsibilities for the entire team and allow discretion with respect to the way employees complete work assignments (Mello, 2007). Thus, it can be said that flexible workplace programs lead to positive outcomes when *supervisors empower their workers.*

Fifth, flexible workplace programs tend to produce more negative effects on work relationships when employees use the programs too frequently. A meta-analytic study (Gajendran & Harrison, 2007) indicated that frequently using flexible workplace programs (e.g., telecommuting) took a toll on the quality of co-worker relationships. Thus, it can be argued that flexible workplace programs led to positive relationship outcomes only when the programs are *used selectively and intermittently.* It is important for employees in flexible workplace programs to manage boundaries between work and personal lives. That is, frequent telecommuting (e.g., more than 2.5 days a week) accentuated telecommuting's beneficial effects on work-family conflict but harmed relationships with coworkers (Gajendran & Harrison, 2007). Thus, it can be said that flexible workplace programs lead to positive outcomes in terms of work relationships only when the programs are *used selectively and intermittently.*

Finally, research indicates that the benefits of flexible workplace programs such as reduced work-family conflict can be enhanced when the program is *used conjointly with a flexible schedule program (*Hill et al., 2010). Specifically, through an analysis of data from the International Business Machines Survey administered in 75 countries (N = 24,436), Hill et al. (2010) found that work-at-home and schedule flexibility are generally related to less work-life conflict and that the benefit of work-at-home is increased when combined with schedule flexibility. In other words, the benefits of workplace flexibility are enhanced when work-at-home is combined with the ability to schedule one's hours to best reflect both work and personal life needs.

7.5.3 Environmental Moderators

Evidence shows the moderating effects of individualism versus collectivism. Specifically, research indicates that flexible workplace programs (e.g., telecommuting) tend to be more effective in individualistic countries compared to collectivistic ones (Hill et al., 2010). This may be due to several factors, which we break down below.

First, telecommuting is more effective in individualistic (than collectivistic) cultures because telecommuting better aligns with the values of individualism (i.e., independent self-concept). In highly individualist countries, people prioritize individual goals over group goals and prefer loose than close personal ties. They tend to focus more on their own needs. Conversely, people in collectivistic cultures tend to express pride in being part of a group, community, or family (Hofstede, 2001) and they focus less on individual needs.

Second, telecommuting may be more effective in individualistic (than collectivistic) cultures because family-to-work interruptions are likely to be less. Employees in an individualistic culture can work more efficiently at home without interruptions from family members because the size of most households in individualistic countries tend to be smaller than those in collectivist countries. Interruptions would be rampant in countries with a collectivistic culture because households tend to be larger and include extended family—relatives such as grandparents, siblings, and aunts/uncles all residing in one homestead. When extended family members share the same household, the house becomes a busy place for socializing and information sharing (Hofstede, 2001). Thus, employees who work from home are more likely to experience family-to-work interference in collectivistic countries. Additionally, in a collectivistic society, there is a stronger cultural expectation that employees work long hours away from home. As such, workers in a collectivistic society rarely use flexible workplace home programs when they are offered (Masuda et al., 2012).

Several studies have documented the moderation effect of individualism versus collectivism. Through a survey study involving 604 teleworkers from different countries, Adamovic (2022) found that individualism is positively related to an employee's belief about telework effectiveness. The results indicate that this relationship is positive and significant ($\beta = 0.13, p < 0.05$). Further, Masuda et al. (2012) found that culture moderated the relationship between telecommuting and turnover intentions. Specifically, the authors reported a significant negative association between telecommuting and turnover intentions in individualistic culture (i.e.,

English-speaking countries) but no effect in collectivistic culture (i.e., Latin countries). This evidence indicates that telecommuting is more effective in countries dominated by individualism than collectivism.

7.6 Summary and Conclusion

We covered much of the research on flexible workplace and its effects on work-life balance. We defined flexible workplace practices as any form of work conducted during normal business hours but performed outside of the physical workplace. Flexible workplace arrangements include telecommuting, home working, and e-working.

Flexible workplace policies have many positive benefits, as well as several negative ones. With respect the positive consequences of flexible workplace programs, research has shown that flexible workplace programs are associated with increased job performance, increased employee productivity, increased organizational commitment and employee retention, increased employee morale and job satisfaction, and decreased work-life conflict.

Research has also documented some negative consequences of the programs, such as high work-family conflict due to blurred boundaries between work and family roles. Flexible workplace programs may also take a toll on WLB by weakening social bonds with coworkers or supervisors, which may result in career stagnation. Furthermore, such programs may increase workload and work hours by the greater penetration of work into home time and increased pressure to be constantly available. Resulting negative organizational consequences include limited interactions with co-workers and management, decreased citizenship behaviors, and reduced organizational commitment.

We also explored how flexible workplace programs help increase work-life balance. These include reduced employee cost of working, time savings, perceived autonomy, boundary flexibility, signaling management trust and support for employees, and increased comfort and ambiance of the workplace.

We then described customary flexible workplace programs that include telecommuting (i.e., having employees perform all or part of their work outside of the physical office), working from home, and e-working (i.e., working online with locational flexibility—remote working using information and communication technology such as videoconferencing).

Following this discussion, we transitioned to exploring several moderator effects on flexible workplace programs. Specifically, we discussed the research on flexible workplace programs dealing with conditions under which these programs were found to be more effective—personal, organizational, and environmental moderators. With respect to personal moderators, workplace flexibility programs tend to be more effective for creative personnel, managers and high-level professionals, low family responsibilities, high family responsibilities, female employees, and those with experience using workplace flexibility programs.

With respect to organizational moderators, research has shown that flexible workplace programs are more effective when the organization allows employees to voluntarily participate in the program, when involving cooperative work, when there is a close and trusting relationship with supervisors, when supervisors make a concerted effort to empower their subordinates, when the program is used selectively and intermittently, and when the program is used conjointly with a flexible schedule program.

With respect to environmental moderators, research has provided evidence suggesting that cultural individualism, versus collectivism, may moderate the effectiveness of flexible workplace programs. Specifically, programs such as telecommuting tend to be more effective in highly individualistic countries compared to collectivistic ones. Households in individualist countries tend to be smaller and more nuclear, meaning that employees can work more efficiently at home without interruptions from family. Interruptions tend to be rampant in countries with a collectivistic culture because of typically larger households which include extended family.

See Box 7.3 for "practical recommendations" from practitioners.

Box 7.3 Practical Recommendations from Industry Practitioners About Flexible Workplace

Flexible work programs such as telework work best when managers allow discretion in the way their team members complete work assignments. These programs serve to increase trust between employer and employee—employees are likely to perceive that management is not micromanaging their every move and looking over their shoulder; that management has faith that the staff will complete their work on their own. Letting employees work "on their honor" is a good way to build a sense of accountability and responsibility. Flexible workplace programs lead to positive outcomes when there is a close relationship and trust between the supervisors and employees.

One way to implement the flexplace program is to provide employees with equipment (e.g., laptops) to work from home or anywhere they choose to be (e.g., coffee shop down the street). As such, managers should invest in good mobile equipment and train their employees to properly use this equipment.

Another tactic is to make sure that offline office space is as inviting as possible. We should recognize that a motivational open space makes for productive staff. Try to identify types of colors that are most inspirational for different moods; type of art and design that could help make the company's workplace more inviting. Consider having separate breakout rooms and make sure to soundproof rooms to encourage team members to get down to business. This is particularly important if the workplace is an open space— not everyone works well with a wide-open space.

We also must acknowledge that in many cases, flexible workplace programs (e.g., telecommuting) often take a toll on social relationships at work. In other words, although these programs can help employees achieve greater work-life balance, the same programs undermine the quality of connections with co-workers and managers. Thus, it is important to implement flexible workplace programs while trying to strengthen social connection among the team members as well as between staff and managers. Examples of efforts to strengthen social connections at work may include having social committees that organize social events (e.g., movie nights, sports teams, or after-work dinners). Social activities can help employees feel more at home in the workplace by fostering friendships with their colleagues.

Source: Adapted from https://www.frontstream.com/blog/work-life-balance-strategies

In the next chapter, we will describe the research dealing with alternative job arrangements, including both the positive and negative consequences of this WLB practice. We will explain how this WLB practice influences employee WLB. We will then describe how alternative job arrangements are commonly implemented, followed by research that indicates conditions that qualify the overall effectiveness of this WLB practice.

References

Adamovic, M. (2022). How does employee cultural background influence the effects of telework on job stress? The roles of power distance, individualism, and beliefs about telework. *International Journal of Information Management, 62*(February), 102437.

Allen, D. G., Renn, R. W., & Griffeth, R. W. (2003). The impact of telecommuting design on social systems, self-regulation, and role boundaries. In *Research in personnel and human resources management* (Vol. 22, pp. 125–163). Emerald Group Publishing Limited.

Allen, T. D., Johnson, R. C., Kibbutz, K. M., & Shockley, K. M. (2013). Work-family conflict and flexible work arrangements: Deconstructing flexibility. *Personnel Psychology, 66*(2), 345–376.

Allen, T. D., Golden, T. D., & Shockley, K. M. (2015). How effective is telecommuting? Assessing the status of our scientific findings. *Psychological Science in the Public Interest, 16*(2), 40–68.

Ashforth, B. E., Kreiner, G. E., & Fugate, M. (2000). All in a day's work: Boundaries and micro role transitions. *Academy of Management Review, 25*(3), 472–491.

Bartel, C. A., Wrzesniewski, A., & Wiesenfeld, B. M. (2012). Knowing where you stand: Physical isolation, perceived respect, and organizational identification among virtual employees. *Organization Science, 23*(3), 743–757.

Baruch, Y., & Nicholson, N. (1997). Home, sweet work: Requirements for effective home working. *Journal of General Management, 23*(2), 15–30.

Beauregard, T. A., & Henry, L. C. (2009). Making the link between work-life balance practices and organizational performance. *Human Resource Management Review, 19*(1), 9–22.

Bono, J. E., & Yoon, D. (2012). Positive supervisory relationships. In L. Eby & T. Allen (Eds.), *Personal relationships: The effect on employee attitudes, behavior and well-being* (pp. 43–66). Taylor & Francis.

Bureau of Labor Statistics. (2010). *www.bls.gov/opub*. US Bureau of Labor Statistics.

Coenen, M., & Kok, R. A. (2014). Workplace flexibility and new product development performance: The role of telework and flexible work schedules. *European Management Journal, 32*(4), 564–576.

Crosbie, T., & Moore, J. (2004). Work-life balance and working from home. *Social Policy and Society, 3*(3), 223–233.

Desrochers, S., Hilton, J. M., & Larwood, L. (2005). Preliminary validation of the work-family integration-blurring scale. *Journal of Family Issues, 26*(4), 442–466.

DuBrin, A. J. (1991). Comparison of the job satisfaction and productivity of telecommuters versus in-house employees: A research note on work in progress. *Psychological Reports, 68*(3_suppl), 1223–1234.

Dutcher, E. G. (2012). The effects of telecommuting on productivity: An experimental examination. The role of dull and creative tasks. *Journal of Economic Behavior & Organization, 84*(1), 355–363.

Edwards, J. R., & Rothbard, N. P. (2000). Mechanisms linking work and family: Clarifying the relationship between work and family constructs. *Academy of Management Review, 25*(1), 178–199.

Elsbach, K. D., Cable, D. M., & Sherman, J. W. (2010). How passive 'face time 'affects perceptions of employees: Evidence of spontaneous trait inference. *Human Relations, 63*(6), 735–760.

Felstead, A., & Jewson, N. (2000). *In work, at home*. Routledge.

Fonner, K. L., & Roloff, M. E. (2010). Why teleworkers are more satisfied with their jobs than are office-based workers: When less contact is beneficial. *Journal of Applied Communication Research, 38*(4), 336–361.

Gajendran, R. S., & Harrison, D. A. (2007). The good, the bad, and the unknown about telecommuting: Meta-analysis of psychological mediators and individual consequences. *Journal of Applied Psychology, 92*(6), 1524–1541.

Gajendran, R. S., Harrison, D. A., & Delaney-Klinger, K. (2015). Are telecommuters remotely good citizens? Unpacking telecommuting's effects on performance via i-deals and job resources. *Personnel Psychology, 68*(2), 353–393.

Golden, T. D. (2006). The role of relationships in understanding telecommuter satisfaction. *Journal of Organizational Behavior, 27*(3), 319–340.

Golden, T. (2007). Co-workers who telework and the impact on those in the office: Understanding the implications of virtual work for co-worker satisfaction and turnover intentions. *Human Relations, 60*(11), 1641–1667.

Golden, T. D., & Raghuram, S. (2010). Teleworker knowledge sharing and the role of altered relational and technological interactions. *Journal of Organizational Behavior, 31*(8), 1061–1085.

Golden, T. D., & Veiga, J. F. (2005). The impact of extent of telecommuting on job satisfaction: Resolving inconsistent findings. *Journal of Management, 31*(2), 301–318.

Golden, T. D., Veiga, J. F., & Simsek, Z. (2006). Telecommuting's differential impact on work-family conflict: Is there no place like home? *Journal of Applied Psychology, 91*(6), 1340–1350.

Grant, C. A., Wallace, L. M., & Spurgeon, P. C. (2013). An exploration of the psychological factors affecting remote e-worker's job effectiveness, Well-being and work-life balance. *Employee Relations, 35*(5), 527–546.

Grant, C. A., Wallace, L. M., Spurgeon, P. C., Tramontana, C., & Charalambous, M. (2019). Construction and initial validation of the E-work life scale to measure remote e-working. *Employee Relations, 41*(1), 16–33.

Greenhouse, J. H., & Buetel, N. J. (1985). Sources of conflict between work and family roles. *Academy of Management Review, 10*(1), 76–88.

Hill, E. J., Miller, B. C., Weiner, S. P., & Colihan, J. (1998). Influences of the virtual office on aspects of work and work/life balance. *Personnel Psychology, 51*(3), 667–683.

Hill, E. J., Erickson, J. J., Holmes, E. K., & Ferris, M. (2010). Workplace flexibility, work hours, and work-life conflict: Finding an extra day or two. *Journal of Family Psychology, 24*(3), 349–358.

Hofstede, G. (2001). *Culture's consequences: Comparing values, behaviors, institutions and organizations across nations*. Sage publications.
Kelliher, C., & Anderson, D. (2010). Doing more with less? Flexible working practices and the intensification of work. *Human Relations, 63*(1), 83–106.
Kirchmeyer, C. (1995). Demographic similarity to the work group: A longitudinal study of managers at the early career stage. *Journal of Organizational Behavior, 16*(1), 67–83.
Kossek, E. E., & Lautsch, B. A. (2018). Work-life flexibility for whom? Occupational status and work-life inequality in upper, middle, and lower-level jobs. *Academy of Management Annals, 12*(1), 5–36.
Kossek, E. E., Lautsch, B. A., & Eaton, S. C. (2006). Telecommuting, control, and boundary management: Correlates of policy use and practice, job control, and work-family effectiveness. *Journal of Vocational Behavior, 68*(2), 347–367.
Lautsch, B. A., Kossek, E. E., & Eaton, S. C. (2009). Supervisory approaches and paradoxes in managing telecommuting implementation. *Human Relations, 62*(6), 795–827.
Martin, B. H., & MacDonnell, R. (2012). Is telework effective for organizations? A meta-analysis of empirical research on perceptions of telework and organizational outcomes. *Management Research Review, 35*(7), 602–616.
Masuda, A. D., Poelmans, S. A., Allen, T. D., Spector, P. E., Lapierre, L. M., Cooper, C. L., et al. (2012). Flexible work arrangements availability and their relationship with work-to-family conflict, job satisfaction, and turnover intentions: A comparison of three country clusters. *Applied Psychology, 61*(1), 1–29.
McCarthy, A., Darcy, C., & Grady, G. (2010). Work-life balance policy and practice: Understanding line manager attitudes and behaviors. *Human Resource Management Review, 20*(2), 158–167.
Mello, J. A. (2007). Managing telework programs effectively. *Employee Responsibilities and Rights Journal, 19*(4), 247–261.
Nardi, B. A., & Whittaker, S. (2002). The place of face-to-face communication in distributed work. In P. J. Hinds & S. Kisler (Eds.), *Distributed work* (pp. 83–112). The MIT Press.
Niles, J. M. (2007). The future of e-work. *The Journal of E-working, 1*, 1–12.
Noonan, M. C., & Glass, J. L. (2012). The hard truth about telecommuting. *Monthly Labor. Review., 135*(6), 38–45.
Peters, P., & Van der Lippe, T. (2007). The time-pressure reducing potential of tele homeworking: The Dutch case. *The International Journal of Human Resource Management, 18*(3), 430–447.
Raghuram, S., & Wiesenfeld, B. (2004). Work-nonwork conflict and job stress among virtual workers. *Human Resource Management, 43*(2–3), 259–277.
Rhoades, L., & Eisenberger, R. (2002). Perceived organizational support: A review of the literature. *Journal of Applied Psychology, 87*(4), 698–714.
Schieman, S., & Young, M. (2010). Is there a downside to schedule control for the work-family interface? *Journal of Family Issues, 31*(10), 1391–1414.
Shockley, K. M., & Allen, T. D. (2007). When flexibility helps: Another look at the availability of flexible work arrangements and work-family conflict. *Journal of Vocational Behavior, 71*(3), 479–493.
Shockley, K. M., & Allen, T. D. (2012). Motives for flexible work arrangement use. *Community, Work & Family, 15*(2), 217–231.
Society for Human Resource Management. (2014). *2014 employee benefits: An overview of employee benefit offerings in the U.S.* Author.
Solís, M. (2017). Moderators of telework effects on the work-family conflict and on worker performance. *European Journal of Management and Business Economics, 26*(1), 21–34.
Standen, P., Daniels, K., & Lamond, D. (1999). The home as a workplace: Work-family interaction and psychological Well-being in telework. *Journal of Occupational Health Psychology, 4*(4), 368–381.

ten Brummellian, L. L., & Van der Lippe, T. (2010). Effective work-life balance support for various household structures. *Human Resource Management, 49*(2), 173–193.
Tsipursky, G. (2022). Does remote work hurt wellbeing and work-life balance? *Forbes*, November 1, 2022. Retrieved from September 29, 2023 https://www.forbes.com/sites/glebtsipursky/2022/11/01/does-remote-work-hurt-wellbeing-and-work-life-balance/?sh=6d649f004b20
Virick, M., DaSilva, N., & Arrington, K. (2010). Moderators of the curvilinear relation between extent of telecommuting and job and life satisfaction: The role of performance outcome orientation and worker type. *Human Relations, 63*(1), 137–154.

Chapter 8
Alternative Job Arrangements

"Cars and decision makers, both need a service break, for better performance and long life."—Harjeet Khanduja (https://teambuilding.com/blog/work-life-balance-quotes)

Abstract In this chapter we describe the research dealing with alternative job arrangements. We start by highlighting the positive and negative consequences of this type of work-life balance (WLB) strategy in terms of employees and organizational outcomes. We explain how this WLB practice influences employee and organizational outcomes in terms of person-job fit, job demands and resources, job demands and control, and role conflict. We then describe how this WLB strategy is commonly implemented: part-time work, job sharing, career breaks, and contract work. Finally, we describe conditions under which alternative job arrangements are most effective in terms of personal, organizational, and environmental moderators.

8.1 Introduction

A traditional job pays a wage or a salary, often has an implicit or explicit contract for continuing employment, a predictable work schedule, predictable earnings, and work supervised by the organization paying the salary (Abraham et al., 2018). Alternative job arrangements mean non-traditional jobs in one or more of these criteria (Mas & Pallais, 2020). In other words, alternative job arrangements symbolize flexibility in employee relationships with their employer (Spreitzer et al., 2017).

Alternative job arrangements often entail a non-traditional work week with the flexibility to take time off without pay for hours not physically at work. Such programs reflect the ability to change the temporal and spatial boundaries of one's job. In other words, alternative job arrangements are designed to allow total life resources to be adapted to promote equilibrium in one's life over time. These programs and practices allow employees to maintain sustainable career development and achieve

D.-J. Lee, M. J. Sirgy, *Organizational Strategies for Work-Life Balance*, Human Well-Being Research and Policy Making,
https://doi.org/10.1007/978-3-031-56314-0_8

work-life balance (WLB). Alternative job arrangements include part-time jobs, job sharing, contract work, and career breaks such as sabbaticals (Allen, 2001; Galinsky et al., 1993). These alternative job arrangements help increase job autonomy and reduce work-family conflict (Batt & Valcour, 2003).

In a global economy in which short-term financial results drive decision-making, management seeks flexibility through employment at will to meet changing market demand—sometimes referred to as a workforce on demand or an open talent economy (Bidwell, 2013; Kalleberg, 2012). As such, an increasing number of organizations have changed from offering standard employment to shorter-term work assignments (Johnson & Ashforth, 2008). In addition, technological innovation has enabled the rise of online talent platforms (i.e., online employment agencies specializing in locating special talent interested in nontraditional jobs), which instantaneously link workers with employers across different countries and time zones (i.e., Indeed). That is, technology is enabling work to be disaggregated to the level of the task, making it easier to outsource specific tasks (Boudreau & Jeppesen, 2015). The internet and advances in information and communication technologies have reduced the costs of offering work arrangements, making it easier for employers to allow workers to work remotely and to provide workers with flexible schedules or schedule workers on-demand. The advent of online platforms has allowed firms to contract out the work for specific tasks for an increasing number of activities. Alternative job arrangements are also driven by the preferences of workers in the new economy. More people are choosing self-employment for the freedom and flexibility it provides (Spreitzer et al., 2017). Katz and Krueger (2019) found that the percentage of workers engaged in alternative job arrangements (defined as temporary help agency workers, on-call workers, contract workers, and independent contractors or freelancers) increased from 10.1% of all workers in 2005 to 15.8% in 2015.

8.2 Consequences of Alternative Job Arrangements

Alternative job arrangements have both positive and negative consequences, as we will discuss below. See Table 8.1 for a summary.

8.2.1 Positive Consequences

Evidence suggests that alternative job arrangements (e.g., part-time work) serve to reduce employees' *workload* and help them cope with *work-life conflict*. The organizational effects of these personal consequences include reduced *absenteeism* and increased *staff retention* (Gholipour et al., 2010). Furthermore, alternative job arrangements (e.g., job sharing) involve approaching job-related tasks from multiple perspectives, which in turn helps improve *job creativity and performance* (Freeman & Coll, 2009). Ultimately, alternative job arrangements (e.g., part-time

Table 8.1 Positive and negative consequences of alternative job arrangements

Type of consequence	Specific consequences
Positive consequences	Reduced workload Reduced work-life conflict Reduced absenteeism Increased staff retention Improved job creativity Improved job performance Successful integration of work and family responsibilities Increased work-life balance Perceived attractiveness of the organization Increased recruitment and retention Increased job attractiveness
Negative consequences	Less opportunity for upward mobility Fewer institutional protections Declining union memberships Low job satisfaction Increased job insecurity Lower perceived employability Lower pay Lower continuance commitment toward customers Less customer oriented Less likely to engage in extra-role behaviors

work) reduce work-life conflict (Hill et al., 2004; Van Rijswijk et al., 2004; Walsh, 2007). Though a survey of full-time vs. part-time working mothers (n = 687), Hill et al. (2004) investigated how part-time work influences the ability of mothers of preschool children working in professional occupations to successfully *integrate work and family responsibilities*. Compared to their counterparts who worked full time, mothers who worked in part-time positions reported significantly greater work-family balance and did not report significantly less career mobility. As such, the data supports that part-time work is a viable option to assist women in professional careers to successfully integrate their family and career.

Study results also indicate that alternative job arrangements increase *perceived attractiveness of the organization*. Organizations offering alternative career paths (with family-supportive policies available to all employees) and dual career paths[1] (with the option to either prioritize career, or balance career and family) are perceived as significantly more attractive than those offering only traditional career paths (Carless & Wintle, 2007). Furthermore, alternative job arrangements (e.g., offering voluntary reduced hours) are associated with increased *recruitment and retention* (Williams et al., 2000). Carless and Wintle (2007) examined the impact of flexible career paths on perceptions of organizational attraction with a sample of young, inexperienced job seekers. A total of 201 participants responded to a

[1] Employees with highly technical skills whose promotion does not involve climbing into a management position but a higher-level technical position with an increase in pay and benefits comparable to the management position.

questionnaire and rated their attraction to two different job advertisements. The results indicate that applicants perceived a job opportunity in an organization that offered either a flexible career path or a dual career path as significantly more attractive than a position in an organization that offered a traditional career path.

8.2.2 Negative Consequences

As we have established, workers choose independent work for freedom and flexibility (Johnson & Ashforth, 2008). Despite the benefits of flexibility, the fact remains that part-time contractual workers have less *opportunity for upward mobility*, fewer *institutional protections* such as *health and retirement benefits*, and declining *union membership* (Bidwell et al., 2013; Bidwell & Mollick, 2015).

Bidwell et al. (2013) reviewed changes to U.S. employment, focusing on the causes of those changes and their consequences. According to these scholars, the U.S. employment model has moved from a closed, internal system to one more open to external markets and institutional pressures. Changes to employment include the growth of short-term employment, contingent work, outsourcing, and performance pay. These part-time contractual workers usually have less opportunity for upward mobility (Bidwell et al., 2013).

Furthermore, employees with alternative job arrangements (e.g., temporary agency workers) are reported to have low *job satisfaction*, compared to permanent employees. Temporary agency workers experience higher dissatisfaction due to increased *job insecurity*, lower *perceived employability*, and lower *pay* (De Cuyper et al., 2009a, b; Wilkin, 2013). Evidence also shows that that they are more *financially insecure* and not *satisfied with their work-life* (Warren, 2004). As a result, they tend to feel less commitment to their employer (De Cuyper et al., 2009b). Other negative consequences of alternative job arrangements include the tendency to have lower *continuance commitment toward customers*, being less *customer oriented*, and being less likely to *engage in extra-role behaviors* (Broschak et al., 2008; Johnson & Ashforth, 2008). Broschak et al. (2008) investigated how nonstandard work arrangements shape work attitudes and behaviors. They found that attitudes and behaviors vary across different types of nonstandard work arrangements. As expected, part-time workers who are retained long-term have more positive *attitudes toward their work arrangements* than do standard workers. In contrast, temporary agency workers have a more negative attitude toward their work arrangement than those part-time workers. But contrary to conventional wisdom about temporary work arrangements, agency temporary workers who have opportunities to transition to standard employment arrangements have more positive *attitudes toward supervisors and coworkers* and perform better than their peers in standard work arrangements. Part-time arrangements designed to retain valued workers do not produce increased commitment or other attitudinal benefits consistent with retention. In addition, De Cuyper et al. (2009a, b) investigated how transitioning between temporary and permanent employment relates to several psychological consequences (e.g., *work engagement*, *affective organizational commitment*, *life satisfaction*, and *turnover intention*). Through a survey on a sample of 1475 workers, continuous temporary employment was found to not relate to negative outcomes over time. In contrast, gaining permanent employment is associated with increased work engagement.

8.3 How Do Alternative Job Arrangements Help with Work-Life Balance

Alternative job arrangements contribute to work-life balance in the following ways: (1) person-job fit, (2) job demands and resources, (3) job demand and job control, and (4) role conflict. See Table 8.2 for summary.

8.3.1 Person-Job Fit

Alternative job arrangements allow employees to work on job-related tasks in a manner consistent with their values in work and nonwork domains. WLB can be achieved with a good fit between the individual and the organization (Greenhaus & Allen, 2011). Specifically, balance means a match between the demands of a situation and the individual's values, needs, and/or resources available to meet that demand. As such, alternative job arrangements (e.g., part time, job sharing, contractual work) allow employees to match role demands with personal values, needs, and resources.

Table 8.2 Theories explaining the impact of alternative job arrangements on work-life balance

Theory	Brief description
Person-job fit	Alternative job arrangements allow employees to work on job-related tasks in a manner consistent with their values in work and nonwork domains. WLB can be achieved with a good fit between the individual and the organization
Job demands and resources	Alternative job arrangements provide employees with additional resources to handle role demand, thus this program serves to reduce work-life conflict
Job demand and job control	Alternative job arrangements provide employees with more control over both family and work duties. Control is a result of flexibility in the employment relationship
Role conflict	Alternative job arrangements help employees reduce time-based conflict resulting from full time work engagement. The program also helps employees reduce *strain-based conflict* by reducing workload, providing opportunities for recovery, and/or reducing strain related to commuting or face-to-face interactions

For example, Sarah is an attorney who is 6 months pregnant. She decides that based on her professional and family needs, she needs to decrease her work hours. She negotiates with the firm's general manager to decrease her work hours (essentially to part-time work) until she delivers, after which she would take maternity leave. In this situation, the part-time hours allow her to keep in touch with her current clients while preparing for the birth of her baby—a match between her personal needs and job demand.

8.3.2 *Job Demands-Resources Theory*

The Job Demands-Resources theory explains how alternative job arrangements contribute to WLB (Bakker & Demerouti, 2007). Specifically, alternative job arrangements provide employees with additional resources to handle role demand, thus this program serves to reduce work-life conflict. For example, part-time work or leave programs reduce job demand and provide employees with additional resources such as time to combat job strain or work overload. Job strain develops when job demands are high and when job resources are limited. To reiterate, alternative job programs provide employees with resources (time) to help manage the demands of work and family.

Using the previous example, transitioning into a part-time job allows Sarah to keep in touch with her current clients (meet job demand) with enough resources left to also prepare for the birth of her baby.

8.3.3 *Job Demands-Control Theory*

Job Demands-Control theory can help explain the effect of alternative job arrangements on work-life balance. Alternative job arrangements provide employees with more control over both family and work duties. Control is a result of flexibility in the employment relationship (Allen et al., 2013; Ashford et al., 2007). When an individual is unable to maintain regular employment due to family demand, instead of leaving the organization, the individual can use alternative job arrangements to achieve work-life balance. Alternative job arrangements provide employees with flexibility on how and when they can meet life's demands. In sum, alternative job arrangements provide employees with more control over their role duties and obligations.

In Sarah's case, transitioning to part-time allows her to maintain control over her job situation with her clients as well as do the many personal things necessary for the delivery of her baby.

8.3.4 Role Conflict

Alternative job arrangements can help employees reduce role conflict. The standard work schedule may create stress for employees who need to find an optimal balance between time for work and time for household responsibilities. Alternative job arrangements help employees reduce time-based conflict resulting from full time work engagement. Alternative job arrangements also help employees reduce *strain-based conflict* by reducing workload (e.g., alternative job arrangements), providing opportunities for recovery, and/or reducing strain related to commuting or face-to-face interactions (Greenhaus & Beutell, 1985).

Considering Sarah, one can easily make the case that requesting management to transition her to part-time helps reduce conflict between her work role and her family role. As such, her part-time job allows her to reduce any time-based conflict as well as strain-based conflict. Her part-time job would also allow her to meet the time demands of her current clients, without taking on new clients. And doing so should reduce strain arising from time-based conflict.

8.4 Implementing Alternative Job Arrangements

Alternative job arrangements allow more control over how much work is done—practices such as part-time, term-time, and job sharing (Chung & Van der Horst, 2018; Timms et al., 2015). That is, alternative job arrangements reflect flexibility in employment (Spreitzer et al., 2017).

The percentage of workers in alternative job arrangements continues to increase (Katz & Krueger, 2019; Spreitzer et al., 2017). Several factors are thought to have contributed to the increased use of alternative job arrangements. These include: (1) financialization of the economy, (2) precarious work, (3) innovations in information and communication technology, and (4) workers' preference. See summary of how these factors contributed to the increased use of alternative job arrangements in Table 8.3.

First, organizations are operating in a global economy where financial markets, institutions, and actors play a more prominent role in shaping economic outcomes and driving economic decision-making. As such, they seek flexibility through alternative employment to meet changing demands. This *financialization of the economy* has led to a stakeholder model of corporate governance being replaced by a shareholder model that privileges the interests of investors and where corporations are much less likely to hire workers into traditional full-time jobs with job security. Organizations are increasingly hiring contract workers who receive no long-term job security, benefits, or often even training (Bidwell & Briscoe, 2009).

Table 8.3 Factors contributing to the increased use of alternative job arrangements

Factors	How?
Financialization of the economy	Trend: The stakeholder model of corporate governance has been replaced by the shareholder model. To increase shareholder's return on investment management hire contract workers with no long-terms job security and benefits
Precarious work	Trend: Firms have increasingly reduced institutional protections and benefits for employees to exert more management control
Innovations in information and communication technology	Trend: Increased innovations in information and communication technology allowed management to hire employees who can work remotely and on a project basis. Doing so, management saves money and exerts more control
Workers' preference	Trend: A growing number of individuals prefer alternative job arrangements when given a choice because the program provides increased freedom and flexibility

Second, firms have increasingly limited employee opportunities for upward mobility; they have also reduced institutional protections and benefits for employees. The result is *precarious work*, in which the power differentials between workers and employers are amplified. Doing so allows management to exert more control over employees and job performance in the short run. Although precarious work is not new, it has dramatically increased in the past decade (Bidwell & Mollick, 2015).

Third, *innovations in information and communication technology* (ICT) allow work to be conducted anytime, anywhere. This trend affects full-time employees as well as contract and gig workers. Cloud technology makes it possible for people to work in any location by logging into their organization's server to access shared documents and use email. Knowledge sharing tools (e.g., instant messaging software, online discussion boards, Q&A forums, or other community websites) are also becoming increasingly common. In addition, ICT enables work to be disaggregated to the level of the task, making it easier to outsource specific tasks (Spreitzer et al., 2017).

Fourth, *workers' preference* is another factor fueling the growth of alternative job arrangements. The levels of self-employment have continued to rise, indicating that a growing number of individuals prefer alternative job arrangements when given a choice. Workers are increasingly choosing to work independently for increased freedom and flexibility. In addition, today there are more dual-career families and single parents in the workforce than ever, lacking a stay-at-home partner to take care of domestic responsibilities. These individuals may value flexibility in where and when they do their work so that they can better manage home commitments. In addition, more workers seek work that is personally meaningful and aligned with their values, passions, and strengths, making independent work attractive (Spreitzer et al., 2017).

As discussed above, alternative job arrangements involve part-time, job sharing, career breaks, and contract work. We will next discuss these in some depth.

8.4.1 Part-Time Work

Some organizations provide employees with the opportunity to work part-time to help them achieve work-life balance. That is, by offering access to part-time jobs and part-year work, management allows employees to voluntarily choose their labor intensity and work time. Part-time work helps the organization expand the available labor pool to include those with restricted schedules such as retirees and students (Beham et al., 2012).

Part-time workers are workers who work less than 35 h on-site with a fixed schedule (Mayfield, 2006; McComb et al., 2003; Spreitzer et al., 2017). Technically speaking, part-time employees are often classified in the category of *contingent work*. They constitute almost 20% of the U.S. workforce, and most part-time employment is concentrated in the service industries.

Some employees prefer part-time work to accommodate family responsibilities or educational commitments, or to remain mentally engaged while retired (Dingemans & Henkens, 2014). In many cases, management tries to convert full-time positions into part-time to retain high performing employees, to reduce wage and benefits costs, and to help schedule shifts (Wittmer & Martin, 2010).

Thorsteinson (2003) conducted a meta-analysis (k = 38, n = 51,231) to examine the difference between full-time and part-time employees in relation to job attitudinal constructs. Results indicated that there was little difference between full-time and part-time employees in relation to job satisfaction, organizational commitment, intentions to leave, and facets of job satisfaction. Yet, full-time employees were found to be more involved with their jobs than part-time employees. Broschak et al. (2008) found that *retention part-timers* (e.g., part-timers that the firm seeks to retain them) who voluntarily worked part-time had similar affective commitment, supervisor satisfaction, and social integration as full-time employees. Retention part-timers were as satisfied with their jobs and pay as full-time employees and just as committed. They received higher performance evaluations than full-time employees. Yet, when workers are forced into part-time status because they cannot obtain full-time employment, the work experience is more negative.

Relatedly, part-time workers are made up of many on-call workers and seasonal employees. *On-call workers* refer to workers having certain days or hours in which they are not at work but are on standby in case they are needed. On-call workers do not have a regular work schedule but are required to be available during on-call periods. They work less than full-time workers on site with less predictable schedules (Spreitzer et al., 2017). Examples of on-call workers include workers with unpredictable schedules (e.g., substitute teachers) and seasonal employees (e.g., agricultural workers, retail clerks during busy holiday periods). In many cases, on-call and seasonal employees have little power over the conditions under which they are hired. Although they may have the freedom to accept or reject requests to work, they have little influence over the conditions under which the work is done. They often have considerable tenure with the hiring organization, for example they come back season after season or remain in the ranks of substitute teachers until their own children have grown (Spreitzer et al., 2017).

Caveat: Part-time employees may find that the actual amount of work was not decreased proportionally. They often end up with similar workloads to full-time employees. Management should ensure that the workload is also reduced proportionally for part-time workers.

8.4.2 Job Sharing

Alternative job arrangements can also involve job sharing. Job sharing means that a full-time position is shared by two people, each working part-time hours, which means that both employees also share a single salary and the same benefits (Allen, 2001; Freeman & Coll, 2009; Galinsky et al., 1993). Job sharing brings a broader range of knowledge, skills, and experiences to a position while providing cross-training and skill enhancement opportunities for each partner.

There are types of several job-sharing: (1) In the responsibility *participation* type of job sharing, there is no sharing in responsibilities, but it requires high cooperation. Although there is regular communication between the participants, all of them are equally responsible for doing the work correctly. This job-sharing method is best for jobs that are continuously active and demand both high communication and cooperation. (2) In the responsibility *sharing* type of job sharing, each participant is only responsible for their own tasks, and do not often work together. This method works best when the job can be divided into different projects and participants do not need to communicate frequently. (3) In the *unrelated* responsibility type of job sharing, participants do totally different jobs that require no cooperation while they are physically in the same place or on the same team (Gholipour et al., 2010).

Job sharing allows for part-time hours in jobs not typically available as part-time positions, such as office or administrative positions. For example, in the simplest of setups, two employees would share a typical full-time position, each working 20 h per week. In some situations, workers will each work 2.5 days and possibly meet for lunch on the split day. Other options include working 2 days per week and rotating working alternate Wednesdays or working 4 h a day, every day. In most cases, the salaries and benefits of the employees participating in the job sharing would be prorated based on the hours each employee worked.

The organizational benefits of job-sharing arrangements have been linked to increased retention of valued employees, increased work and non-work attitudes, cost savings, and improved recruitment. Job sharing also allows for greater flexibility that can help improve work-life balance for employees. The two employees can complement each other's skills and knowledge, and potentially solve problems that one person may not be able to solve alone. The benefits for employees from job sharing arrangements generally far outweigh any negative aspects (Griffin et al., 2014). It is important for management to coordinate job sharing to make sure that two employees generate synergies while minimizing role ambiguity and conflict.

Caveat: In job sharing, the benefits of the full-time post are retained by the organization whereas the part-time employees typically receive lower wage rates, receive fewer benefits, and have fewer opportunities for training and promotion (Harris, 1997).

8.4.3 Career Breaks

Some organizations offer alternative job arrangements for their employees by permitting career breaks without losing one's job (i.e., sabbatical). In some cases, management offers opportunities such as part-time and job sharing, and treats those as regular career breaks (Allen, 2001; Galinsky et al., 1993). In other words, these alternative job arrangements are not held against the employee for when considering promotion and career advancement within the organization.

Caveat: As we have previously mentioned, women often assume a disproportionately large share of household responsibility, which often necessitates leaving the workforce for periods at a time. The difficulties identified among women returning to employment after an unsanctioned career break (not supported by the organization) include finding suitable and affordable childcare, and often overcoming loss of confidence and self-esteem. In a study on the effect of breaks in employment on the working life of women in Australia, Arun et al. (2004) found that women who leave the workforce interrupt their accumulation of human and financial capital, and that they often were not able to return to the same type of job at comparable pay. As such, career break programs that do not penalize employees (i.e., little negative career consequences) should help firms retain talented workers while maintaining job satisfaction and organizational commitment. It is also important for firms to maintain contact with employees during career breaks and update them periodically regarding work-related issues.

8.4.4 Contract Work

Contract workers refer to workers who work for themselves based on a short-term contract. They are hired to apply their knowledge and skills based to a specific and short-term project. Rather than a salary, they are paid by the hour or project that a client specifies in a contract written before the work begins (Spreitzer et al., 2017). Examples of contract workers include freelancers, gig workers, and temporary agency workers. *Freelancers* are highly skilled contractors that include not only writers and editors but also computer programmers, engineers, or even film producers (Cappelli & Keller, 2013).

Gig workers are independent workers who find work that is mediated through online platforms such as Uber, Upwork, and Care.com. Gig work contracts tend to be very short—minutes, hours, or days (Farrell & Greig, 2016).

Temporary agency workers are workers employed by an agency who assigns them to perform client work, usually full-time and on-site, after which they return to the agency for their next assignment (Spreitzer et al., 2017). Temporary agency workers who are assigned work through an agency on a short-term contract are often clerical, and longer-term contracts tend to be IT specialists (Barley & Kunda, 2006).

Caveat: Temporary agency workers are not considered members of the organization for which they perform work. They are under the administrative control of a temporary help agency and typically do not have access to the same resources, training, and promotion opportunities as standard workers. Their work arrangement limits the duration of their employment. As a result, although they may work in the same jobs as regular workers, temporary agency workers are afforded lower status and are likely to have far more negative work experiences (Broschak et al., 2008). De Cuyper et al. (2009a) found that temporary agency workers had lower levels of job satisfaction and affective organizational commitment compared to permanent employees due to increased feelings of job insecurity and lower perceived employability. A meta-analysis concluded that temporary agency workers experienced the least amount of job satisfaction, in comparison to both direct contract workers and permanent employees (Wilkin, 2013).

8.5 Under What Conditions Is an Alternative Job Arrangement Most Effective

In this section we will describe the research related to moderator effects—that is, those personal, organizational, and environmental factors that affect the efficacy of alternative job arrangements on work-life balance. See Table 8.4 for a summary.

Table 8.4 Factors moderating the effectiveness of alternative job arrangements policies and programs

Type of moderators	Specific conditions
Personal moderators	Those who participate in the program voluntarily Those who perceive the program as useful Those with childcare responsibilities and post-retirement adults Person-program fit Those with a sense of workplace inclusion
Organizational moderators	Divisibility of job tasks Pre-specified job arrangements Managerial support
Environmental moderators	Organizations operating in countries with an individualistic culture Countries high on gender equality

8.5.1 Personal Moderators

Alternative job arrangements are most likely to produce positive outcomes for employees with the following individual characteristics: (1) those who participate in the program voluntarily, (2) those who perceive the program to be useful, (3) those with childcare responsibilities and post-retirement adults, (4) person-program fit, and (5) those with a sense of workplace inclusion.

First, alternative job arrangements are most likely to produce positive WLB effects if employees *voluntarily participate in the program* (Kossek & Ruderman, 2012). For example, research has shown that voluntarily reduced hours and part-time work are associated with higher levels of job satisfaction, organizational commitment (Thorsteinson, 2003; Williams et al., 2000), and greater self-reported productivity and efficiency (Lewis, 1997; Williams et al., 2000). The Bureau of Labor Statistics classifies part time employment in two categories, part-time workers working part time voluntarily (i.e., for non-economic reasons) and part-time workers working part time involuntarily (i.e., for economic reasons). Most part-time workers are classified as working part time voluntarily (Nardone, 1995). Part-time workers who voluntarily chose to work part time have greater job satisfaction than part-time workers who are working part-time involuntarily due to an inability to find a full-time position or because of a reduction in hours at work (Keil et al., 2000). As previously described, Thorsteinson (2003) conducted a meta-analysis ($k = 38$, $n = 51{,}231$) to examine the difference between full- and part-time employees on job attitudes and examined whether the relationship is moderated by voluntary vs. involuntary part-time work. Results indicated that there was little difference between full-time and voluntary part-time employees in relation to job satisfaction, organizational commitment, intentions to leave and facets of job satisfaction. Employees working part-time voluntarily reported higher job satisfaction than employees working part-time involuntarily, although the effect is small (corrected $d = 0.19$). Also, employees working part-time voluntarily reported higher job satisfaction than full-time employees (corrected $d = 0.09$), although this difference was not statistically significant. Furthermore, the study found that part-time work results in positive outcomes when the workers volunteer to do so for non-economic reasons. Thus, it can be said that alternative job arrangements are most likely to produce positive effects for those employees who voluntarily participate in the program and given that their choice to work part time is based on non-economic reasons.

Second, alternative job arrangements are most likely to produce positive effects for those employees who *perceive the program to be useful*. Data suggests that employees in flexible work arrangement are satisfied with their job when they perceive the program to be useful (Lambert, 2000). Female employees with high family demand are more likely to perceive alternative work schedules to be useful in reducing work-family conflict, as they often are responsible for a greater share of household responsibility (Kim & Wiggins, 2011). Based on social exchange theory, the more useful workers find the extra benefits provided by the organization, the more they should want to give something extra back to it. Consider the study conducted by Lambert (2000). Through a survey of a 884 randomly selected employees (667 workers and 217 supervisors and managers) this WLB scholar found that the more useful workers perceived the company's work-life benefits to be in terms of helping them and their families, the more likely they were to submit suggestions for improvement, to voluntarily attend meetings on quality methods, and to report that they assisted others with their job duties. The findings support the basic premise of social exchange theory that positive actions on the part of an organization propels workers to reciprocate in beneficial ways. Thus, it can be said that alternative job arrangements are most likely to produce positive effects for those employees who *perceive the program to* be beneficial and useful to them.

Third, alternative job arrangements allow *married women and retired employees* to continue to maintain or further develop their careers. For both married women with domestic responsibilities and retired adults, an alternative job arrangement is an effective mean to re-enter into the labor force and continue their career development (Straughan & Tadai, 2018). A popular alternative job arrangement for parents with childcare responsibilities as well as post-retirement adults who seek extended employment is part-time work. Straughan and Tadai (2018) conducted in-depth interviews with Singapore employees who successfully negotiated for part-time work. The results indicate that people want to do part time because they want to take care of young children, to have time for themselves (e.g., nurturing hobbies or interests), and to remain economically active and engaged. For both married women with childcare responsibilities and older adults, an alternative job arrangement is often central to their continued economic participation. Part-time work enables mothers to meaningfully integrate work and family responsibilities and allows older adults to reap the benefits of economic engagement post-retirement. Thus, it can be said that alternative job arrangements are most likely to be most effective in contributing to WLB for *married women and retired employees* alike.

Fourth, alternative job arrangements are most likely to generate positive outcomes given a match between the type of alternative job arrangement program and the employee preference for that program (i.e., *person-program fit*). When work arrangements match employee preference, a strong person-program fit leads to increased job satisfaction and elevated job performance (Thorsteinson, 2003). For example, alternative job arrangements (e.g., part-time work) may fit well with upper-level managers who work independently and who can afford a reduced income. In contrast, flexible work arrangements (e.g., part-time work) may not fit well with low-level employees who are engaged in interdependent tasks (i.e., must work with others) and who cannot afford an income decrease. Consider the following study conducted by Kossek and Lautsch (2018). These investigators reviewed how occupational status and flexibility experiences vary and shape work-life inequality. They found that employees across occupational groups experience different work-life flexibility outcomes. Specifically, they found that part-time work permits control over work volume and workload but hurts lower-level employees the most because of the involuntary loss of income and benefits. Leave may benefit upper and middle-level employees but not lower-level workers. Thus, it can be said that alternative job arrangements are most likely to generate positive outcomes when there is *person-program fit*.

Lastly, alternative job arrangements are most likely to have positive effects when participating employees have a strong *sense of workplace inclusion*. Workplace inclusion refers to one's sense of belonging to the organization. It entails being invited to participate and perceptions that one's input matters (Hayes et al., 2002). Employees taking advantage of an alternative job arrangement tend to feel insecure about aspects of their organizational membership (Morganson et al., 2010). As such, alternative job arrangements may be most effective when participating employees feel that they are treated comparably to full-time, regular employees (i.e., they feel a sense of inclusion in the organization). *Workplace exclusion* (or lack of inclusion) is associated with adverse outcomes such as higher turnover, reduced organizational commitment, lower job satisfaction, burnout, and disinterest in and rejection by co-workers (Golden, 2006). Likewise, professionally isolated workers report anxiety, loneliness, and physiological health symptoms (DeWall & Baumeister, 2006). Research has demonstrated that professional isolation is negatively associated with job performance and is stronger for those with alternative job arrangements who have limited interactions with others. To examine the effect of perceived inclusion on job satisfaction, Morganson et al. (2010) conducted a web-based survey involving 578 telework employees. Their study results indicate that strong feelings of inclusion and organizational support significantly influence job satisfaction. Thus, it can be said that alternative job arrangements are most likely to be most effective when participating employees have a strong *sense of workplace inclusion*.

8.5.2 Organizational Moderators

Alternative job arrangements are most likely to produce positive outcomes for organizations with the following characteristics: (1) divisibility of job tasks (discrete/self-contained/divisible tasks), (2) pre-specified job arrangements, and (3) managerial support.

First, alternative job arrangements (e.g., part-time, job sharing, contractual work) are likely to be effective when tasks are *discrete, self-contained, and divisible*. Jobs which are task-related (discrete or self-contained) are considered most suitable for alternative job arrangements. In contrast, managerial, supervisory, and marketing jobs are unsuitable because they depend on personal contact, frequent communication, continuity, and ad hoc problem solving (Harris, 1997). In other words, employees may not be in an optimal position to participate in alternative job arrangements if the job requires close collaboration with co-workers or interaction with customers. Harris (1997) conducted a survey of directors of personnel in each of the 117 U.K. universities to identify their perceptions on job sharing. Questions were asked concerning the principal perceived advantages and problems of job-sharing arrangements. Results showed that key advantages of job sharing include:

- greater flexibility and continuity that job sharing allows (e.g., at least part of the job is covered when one person is away sick or on holiday, and both employees may be available during peak periods);
- the possibility of retaining skilled personnel who might otherwise be lost, with potential savings in respect to recruiting and assimilating new staff; and
- greater productivity.

The potential or actual problems identified were:

- the necessity of close liaison and good communication between the job sharers; and
- the potential difficulties of finding an appropriate replacement if one job sharer leaves.

Given the difficulties between job sharers, alternative job arrangements (e.g., part time, job sharing, contractual work) are likely to be most effective when tasks are *discrete, self-contained, and divisible* (Harris, 1997).

Second, alternative job arrangements are likely to be most effective when the arrangements help the employee cope with work-life conflict and the *work hours are specified in advance*—instead of a work schedule that is highly variable and imposed in an ad hoc manner (Chow & Chew, 2006; Kossek & Ozeki, 1999; Scholarios et al., 2017). Consider the following study. Scholarios et al. (2017) examined whether unpredictability in scheduling is associated with greater employee work-life conflict and perceived stress. Through a survey of 1207 police officers, they were able to confirm this hypothesis in relation to work-life conflict ($\beta = 0.13$, $p < 0.05$), which in turn was found to have an impact on health and well-being. Alcohol consumption increased for those with an unpredictable schedule, thereby intensifying the negative effects of unpredictability on wellbeing and health outcomes. Therefore, in designing flexible working arrangements (e.g., part-time work, shift work), it is important for managers to share the schedule in advance and to reduce unpredictability in scheduling.

Lastly, alternative job arrangements are likely to be more effective when the *organization is perceived to have a culture that is pro work-life balance* (Callan, 2007; Timms et al., 2015). Employees are likely to reject an alternative job arrangement if they perceive that participation is not properly supported by management (Shockley & Allen, 2007). The managerial implication is that to support alternative job arrangements, managers should provide clear guidelines about performance evaluation and promotion for employees with an alternative job arrangement (Straughan & Tadai, 2018). Employee's perceptions about the extent to which management is supportive influence the effectiveness of work-family programs, including alternative job arrangements. Perceived organizational support for the programs serves to reduce work-family conflict and facilitates the actual use of alternative work programs. Through a survey of 230 employed women, Shockley and Allen (2007) found that employee's family-supportive organizational perceptions correlated negatively with work-family conflict ($r = -0.49$. $p < 0.01$) and family-work conflict ($r = -0.37$, $p < 0.01$). These study findings reinforce the importance of developing an organizational culture that is family supportive.

8.5.3 Environmental Moderators

Research has also identified the following environmental moderators associated with optimal alternative job arrangements: (1) organizations operating in countries with an individualistic culture, and (2) countries that are high on gender equality.

First, evidence suggests that alternative job arrangements are more effective in organizations operating in highly individualistic countries (i.e., low on collectivism). In his cultural values framework, Hofstede (2001) argued that employees who are high in individualism tend to prefer working independently instead of working in groups. Employees high in individualism also tend to place a higher value on the achievement of personal goals than on goals of the group. That is, an employee's cultural background influences the effectiveness of alternative job arrangements (Adamovic, 2022). In other words, individualistic employees like working the way they want to and focus more on individual goal achievement. They like to work in non-traditional work arrangements (e.g., job sharing) which better accommodates their individual needs and preferences. In contrast, collectivist employees like to work in groups and worry more about social isolation. Employees in countries high on collectivism also tend to conform to customs and traditions.

Second, alternative job arrangements are more effective in organizations operating in countries with a culture that promotes gender equality. This is because female employees working in societies with strong adherence to traditional gender roles (i.e., countries that lack a gender egalitarian culture) are likely to encounter obstacles when seeking roles associated with alternative job arrangements. Gender egalitarianism is a measure of national culture that reflects the degree of differentiation in prescribed gender roles for men and women. Cross-national variations in societal beliefs about gender roles (e.g., gender egalitarianism) shape not only women's and men's behaviors (and ability to achieve work-life balance) but also corresponding stereotypical beliefs about the attributes of women and men (Lyness & Judiesch, 2014). In low gender egalitarian cultures men are expected to prioritize work over family, and women are expected to prioritize family over work, whereas in more egalitarian cultures there is less differentiation between gender roles and expected priorities based on gender (McDaniel, 2008). Consider the following study. Based on the survey of 40,921 managers in 36 countries, Lyness and Judiesch (2014) found that women reported lower work-life balance than men in low egalitarian countries, and that gender did not have a significant impact on work-life balance in high egalitarian countries.

8.6 Summary and Conclusion

In this chapter, we discussed much of the research on alternative job arrangements. Programs involving alternative job arrangements are essentially a nontraditional work week and the flexibility to take time off without pay for hours not physically at work. Alternative job arrangements include part-time jobs, job sharing, and career breaks such as sabbaticals.

Research indicates that alternative job arrangements have both positive and negative consequences. Positive consequences include reduction of employees' workload to help them cope with work-life conflict. Positive organizational effects include reduced absenteeism, increased staff retention, diversity of organizational solutions to job-related tasks, and improved job performance. Additionally, alternative job arrangements tend to increase perceived attractiveness of the organization. This translates into increased employee recruitment and retention.

That is not to say that alternative job arrangements do not have a downside. For example, part-time contractual workers have less opportunity for upward mobility, fewer institutional protections such as health and retirement benefits, and declining union membership. Temporary agency workers tend to experience lower job satisfaction compared to permanent employees. This may be due to feelings of job insecurity, perceptions of lower employability, lower pay, and low organizational commitment. One way to address these problems is to offer part-time employees the ability to transition into full-time positions within the organization given a good job performance.

There are many forms of alternative job arrangements including part time, job sharing, career breaks, on-call work, and contract work.

Research also indicates the effectiveness of alternative job arrangements is moderated by personal, organizational, and environmental factors. Specifically, alternative job arrangements are most likely to produce positive outcomes for employees with the following individual characteristics: those who participate in the program voluntarily, those who perceive the program to be useful, those with childcare responsibilities and post-retirement adults, those experiencing a good person-program fit, and those with a strong sense of workplace inclusion.

With respect to organizational factors moderating the effectiveness of these programs, research indicates that the following conditions are important. That is, alternative job arrangements are most likely to produce positive outcomes for jobs with the following organizational characteristics: divisibility of job tasks (discrete/self-contained/divisible tasks), pre-specified job arrangements, and managerial support.

Research has also identified the following cultural factors associated with optimal alternative job arrangements. These include organizations operating in countries with an individualistic culture and countries that are high on gender equality.

Management can enhance the effectiveness of alternative job arrangements by promoting those programs to employees who:

- believe that such programs have significant benefits to themselves and their families.
- express interest in applying to a specific program voluntarily.
- report that they have significant childcare responsibilities.
- identify themselves as post-retirement adults with expressed interest in sustaining their careers.

- desire to be identified with the organization and maintain a sense of workplace inclusion.

Management should offer alternative job arrangements for jobs, projects and tasks characterized as discrete, self-contained, and divisible. The job expectations and requirements must be pre-specified and well supported by management.

Furthermore, management should realize that alternative job arrangements can be best implemented in units or divisions located in highly individualistic countries (e.g., English speaking Western countries) because of cultural congruency—these countries place more value on individualism and gender equality. Individualism and gender equality are cultural characteristics serving as catalysts enhancing the effectiveness of alternative job arrangements.

See Box 8.1 for "practical recommendations" from practitioners.

Box 8.1 Practical Recommendations from Industry Practitioners About Alternative Jon Arrangements

An alternative job arrangement such as job sharing usually brings much knowledge, skills, and experiences to a position. This arrangement also provides cross-training and skill enhancement opportunities to those who are sharing the position. Of course, such an arrangement requires management to maintain close coordination and use effective means to ensure good teamwork.

Talking about team building, management should assign the partners to engage in activities that have the specific purpose to bring the partners closer together. Examples of activities include escape rooms, trust exercises, problem-solving puzzles, etc.

The same may apply to other job arrangements such as part-time work. Again, the goal here is to provide support to ensure good teamwork. This may take form in a range of activities such as signing up the team to run a marathon or getting together to sort canned goods at the local food bank. These activities allow the team members to bond. Management could even offer to give employees a bonus day off per year for them to partake in a volunteering activity of their choice. Encouraging volunteering in the workplace helps build team spirit and mutual trust among participating employees.

Source: Adapted from https://www.frontstream.com/blog/work-life-balance-strategies

In the next chapter, we will discuss the research related to family care policies and programs. Specifically, we will discuss the personal and organizational consequences of family care practices. We will explain how these practices influence WLB and how they are commonly implemented. We will then examine conditions that moderate the overall effectiveness of family care practices.

References

Abraham, K. G., Haltiwanger, J. C., Sandusky, K., & Spletzer, J. R. (2018). *Measuring the gig economy: Current knowledge and open issues. Technical report working paper 24950*. National Bureau of Economic Research.

Adamovic, M. (2022). How does employee cultural background influence the effects of telework on job stress? The roles of power distance, individualism, and beliefs about telework. *International Journal of Information Management, 62*(February), 102437.

Allen, T. D. (2001). Family-supportive work environments: The role of organizational perceptions. *Journal of Vocational Behavior, 58*(3), 414–435.

Allen, T. D., Johnson, R. C., Kiburz, K. M., & Shockley, K. M. (2013). Work-family conflict and flexible work arrangements: Deconstructing flexibility. *Personnel Psychology, 66*(2), 345–376.

Arun, S. V., Arun, T. G., & Borooah, V. K. (2004). The effect of career breaks on the working lives of women. *Feminist Economics, 10*(1), 65–84.

Ashford, S. J., George, E., & Blatt, R. (2007). 2 old assumptions, new work: The opportunities and challenges of research on nonstandard employment. *Academy of Management Annals, 1*(1), 65–117.

Bakker, A. B., & Demerouti, E. (2007). The job demands-resources model: State of the art. *Journal of Managerial Psychology, 22*(3), 309–328.

Barley, S. R., & Kunda, G. (2006). Contracting: A new form of professional practice. *Academy of Management Perspectives, 20*(1), 45–66.

Batt, R., & Valcour, P. M. (2003). Human resources practices as predictors of work-family outcomes and employee turnover. *Industrial Relations, 42*(2), 189–220.

Beham, B., Präg, P., & Drobnič, S. (2012). Who's got the balance? A study of satisfaction with the work-family balance among part-time service sector employees in five western European countries. *The International Journal of Human Resource Management, 23*(18), 3725–3741.

Bidwell, M., Briscoe, F., Fernandez-Mateo, I., & Sterling, A. (2013). The employment relationship and inequality: How and why changes in employment practices are reshaping rewards in organizations. *Academy of Management Annals, 7*(1), 61–121.

Bidwell, M., & Mollick, E. (2015). Shifts and ladders: Comparing the role of internal and external mobility in managerial careers. *Organization Science, 26*(6), 1629–1645.

Bidwell, M. J. (2013). What happened to long-term employment? The role of worker power and environmental turbulence in explaining declines in worker tenure. *Organization Science, 24*(4), 1061–1082.

Bidwell, M. J., & Briscoe, F. (2009). Who contracts? Determinants of the decision to work as an independent contractor among information technology workers. *Academy of Management Journal, 52*(6), 1148–1168.

Boudreau, K. J., & Jeppesen, L. B. (2015). Unpaid crowd complementors: The platform network effect mirage. *Strategic Management Journal, 36*(12), 1761–1777.

Broschak, J. P., Davis-Blake, A., & Block, E. S. (2008). Nonstandard, not substandard: The relationship among work arrangements, work attitudes, and job performance. *Work and Occupations, 35*(1), 3–43.

Callan, S. (2007). Implications of family-friendly policies for organizational culture: Findings from two case studies. *Work, Employment and Society, 21*(4), 673–691.

Cappelli, P., & Keller, J. R. (2013). Classifying work in the new economy. *Academy of Management Review, 38*(4), 575–596.

Carless, S. A., & Wintle, J. (2007). Applicant attraction: The role of recruiter function, work-life balance policies and career salience. *International Journal of Selection and Assessment, 15*(4), 394–404.

Chow, I. H. S., & Chew, I. K. H. (2006). The effect of alternative work schedules on employee performance. *International Journal of Employment Studies, 14*(1), 105–130.

Chung, H., & Van der Horst, M. (2018). Women's employment patterns after childbirth and the perceived access to and use of flexitime and teleworking. *Human Relations, 71*(1), 47–72.

De Cuyper, N., Notelaers, G., & De Witte, H. (2009a). Transitioning between temporary and permanent employment: A two-wave study on the entrapment, the steppingstone and the selection hypothesis. *Journal of Occupational and Organizational Psychology, 82*(1), 67–88.

De Cuyper, N., Notelaers, G., & De Witte, H. (2009b). Job insecurity and employability in fixed-term contractors, agency workers, and permanent workers: Associations with job satisfaction and affective organizational commitment. *Journal of Occupational Health Psychology, 14*(2), 193–205.

DeWall, C. N., & Baumeister, R. F. (2006). Alone but feeling no pain: Effects of social exclusion on physical pain tolerance and pain threshold, affective forecasting, and interpersonal empathy. *Journal of Personality and Social Psychology, 91*(1), 1–15.

Dingemans, E., & Henkens, K. (2014). Involuntary retirement, bridge employment, and satisfaction with life: A longitudinal investigation. *Journal of Organizational Behavior, 35*(4), 575–591.

Farrell, D., & Greig, F. (2016). Paychecks, paydays, and the online platform economy. In *Proceedings. Annual conference on taxation and minutes of the annual meeting of the National tax Association* (Vol. 109 (January), pp. 1–40). National Tax Association.

Freeman, B. J., & Coll, K. M. (2009). Solutions to faculty work overload: A study of job sharing. *The Career Development Quarterly, 58*(1), 65–70.

Galinsky, E., Bond, J. T., & Friedman, D. E. (1993). *The changing workforce: Highlights of the national study*. Diane Publishing.

Gholipour, A., Bod, M., Zehtabi, M., Pirannejad, A., & Kozekanan, S. F. (2010). The feasibility of job sharing as a mechanism to balance work and life of female entrepreneurs. *International Business Research, 3*(3), 133–140.

Golden, T. D. (2006). The role of relationships in understanding telecommuter satisfaction. *Journal of Organizational Behavior, 27*(3), 319–340.

Greenhaus, J. H., & Allen, T. D. (2011). Work-family balance: A review and extension of the literature. In J. C. Quick & L. E. Tetrick (Eds.), *Handbook of occupational Health Psychology* (pp. 165–183). American Psychological Association.

Greenhaus, J. H., & Beutell, N. J. (1985). Sources of conflict between work and family roles. *Academy of Management Review, 10*(1), 76–88.

Griffin, B., Vest, K., Pohl, S., Mazan, J., & Winkler, S. (2014). Part-time and job-share careers among pharmacy practice faculty members. *American Journal of Pharmaceutical Education, 78*(3), 49–62.

Harris, G. (1997). Is job sharing worthwhile? A cost-benefit analysis in UK universities. *Higher Education, 33*(1), 29–38.

Hayes, B. C., Bartle, S. A., & Major, D. A. (2002). Climate for opportunity: A conceptual model. *Human Resource Management Review, 12*(3), 445–468.

Hill, E. J., Märtinson, V. K., Ferris, M., & Baker, R. Z. (2004). Beyond the mommy track: The influence of new-concept part-time work for professional women on work and family. *Journal of Family and Economic Issues, 25*(1), 121–136.

Hofstede, G. (2001). *Culture's consequences: Comparing values, behaviors, institutions and organizations across nations*. Sage publications.

Johnson, S. A., & Ashforth, B. E. (2008). Externalization of employment in a service environment: The role of organizational and customer identification. *Journal of Organizational Behavior, 29*(3), 287–309.

Kalleberg, A. L. (2012). Job quality and precarious work: Clarifications, controversies, and challenges. *Work and Occupations, 39*(4), 427–448.

Katz, L. F., & Krueger, A. B. (2019). The rise and nature of alternative job arrangements in the United States, 1995–2015. *ILR Review, 72*(2), 382–416.

Keil, M. J., Armstrong-Stassen, M., Cameron, S., & Horsburgh, M. (2000). Part-time nurses: The effect of work status congruency on job attitudes. *Applied Psychology, 49*(2), 227–236.

Kim, J., & Wiggins, M. E. (2011). Family-friendly human resource policy: Is it still working in the public sector? *Public Administration Review, 71*(5), 728–739.

Kossek, E. E., & Lautsch, B. A. (2018). Work-life flexibility for whom? Occupational status and work-life inequality in upper, middle, and lower-level jobs. *Academy of Management Annals, 12*(1), 5–36.
Kossek, E. E., & Ozeki, C. (1999). Bridging the work-family policy and productivity gap: A literature review. *Community, Work & Family, 2*(1), 7–32.
Kossek, E. E., & Ruderman, M. N. (2012). Work-family flexibility and the employment relationship. In L. M. Shore, J. A.-M. Coyle-Shapiro, & L. E. Tetrick (Eds.), *The employee-organization relationship* (pp. 265–296). Routledge.
Lambert, S. J. (2000). Added benefits: The link between work-life benefits and organizational citizenship behavior. *Academy of Management Journal, 43*(5), 801–815.
Lewis, S. (1997). 'Family friendly' employment policies: A route to changing organizational culture or playing about at the margins? *Gender, Work and Organization, 4*(1), 13–24.
Lyness, K. S., & Judiesch, M. K. (2014). Gender egalitarianism and work-life balance for managers: Multisource perspectives in 36 countries. *Applied Psychology, 63*(1), 96–129.
Mas, A., & Pallais, A. (2020). *Alternative job arrangements., Technical Report Working Paper* 26605,. National Bureau of Economic Research.
Mayfield, J. (2006). The benefits of leader communication on part-time worker outcomes: A comparison between part-time and full-time employees using motivating language. *Journal of Business Strategies, 23*(2), 131–154.
McComb, S. A., Bourne, K. A., & Barringer, M. W. (2003). Reconciling the paradox of part-time service work-strategies for managers. *Organizational Dynamics, 4*(32), 342–356.
McDaniel, A. E. (2008). Measuring gender egalitarianism: The attitudinal difference between men and women. *International Journal of Sociology, 38*(1), 58–80.
Morganson, V. J., Major, D. A., Oborn, K. L., Verive, J. M., & Heelan, M. P. (2010). Comparing telework locations and traditional work arrangements: Differences in work-life balance support, job satisfaction, and inclusion. *Journal of Managerial Psychology, 25*(6), 578–595.
Nardone, T. (1995). Part-time employment: Reasons, demographics, and trends. *Journal of Labor Research, 16*(3), 275–292.
Scholarios, D., Hesselgreaves, H., & Pratt, R. (2017). Unpredictable working time, well-being and health in the police service. *The International Journal of Human Resource Management, 28*(16), 2275–2298.
Shockley, K. M., & Allen, T. D. (2007). When flexibility helps: Another look at the availability of flexible work arrangements and work-family conflict. *Journal of Vocational Behavior, 71*(3), 479–493.
Spreitzer, G. M., Cameron, L., & Garrett, L. (2017). Alternative job arrangements: Two images of the new world of work. *Annual Review of Organizational Psychology and Organizational Behavior, 4*, 473–499.
Straughan, P. T., & Tadai, M. E. (2018). Addressing the implementation gap in flexiwork policies: The case of part-time work in Singapore. *Asia Pacific Journal of Human Resources, 56*(2), 155–174.
Thorsteinson, T. J. (2003). Job attitudes of part-time vs. full-time workers: A meta-analytic review. *Journal of Occupational and Organizational Psychology, 76*(2), 151–177.
Timms, C., Brough, P., O'Driscoll, M., Kalliath, T., Siu, O. L., Sit, C., & Lo, D. (2015). Flexible work arrangements, work engagement, turnover intentions and psychological health. *Asia Pacific Journal of Human Resources, 53*(1), 83–103.
Van Rijswijk, K., Bekker, M. H., Rutte, C. G., & Croon, M. A. (2004). The relationships among part-time work, work-family interference, and Well-being. *Journal of Occupational Health Psychology, 9*(4), 286–295.
Walsh, J. (2007). Experiencing part-time work: Temporal tensions, social relations and the work-family interface. *British Journal of Industrial Relations, 45*(1), 155–177.
Warren, T. (2004). Working part-time: Achieving a successful work-life balance? *The British Journal of Sociology, 55*(1), 99–122.
Wilkin, C. L. (2013). I can't get no job satisfaction: Meta-analysis comparing permanent and contingent workers. *Journal of Organizational Behavior, 34*(1), 47–64.

Williams, M. L., Ford, L. R., Dohring, P. L., Lee, M. D., & MacDermid, S. M. (2000, August). Outcomes of reduced load work arrangements at managerial and professional levels: Perspectives from multiple stakeholders. In *Annual Meeting of the Academy of Management,* Toronto, ON, Canada.

Wittmer, J. L., & Martin, J. E. (2010). Emotional exhaustion among employees without social or client contact: The key role of nonstandard work schedules. *Journal of Business and Psychology, 25*(4), 607–623.

Chapter 9
Family Care Policies and Programs

"If you want to change the world, go home and love your family."—Mother Teresa (https://teambuilding.com/blog/work-life-balance-quotes)

Abstract In this chapter we discuss the research related to family care policies and programs. Specifically, we discuss the evidence related to employee and organizational consequences of family care practices. We also explain how these consequences occur using work-life balance theories such as role conflict, family demands and resources, and social exchange. We then describe specific family care practices such as childcare and eldercare services, family-leave policies, time-off programs, assistance programs, and other services. We then examine the conditions that moderate the overall effectiveness of family care practices—personal, organizational, and environmental conditions.

9.1 Introduction

Since 1993 U.S. federal law has required companies with 50 or more employees to allow eligible workers 12 weeks of unpaid leave to care for a newborn or an ailing family member or deal with a medical problem of their own (Kalev & Dobbin, 2022). Unfortunately, not all employers are on board. Today only one in 14 offer this program to new mothers and nearly one in four offer the same to new fathers (Kalev & Dobbin, 2022).

Family care policies and programs involve any form of benefit specifically designed to accommodate employees by providing leave or facilities (or flexibility) to care for children, elders, and/or other family members. Research has demonstrated that availability and utilization of family care programs decreases family-to-work conflict (Thomas & Ganster, 1995; Yuile et al., 2012). Organizational family care practices include, but are not limited to, on-site childcare/eldercare services, employee assistance programs, and family-leave programs.

D.-J. Lee, M. J. Sirgy, *Organizational Strategies for Work-Life Balance*, Human Well-Being Research and Policy Making,
https://doi.org/10.1007/978-3-031-56314-0_9

9.2 Consequences of Family Care Policies and Programs

Research has documented the following positive personal and organizational consequences of family care programs. See Table 9.1 for a list of consequences.

First, family care practices (e.g., family leave, childcare, eldercare) increase employees' perception of control over work and family life (Thomas & Ganster, 1995). They also provide health benefits (Aitken et al., 2015). Aitken et al. (2015) conducted a systematic review of studies that examined the association between paid maternity leave and maternal health through a search of electronic databases. Their results indicate that paid maternity leave provides several maternal health benefits including a positive effect on mental health, general health, and physical well-being.

Second, family care practices increase the extent to which employees view their work environment as being family supportive (O'Driscoll et al., 2003), help employees reduce work-life conflict (Butts et al., 2013), and increase job satisfaction and organizational commitment (Butts et al., 2013; Caillier, 2013, 2016; Roehling et al., 2001; Wang & Walumbwa, 2007). Butts et al. (2013) conducted a meta-analysis to find out whether *availability* and *use* of work-family support policies are related to more positive work attitudes. They found that availability and use of family support programs exhibited small positive relationships with job satisfaction, affective commitment, and intentions to stay. The effects associated with policy availability were generally stronger than those associated with the use of the program. This may be because availability of family care programs may operate through both a symbolic mechanism by signaling corporate concern and an instrumental mechanism by reducing work-family conflict. Specifically, the study shows that policy availability increases employee perceptions of the firm being family supportive (beta = 0.19**), which has a positive influence on positive work attitude. That is, family care programs contribute to positive job attitude by signaling corporate concern (e.g., symbolic mechanism). In addition, the results also indicate that policy availability has a positive association with policy use (beta = 0.48**), which in turn serves to decrease

Table 9.1 Personal and organizational consequences of family care policies and programs

Type of consequence	Specific consequences
Personal consequences	Increased employee perception of control over work and family life Increased health benefits Positive effects on employees' mental health Positive effects on employees' general health Positive effects on employees' physical wellbeing Heightened employees' perceptions that management is family supportive Reduced employees' work-life conflict Reduced employees' personal stressors
Organizational consequences	Increased employees' job satisfaction Increased employees' organizational commitment Increased employees' positive work attitudes Increased employees' intentions to stay Increased employer attractiveness among potential recruits

work-to-family conflict (beta = −14**), contributing to a positive work attitude. That is, family care programs contribute to a positive job attitude by reducing work-family conflict (e.g., instrumental mechanism).

Third, evidence suggests that providing employees with family care programs tends to reduce turnover intention. Consider the study conducted by McDonald et al. (2005). These researchers analyzed family-policy documents and conducted in-depth interviews with women who have dependent children to determine the extent to which the intended goals of formal work-family policies are being achieved at the individual employee level. They found that family care programs significantly increased perception of control in work and family life and served to reduce personal stressors.

Finally, research shows that the availability of family care practices leads to employees perceiving organizations are more family supportive (Butts et al., 2013). These increased perceptions seem to increase intentions to pursue employment with those organizations. Consider the following study. Through an experiment of 371 job applicants, Casper and Buffardi (2004) manipulated the availability of dependent care programs of an organization (i.e., availability of vacation, sick leave, on-site childcare, dependent care referral service) and asked respondents about their perceptions of anticipated organizational support and their intention to pursue employment with the organization. The study findings indicate that the availability of various dependent care programs increased perceptions of anticipated organizational support and intention to pursue employment with the organization.

9.3 How Do Family Care Programs Help with Work-Life Balance

The research literature on family-friendly practices (e.g., on-site childcare services, employee assistance programs, family leave, and time-off for family care) has identified several theoretical explanations tying the availability and use of these programs to increased WLB and other positive outcomes (e.g., organizational commitment) (Beauregard & Henry, 2009; Chiu & Ng, 1999; Grover & Crooker, 1995; Thompson et al., 2004; Wang & Walumbwa, 2007). These include role conflict, family demands and resources, and social exchange. See Table 9.2 for a summary of these mediating dynamics.

Table 9.2 Theories to explain the impact of family care policies and program

Theory	Explanation
Role conflict	Family care programs contribute to WLB by reducing role conflict. More specifically, they do so by providing a measure of control over time
Family demands and resources	Family care programs support employees in maintaining high performance by providing necessary resources to handle role demands
Social exchange	Family care programs serve to create and reinforce a positive attitude toward the workplace, which in turn spills over to satisfaction in the family life domain

9.3.1 Role Conflict

Role conflict theory (Kahn et al., 1964) posits that different roles that individuals assume, such as work and family roles, can be incompatible or sometimes conflict with one another. Family care programs (e.g., leave programs) contribute to WLB by reducing role conflict. They help employees reduce work-life conflict by providing a measure of control over time. By enabling employees to schedule their time to better meet competing demands from work and home, and by helping employees to procure third-party assistance with caregiving responsibilities, family care practices reduce or eliminate work-life conflict, and thereby augment employee performance and organizational effectiveness (Beauregard & Henry, 2009).

9.3.2 Family Demands and Resources

Family care programs (e.g., on-site childcare services) support employees in maintaining high performance by providing necessary resources to handle role demands. As of 2016, the average cost of full-time infant care in the United States was between 7% and 16% of the median income for a married couple and, on average, center-based infant care was more than 24% of the median income for single parents (Child Care Aware, 2016). These costs can place significant financial pressures on families of all income levels. As such, the cost of childcare can be a significant factor in household decisions related to employment decisions of parents. Affordable, quality childcare enables parents to work and to work more hours for higher income, thereby enabling work-life balance (Feeney & Stritch, 2019). Family care programs (e.g., leave programs) contribute to work-life balance by providing resources (financial, physical, psychological resources) to handle role demands.

9.3.3 Social Exchange

Family care programs facilitate positive work attitude (e.g., job satisfaction, organizational commitment), which in turn spills over to satisfaction in the family life domain. Family care programs improve positive job-related attitudes and perceptions of organizational support. Employees who benefit from childcare centers, referral services and other family-supportive practices report higher levels of job satisfaction and commitment to the organization (Grover & Crooker, 1995). Lambert (2000) found that workers' experiences with family-friendly benefits fostered organizational citizenship behaviors, suggesting that workers feel obligated to exert "extra" effort in return for "extra" benefits. These results can be interpreted using social exchange theory (Blau, 1964). When treated favorably by the organization, employees will feel obliged to respond in kind, through positive attitudes or behaviors toward the source of the treatment. Increased satisfaction in the work-life domain spills over to satisfaction in the family life domain, thereby contributing to work-life balance.

9.4 Implementing Family Care Practices

What are common family care practices that have been implemented by many organizations to date? These include: (1) childcare and eldercare programs, (2) family-leave policies and programs, (3) time-off policies and programs, (4) assistance programs and policies, and (5) other services. Let us describe these programs in more detail.

9.4.1 Childcare and Eldercare Policies and Programs

Many companies are providing access to childcare and eldercare facilities for their employees (both part-time and full-time). Many even have childcare and eldercare facilities on site. Some companies even offer IT-based childcare systems, which let parents monitor the activities of their children at work or from home (Allen, 2001; Beauregard & Henry, 2009; Dikkers et al., 2001).

Childcare programs include on-site childcare facilities (i.e., employer sponsored childcare center), employer childcare referral services (i.e., a company provides a list of childcare providers to their employees), subsidized child-care costs (i.e., a company shares part of the childcare costs of their employees). See Box 9.1 for a current snapshot of current reality in the U.S.

Box 9.1 The Current Reality of Childcare Support

Corporate childcare support programs vary greatly. Three programs are discussed below: referral services (the least-expensive option); vouchers (a middle-range option); and company childcare centers (the most expensive option).

Referral Services: Such programs provide contact information for local childcare centers, usually in online listings. Referral services are the most common type of childcare support, offered by about 40% of all U.S. employers and 60% of large employers. These programs provide no financial help, but they signal an employer's disposition to help employees deal with childcare problems.

Childcare Vouchers: Employers also offer vouchers that subsidize childcare, usually at independent childcare centers.

Company Childcare Centers: Consider the Patagonia example. This company now has a child-learning center at its headquarters, in Ventura, California, and another at its distribution center in Reno. It is reported that the company recoups 91% of calculable costs for its centers through tax refunds, decreased turnover, increased engagement, and heightened employee loyalty and trust. Today about one out of every six large companies has at least one childcare center (e.g., Fannie Mae, Walgreens, Boeing, and Home Depot).

It should be noted that vouchers accommodate changes in demand better than company centers. Vouchers tend to be administered through flexible spending accounts, both employers and employees save on payroll taxes, and employees save on income taxes.

Source: Adapted from Kalev and Dobbin (2022).

Similar arrangements are made for eldercare programs. However, eldercare programs are not as popular compared to childcare services.

9.4.2 Family-Leave Policies and Programs

Popular family-leave programs that many organizations have in place include maternity leave (employment-protected leave of absence for employed women directly after childbirth/adoption), paternity leave (employment-protected leave of absence for employed men directly after childbirth), parental leave (employment-protected leave of absence for employed parents, which is often supplementary to specific maternity and paternity leave periods), and home/child care leave (employment-protected leaves of absence that sometimes follow parental leave and that typically allow at least one parent to remain at home to provide care until the child is 2 or 3 years old) (Allen, 2001; Beauregard & Henry, 2009; Dikkers et al., 2001). See Box 9.2 for example companies offering payment to employees on family leave.

Box 9.2 The New Trend of Paying Staff Members on Family Leave

The current reality is that fewer than 10% of low-wage workers are eligible for any pay during family and medical leaves. However, there is a trend promising change. For example, retailers such as Nordstrom and Walmart offer new parents 6 weeks of pay, with birth mothers getting another six. Target offers new parents 4 weeks, with birth mothers getting another six to eight. Tech firms are doing better than retailers. For example, since 2015, Netflix has offered salaried workers up to a year of paid parental leave. Meta provides full pay for 4 months. Google (now Alphabet) extended its 12-week paid leave to 24 weeks for new mothers.

Source: Adapted from Kalev and Dobbin (2022).

Family-leave policies are designed to provide time off from work so that new mothers can prepare for and recover from childbirth, parents can care for their newborn or newly adopted children, and individuals can care for seriously ill family members. For maternity leave, most countries around the world guarantee some type of paid maternity leave to new working mothers. The International Labor Organization (ILO) set a standard maternity benefit that amounts to at least two-thirds of a woman's previous earnings for at least 14 weeks (Rossin-Slater, 2017). In addition, most developed countries also provide access to other types of family leave: paternity leave (i.e., leave designated specifically for new fathers), parental leave (i.e., leave that can be taken by both new mothers and fathers), or family leave (i.e., leave that can be taken to care for ill family members in addition to new children). Parental leave is relatively long-term leave that is typically available to either or both parents (although some countries have dedicated non-transferrable portions specifically for fathers) and is meant to allow them to care for an infant or young child after the end of the maternity or paternity leave period. In the U.S., the Family and Medical Leave Act (FMLA) of 1993 mandated that employers grant 12 weeks of unpaid job-protected family leave with continued coverage by the employer's health insurance (if such coverage was already offered at the job) to qualifying workers. To be eligible, workers must have worked at least 1250 h in the preceding year for an employer with at least 50 employees.

Family-leave policies significantly contribute to family wellbeing and promoting career continuity. That is, family leave policies are likely to increase leave-taking and job continuity of parents after childbirth. Research has shown that the FMLA and state-level maternity leave policies increase maternal leave-taking by 13% during the birth month, 16% during the month after birth, and a marginally significant 20% during the second month after birth (Han et al., 2009). Evidence also shows that leave entitlements less than 1 year in length can improve job continuity for women and increase their employment rates several years after childbirth, whereas longer leaves can negatively influence women's earnings, employment, and career advancement (Rossin-Slater, 2017).

Access to paid sick leave and the ability to use that sick leave without penalty are particularly important for women, who are more often responsible for caregiving in the home—including caring for sick children and elderly parents (Heymann, 2000). While all public and private organizations with 50 or more employees in the United States are subject to the Family Medical and Leave Act of 1993 (FMLA) and other federal laws regarding family leave, individual states and organizations can go above and beyond to offer more generous leave policies including paid sick leave, pregnancy leave, domestic violence leave, and volunteer emergency services personal leave. More generous leave policies may include offering full or partial pay during family or sick leave, extending leave time, or negotiating special circumstances (Feeney & Stritch, 2019). Although workers in the United States have the option to take unpaid leave under the FMLA, Americans, in general, are reluctant to take sick leave without pay, even when paid leave is available for fear that they might be ostracized.

Some organizations hire replacement workers for employees taking family leave (e.g., maternity and paternity leave for childbirth, family care leave for elderly and childcare). Without replacement workers, the workload of leave workers is usually redistributed among existing workers. Many organizations guarantee their employees who use a family program the ability to return to their original job with no penalty in terms of career development and advancement. They also encourage paternity leave for the dual-income families (Allen, 2001; Beauregard & Henry, 2009; Dikkers et al., 2001). In addition to family leave for full-time employees, management often also provides leave for employees with alternative job arrangements (e.g., maternity leave for part-time workers).

9.4.3 Time-Off Policies and Programs

Many companies have time-off programs. These programs include time off for personal and professional development, paid vacations and sabbaticals, and accrued days off (Allen, 2001; Beauregard & Henry, 2009; Dikkers et al., 2001).

Sabbatical leave is paid leave for personal and professional development that is most offered to those in academic professions (Miller & Kang, 1998). Sabbatical leave is meant to provide relief from routine work duties and is appreciably longer and less frequent than traditional vacations. Though individuals on sabbatical can be expected to perform some parts of the job while on sabbatical, some of the stressors that characterize routine work are diminished (Zahorski, 1994). Davidson et al. (2010) conducted a quasi-experiment to test the effects of sabbatical leave with a sample of 129 faculty members on sabbatical and a sample of 129 matched controls. Among the sabbatees, resource loss declined, and resource gain and wellbeing rose. The comparison group showed no change. Moderation analysis revealed that positive wellbeing effect of sabbatical was higher for those individuals with high self-control, those who had a more positive sabbatical experience, and those who spent their sabbatical outside their home country.

Management can also provide flexible time away from work to meet personal needs. Examples include emergency flexibility (fixed number of days off with pay for emergencies), vacation buying or borrowing, and mini vacation (single day vacation instead of a full week or more). Furthermore, the ideal organization has policies in place to guarantee that those who take advantage of alternative job arrangements (part-time workers and job-sharing employees) maintain sustainable career paths within the organization (Allen, 2001; Beauregard & Henry, 2009; Dikkers et al., 2001).

9.4.4 Assistance Policies and Programs

Some organizations provide information, consultation, and educational services about family care. Some go the extra mile by providing financial assistance for home networks that employees can use at work (e.g., remote control of home temperature, remote control of home appliances) (Allen, 2001; Beauregard & Henry, 2009; Dikkers et al., 2001).

For example, in relation to eldercare, some organizations refer employees to existing eldercare providers, assist them with making arrangements, grant employees financial assistance toward the costs of eldercare, provide information about government programs that address the needs of the aging, offer support to outside eldercare centers, and operate on site eldercare centers (Merrill, 1997).

9.4.5 *Other Services*

There are numerous other family care services often available such as dry-cleaning services, employee counselling, postal and mailing services, onsite fitness facilities, and healthy food options (McCarthy et al., 2010). Some organizations provide health-related assistance such as voluntary, work-based programs that offer free and confidential medical assessments, short-term counseling, referrals, and follow-up services to employees who have health-related problems. Essentially, these family supportive services are offered by organizations to help staff manage the demands associated with both work and nonwork roles (McCarthy et al., 2010).

9.5 Under What Conditions Are Family Care Practices Most Effective

In this section we will describe the research dealing with moderator effects—under what conditions are family care programs most effective. Specifically, we will describe three sets of moderators: personal, organizational, and environmental. See Table 9.3 for a summary.

Table 9.3 Factors moderating the effectiveness of family care policies and programs

Type of moderators	Specific conditions
Personal moderators	When there is a good fit between the program and the specific needs of the employees When employees have experience with the program
Organizational moderators	Family-supportive supervision Transformational leadership Family-supportive organizational culture
Environmental moderators	Individualistic culture for childcare programs Collectivistic culture for eldercare programs Uncertainty avoidance culture

9.5.1 Personal Moderators

Research suggests that family care programs are most effective under two conditions: (1) when there is a good fit between the program and the specific needs of the employees (i.e., need fit), and (2) when employees have experience with the program (i.e., use experience).

First, evidence suggests that family care practices (e.g., family leave, childcare, eldercare) are effective when the programs *fit well with employees' need and preferences* (Ashforth et al., 2000). For example, married parents with young children are more likely than single parents to express satisfaction with childcare policies (Ezra & Deckman, 1996; Frone & Yardley, 1996). According to *gender role theory*, women are traditionally expected to be responsible for a greater share of family responsibility than men, who focus more on work (Blanch & Aluja, 2012; Katz-Wise et al., 2010). Specifically, Petts and Knoester (2019) identified that the length of paternity leave is only positively correlated with relationship satisfaction for mothers but not for fathers. Family care programs (family leave, childcare, eldercare) are effective when the programs fit well with employees' needs and preferences, and these needs and preferences are likely to be influenced by gender norms.

Second, evidence shows that family care practices (family leave, childcare, eldercare) have positive effects on job attitudes for those who have *experience with the program* (Butts et al., 2013). Through a meta-analysis, Butts et al. (2013) examined the relationship between work-family support policies (e.g., policies that provide support for dependent care responsibilities) and employee outcomes. The results indicated that actual use of work-family support policies have a modest positive relationship with job attitudes such as job satisfaction, affective commitment, and intentions to stay.

9.5.2 Organizational Moderators

Studies on family care programs reveal that these practices may be more effective given the following organizational characteristics: (1) family-supportive supervision, (2) transformational leadership, and (3) family-supportive organizational culture.

First, family care programs are effective when there is *family-supportive supervision*. Research demonstrates that family care programs (e.g., dependent care program, leave program) reduce work-life conflict and increase job satisfaction when there is a high level of supervisor support for these programs (Allen et al., 2014; Ko et al., 2013). A family-supportive supervisor is sympathetic to the employee's desire to seek balance between work and family, and who helps employees meet their work and family responsibilities (Allen, 2001). Thus, a family-supportive supervisor may increase the use of, and the satisfaction gained from family care programs. Consider the following study. Ko et al. (2013) examined this moderation relationship using the 2010 Federal Employee Viewpoint Survey ($n = 92{,}000$) and found that supervisor support significantly and positively moderates the association between dependent care programs and job satisfaction. In other words, family care programs are effective when there is family-supportive supervision.

See Box 9.3 for a discussion on how managers can overcome the fear of disruption of operations due to maternity/paternity leave.

Box 9.3 How Managers Can Overcome the Fear of Disruption of Operations

Unfortunately, companies with leave policies often don't advertise them and sometimes discourage new parents from taking advantage of those policies. Why the resistance? Employers often fear the disruption of operations that maternity/paternity leaves may cause.

Here are examples of companies who were successful in minimizing disruption of operations. Consider Tennessee's First Horizon Bank. Managers request a junior staff member to take on a challenging assignment to deal with a person's absence on a team under a deadline. Alternatively, managers look for someone who is coming off another project and may have time to spare. Furthermore, managers prepare for leaves by cross-training workers so that when someone must take time off, others will be ready to step in.

Source: Adapted from Kalev and Dobbin (2022).

Second, research shows that family care practices are more effective if the supervisor is a *transformational leader*. Transformational leaders are inspiring, challenging, and considerate of employees' feelings. In other words, family care programs conjoined with transformational leadership produce higher levels of organizational commitment and reduced the level of work withdrawal (Wang & Walumbwa, 2007). Consider the following study. Using a survey of 475 bank employees in China, Kenya, and Thailand, Wang and Walumbwa (2007) investigated the moderating effect of transformational leadership on the relationships between family-friendly programs, organizational commitment, and work withdrawal. Results support the idea that transformational leadership moderates the relationships between work flexibility benefits and both organizational commitment and work withdrawal, and between childcare benefits and work withdrawal (Wang & Walumbwa, 2007). In other words, family care programs are more effective when supervisors are transformational leaders.

Finally, family care practices are more effective when the organization has a *culture supportive of family care programs* (e.g., managerial support for paid sick leave). Specifically, these programs have been demonstrated to reduce work-life conflict when the organization is perceived as family-supportive (Allen et al., 2014). Consider the following study. With a sample of 643 working married parents with children under the age of 5 across 12 industrialized nations, Allen et al. (2014) examined the effect of paid leave policies (paid parental leave, paid sick leave, paid annual leave) on work-family conflict. Results showed that paid sick leave has a small but significant negative relationship with work-family conflict. In addition, family-supportive organizational perceptions and family-supportive supervision were tested as moderators with some evidence to suggest that paid leave policies are most beneficial when employees' perceptions of support are higher than when they are lower. In other words, a family-supportive organization can enhance the benefits of paid sick leave and family care programs are most effective when the organization has a culture supportive of them.

9.5.3 Environmental Moderators

Family care practices seem to be more effective given the following environmental characteristics: (1) individualistic culture for childcare programs, (2) collectivistic culture for eldercare programs, and (3) uncertainty avoidance culture.

First, childcare programs are more effective in countries with an *individualistic culture* in which employees often cannot rely on extended family members to care for their children (compared to a collectivistic culture). Parents of children in an individualistic culture are more likely to experience high work-life conflict; as such, childcare programs tend to be effective in reducing work-family conflict in a country with an individualistic culture (Spector et al., 2017; Yang et al., 2000). Consider the following study. Yang et al. (2000) found that American employees experienced greater family demand compared to Chinese employees because they usually cannot get help from extended family members. Furthermore, family demand had a greater impact on work-family conflict in the United States than in China. In another study, Spector et al. (2017) found that the negative effect of long work hours on work attitudes is greater for employees in English speaking countries (Australia, Canada, England, New Zealand, and the United States) than employees in China and Latin America. In addition, employees in English speaking Western countries demonstrated a stronger positive relation between work hours and work-family stressors than Chinese and Latin American workers. Thus, it can be said that childcare programs tend to be more effective in countries with an *individualistic culture* because employees view the program as very important and often do not have extended family support (e.g., childcare help from family members).

Second, research has demonstrated that eldercare programs tend to be more effective in countries with a *collectivistic culture*—which often have stronger expectations regarding care for elderly family members. For example, a study found that men in Singapore were systematically more involved in eldercare than men in the United States—perhaps influenced by Confucian values (Kossek et al., 2013). Pyke and Bengtson (1996) classified people providing care to elderly family members as individualistic versus collectivistic. Collectivism highly values the concept of family and prioritizes the needs of the group over the needs of individual family members. Collectivist families typically exhibit closeness and interdependence. Collectivists willingly provide informal family care out of affection and a sense of responsibility, whereas individualists have an independent self-concept and feel less obligated to provide family care (cf. Reher, 1998). Thus, it can be said that eldercare programs are more effective and highly appreciated by employees in a collectivistic culture because employees in that culture feel a strong obligation to care for their elderly family members.

Finally, research shows that family care programs (e.g., taking time off during the working day to take care of personal of family issues) are more effective for employees in countries *high on uncertainty avoidance.*[1] This is because people in a high uncertainty avoidance culture are likely to experience a high level of anxiety and stress under uncertainty; as such, family care programs serve to reduce anxiety and stress (Lucia-Casademunt et al., 2015).

When employees have high uncertainty avoidance values, they exhibit an increased need for control over their future family needs. In contrast, when uncertainty avoidance values are low, uncertain situations do not cause employees significant anxiety; therefore, their need to avoid future uncertainty is low (Hofstede, 1984). A further translation: when employees have low uncertainty avoidance values, they do not have a strong need for family care programs that are not immediately necessary. Consider this additional study. Lucia-Casademunt et al. (2015) conducted an empirical analysis on a sample of 745 employees in tourism firms located in 17 European countries: eight low uncertainty avoidance countries (Denmark, Germany, France, Ireland, Austria, Finland, Sweden, and the United Kingdom) and nine high uncertainty avoidance countries (Greece, Spain, Italy, Hungary, Poland, Portugal, Slovenia, Turkey, and Albania). Their study found that the cultural value of uncertainty avoidance moderated the effect of family care programs on employees' wellbeing. Specifically, the results indicated that family-leave programs (e.g., easy to take off hours during the working day to take care of personal of family issues; working hours fit in with family or social commitments) have a stronger effect on employee wellbeing in the high uncertainty avoidance countries than in the low uncertainty avoidance countries (Lucia-Casademunt et al., 2015).

9.6 Summary and Conclusion

We discussed much of the WLB research focused on family care programs. Examples of family care programs include on-site childcare services, employee assistance programs, family programs, leave and time-off for family care.

We reported on the positive consequences (both personal and organizational consequences) of family care programs. As such, research shows that family care programs serve to increase employees perceived control, provide health benefits, and help employees reduce work-life conflict. Evidence also suggests that these

[1] Some of the highest uncertainty avoidance countries include Finland, Germany, Greece, Guatemala, Japan, Mexico, Portugal, and South Korea.

programs play an important role in increasing job satisfaction and organizational commitment while mitigating the adverse effects of turnover. We explained how family care programs help increase WLB through three well-established theories, namely role conflict, family demand and resources, and social exchange.

We also discussed the variety and types of family care programs. These include programs related to childcare, employee assistance, family leave, time-off, and other services.

We then discussed the moderating effects of family care programs. That is, the research that helps us understand those personal, organizational, and environmental/cultural conditions that make family care programs more effective. Specifically, research shows that family care programs are more effective when the employees perceive a greater fit with their needs and preferences. Research also shows that family care programs tend to be more effective for those who have experience with these programs.

With respect to organizational moderators, family care programs may be more effective given family-supportive supervision, transformational leadership, and family-supportive organizational culture.

Regarding environmental/cultural moderators, research indicates that childcare programs may be more effective in individualistic countries, in which the nuclear family is more common than the extended family. Conversely, eldercare programs tend to be more effective in collectivist countries, in which the extended family is more common than the nuclear family.

As such, we recommend that management develop and implement family care programs such as childcare, employee assistance, family leave, time-off, and other services. However, management should keep in mind that effective implementation of these programs is subject to those personal, organizational, and environmental/cultural moderators. Specifically, we recommend that management make a concerted effort to match programs with the employees' expressed needs and preferences. In other words, allow employees to select their own program that best fit their needs, especially those employees who have had experience with family care programs.

Furthermore, management should make a concerted effort to train supervisors to be supportive of their employees as they select and use one or more family care programs. Management should also signal their support for family care programs from the top echelons of the organization. Supervisors and managers can enhance the effectiveness of family care programs with training in transformational leadership—teaching supervisors to be inspiring, challenging, and individually considerate. This translates into a supportive attitude toward family care programs. Finally, management should also realize that some family care programs are better suited to certain countries than others. Specifically, childcare programs are more suited to countries dominated by an individualistic culture. For example, the nuclear family (traditionally involving a husband, wife, and one or more children) is the dominant demographic in individualistic countries. In such countries, childcare programs are very important nuclear families often do not have the support network of extended families to help with childcare. In contrast, in countries dominated by a collectivistic culture the members of the extended frequently family help with childcare, and thus value childcare programs less. As such, management of organizations operating in English speaking Western countries should invest more resources in developing and implementing childcare programs, perhaps more so than other family care programs.

See Box 9.4 for "practical recommendations" from practitioners.

Box 9.4 Practical Recommendations from Industry Practitioners About Family Care Policies and Programs

Many employers offer benefits to support parents and caregivers including equal maternity and paternity benefits or shared parental leave, catering childcare costs such as school fees, medical cover, and onsite daycare. This type of support for parents and caregivers should greatly increase job satisfaction, reduce burnout, and help retain top talent.

There are other workplace "perks" that can even be a deciding point when it comes to where skilled candidates choose to work. These days, many employers offer free meals or snacks, extra health stipends (e.g., massages, gym memberships), and financial services at no cost. Not only is offering perks like these a great work-life balance strategy for employees, but it's also investing in their health and well-being. Some employers go even further by offering perks like childcare, laundry, or allowing pets at work. As such, management can help relieve some of the stress employees face when it comes to juggling daily responsibilities outside of the office. The result is obvious: more employee engagement at work.

One way of supporting family care programs is an open-door policy. This means communicating that anybody is free to ask anybody else for help. Whether it's regarding professional work or personal matters, it's remarkable how many issues can be worked out if staff feel free to have open discussions. Another program consistent with the open-door policy is to run online survey. Doing so staff can give feedback to management about any given topic related to their workplace. If it's suspected that work-life balance is at stake, that can be a focal point in the employee survey.

Supportive employers can also provide employees with counseling services—whether in person or over the phone—to help employees better balance their life stresses. It's all about making sure your staff are bringing their best possible selves to work each day. Employee health and well-being, corporate social responsibility, and generally making a company a more attractive place to work are good ways to help employees achieve better work-life balance.

Source: Adapted from https://www.frontstream.com/blog/work-life-balance-strategies, https://www.driveresearch.com/market-research-company-blog/work-life-balance-organizational-strategies/, and https://www.timedoctor.com/blog/employee-work-life-balance/.

The next part of the book is the epilogue. In this last part, we will describe conditions (personal, program, organizational, and environmental/cultural characteristics) governing the overall effectiveness of WLB practices. We will then wrap up the book by making specific recommendations on how management can implement WLB practices.

References

Aitken, Z., Garrett, C. C., Hewitt, B., Keogh, L., Hocking, J. S., & Kavanagh, A. M. (2015). The maternal health outcomes of paid maternity leave: A systematic review. *Social Science & Medicine, 130*, 32–41.

Allen, T. D. (2001). Family-supportive work environments: The role of organizational perceptions. *Journal of Vocational Behavior, 58*(3), 414–435.

Allen, T. D., Lapierre, L. M., Spector, P. E., Poelmans, S. A., O'Driscoll, M., Sanchez, J. I., et al. (2014). The link between national paid leave policy and work-family conflict among married working parents. *Applied Psychology, 63*(1), 5–28.

Ashforth, B. E., Kreiner, G. E., & Fugate, M. (2000). All in a day's work: Boundaries and micro role transitions. *Academy of Management Review, 25*(3), 472–491.

Beauregard, T. A., & Henry, L. C. (2009). Making the link between work-life balance practices and organizational performance. *Human Resource Management Review, 19*(1), 9–22.

Blanch, A., & Aluja, A. (2012). Social support (family and supervisor), work-family conflict, and burnout: Sex differences. *Human Relations, 65*(7), 811–833.

Blau, P. (1964). *Exchange and power in social life*. Wiley.

Butts, M. M., Casper, W. J., & Yang, T. S. (2013). How important are work-family support policies? A meta-analytic investigation of their effects on employee outcomes. *Journal of Applied Psychology, 98*(1), 1–25.

Caillier, J. G. (2013). Satisfaction with work-life benefits and organizational commitment/job involvement: Is there a connection? *Review of Public Personnel Administration, 33*(4), 340–364.

Caillier, J. G. (2016). Does satisfaction with family-friendly programs reduce turnover? A panel study conducted in US federal agencies. *Public Personnel Management, 45*(3), 284–307.

Casper, W. J., & Buffardi, L. C. (2004). Work-life benefits and job pursuit intentions: The role of anticipated organizational support. *Journal of Vocational Behavior, 65*(3), 391–410.

Child Care Aware. (2016). *Parents and the high cost of childcare*. Author. http://www.usa.childcareaware.org/advocacy-public-policy/resources/reports-and-research/costofcare/

Chiu, W. C., & Ng, C. W. (1999). Women-friendly HRM and organizational commitment: A study among women and men of organizations in Hong Kong. *Journal of Occupational and Organizational Psychology, 72*(4), 485–502.

Davidson, O. B., Eden, D., Westman, M., Cohen-Charash, Y., Hammer, L. B., Kluger, A. N., et al. (2010). Sabbatical leave: Who gains and how much? *Journal of Applied Psychology, 95*(5), 953–764.

Dikkers, J. S. E., Geurts, S. A. E., den Dulk, L., & Peper, B. (2001). Work-nonwork culture, utilization of work-nonwork arrangements, and employee-related outcomes in two Dutch organizations. In S. A. Y. Poelmans (Ed.), *Work and family: An international research perspective* (pp. 147–172). Lawrence Erlbaum Associates.

Ezra, M., & Deckman, M. (1996). Balancing work and family responsibilities: Flexitime and childcare in the federal government. *Public Administration Review, 56*(2), 174–179.

Feeney, M. K., & Stritch, J. M. (2019). Family-friendly policies, gender, and work-life balance in the public sector. *Review of Public Personnel Administration, 39*(3), 422–448.

Frone, M. R., & Yardley, J. K. (1996). Workplace family-supportive programmes: Predictors of employed pare'ts' importance ratings. *Journal of Occupational and Organizational Psychology, 69*(4), 351–366.

Grover, S. L., & Crooker, K. J. (1995). Who appreciates family-responsive human resource policies: The impact of family-friendly policies on the organizational attachment of parents and non-parents. *Personnel Psychology, 48*(2), 271–288.

Han, W. J., Ruhm, C., & Waldfogel, J. (2009). Parental leave policies and parents' employment and leave-taking. *Journal of Policy Analysis and Management, 28*(1), 29–54.

Heymann, J. (2000). *The widening gap: Why America's working families are in jeopardy and what can be done about it*. Basic Books.

Hofstede, G. (1984). *Culture's consequences: International differences in work-related values*. Sage Publications.

Kahn, R. L., Wolfe, D. M., Quinn, R. P., Snoek, J. D., & Rosenthal, R. A. (1964). *Organizational stress: Studies in role conflict and ambiguity*. John Wiley.

Kalev, A., & Dobbin, F. (2022). The surprising benefits of work/life support. *Harvard Business Review* (September–October). Retrieved from September 29, 2023 https://hbr.org/2022/09/the-surprising-benefits-of-work-life-support

Katz-Wise, S. L., Priess, H. A., & Hyde, J. S. (2010). Gender-role attitudes and behavior across the transition to parenthood. *Developmental Psychology, 46*(1), 18–28.

Ko, J., Hur, S., & Smith-Walter, A. (2013). Family-friendly work practices and job satisfaction and organizational performance: Moderating effects of managerial support and performance-oriented management. *Public Personnel Management, 42*(4), 545–565.

Kossek, E. E., Chang, D., & Zhou, X. (2013). A cross-national exploration of divergence and convergence in objective and subjective assessments of the work-family nexus. In *Work and Family in a Multicultural World Symposium, The 73rd Annual Meeting of Academy of Management.*, Vol. 9 (August), p. 13.

Lambert, S. J. (2000). Added benefits: The link between work-life benefits and organizational citizenship behavior. *Academy of Management Journal, 43*(5), 801–815.

Lucia-Casademunt, A. M., García-Cabrera, A. M., & Cuéllar-Molina, D. G. (2015). National culture, work-life balance, and employee Well-being in European tourism firms: The moderating effect of uncertainty avoidance values. *Tourism & Management Studies, 11*(1), 62–69.

McCarthy, A., Darcy, C., & Grady, G. (2010). Work-life balance policy and practice: Understanding line manager attitudes and behaviors. *Human Resource Management Review, 20*(2), 158–167.

McDonald, P., Guthrie, D., Bradley, L., & Shakespeare-Finch, J. (2005). Investigating work-family policy aims and employee experiences. *Employee Relations., 27*(5), 478–494.

Merrill, D. M. (1997). *Caring for elderly parents: Juggling work, family, and caregiving in middle- and working-class families*. Auburn House.

Miller, M. T., & Kang, B. (1998). A case study of post-sabbatical assessment measures. *Journal of Staff, Program & Organization Development, 15*(1), 11–16.

O'Driscoll, M. P., Poelmans, S., Spector, P. E., Kalliath, T., Allen, T. D., Cooper, C. L., et al. (2003). Family-responsive interventions, perceived organizational and supervisor support, work-family conflict, and psychological strain. *International Journal of Stress Management, 10*(4), 326–344.

Petts, R. J., & Knoester, C. (2019). Paternity leave and parental relationships: Variations by gender and mothers' work statuses. *Journal of Marriage and Family, 81*(2), 468–486.

Pyke, K. D., & Bengtson, V. L. (1996). Caring more or less: Individualistic and collectivist systems of family eldercare. *Journal of Marriage and the Family, 58*(2), 379–392.

Reher, D. S. (1998). Family ties in Western Europe: Persistent contrasts. *Population and Development Review, 24*(2), 203–234.

Roehling, P. V., Roehling, M. V., & Moen, P. (2001). The relationship between work-life policies and practices and employee loyalty: A life course perspective. *Journal of Family and Economic Issues, 22*(2), 141–170.

Rossin-Slater, M. (2017). *Maternity and family leave policy (No. w23069)*. National Bureau of Economic Research.

Spector, P. E., Cooper, C. L., Poelmans, S., Allen, T. D., O'driscoll, M., Sanchez, J. I., et al. (2017). A cross-national comparative study of work-family stressors, working hours, and Well-being: China and Latin America versus the Anglo world. In *International human resource management* (pp. 257–277). Routledge.

Thomas, L. T., & Ganster, D. C. (1995). Impact of family-supportive work variables on work-family conflict and strain: A control perspective. *Journal of Applied Psychology, 80*(1), 6–15.

Thompson, C. A., Jahn, E. W., Kopelman, R. E., & Prottas, D. J. (2004). Perceived organizational family support: A longitudinal and multilevel analysis. *Journal of Managerial Issues*, 545–565.

Wang, P., & Walumbwa, F. O. (2007). Family-friendly programs, organizational commitment, and work withdrawal: The moderating role of transformational leadership. *Personnel Psychology, 60*(2), 397–427.

Yang, N., Chen, C. C., Choi, J., & Zou, Y. (2000). Sources of work-family conflict: A Sino-US comparison of the effects of work and family demands. *Academy of Management Journal, 43*(1), 113–123.

Yuile, C., Chang, A., Gudmundsson, A., & Sawang, S. (2012). The role of life friendly policies on employees' work-life balance. *Journal of Management & Organization, 18*(1), 53–63.

Zahorski, K. J. (1994). *The sabbatical mentor: A practical guide to successful sabbaticals*. Anker Publishing Company, Inc.

Part III
Epilogue

We conclude this book by focusing on the research governing the effectiveness of work-life balance (WLB) policies and programs. That is, we discuss and report on study findings pertaining to personal, program, organizational, and environmental/cultural moderators. By doing so, we identify those conditions that make WLB programs more effective. This information is vitally important to management—managers can use these study findings to make a host of decisions that make the implementation of WLB programs more effective and cost efficient. These decisions involve matching employees with the most optimal WLB program (effects of personal moderators), modifying programs to enhance their effectiveness (effects of program moderators), implementing additional programs within the organization that can enhance program effectiveness (effects of organizational moderators), and implementing programs that are congruent with the culture and environment in which the organization operates (effects of environmental/cultural moderators).

Chapter 10
Conditions Governing the Effectiveness of Work-Life Balance Policies and Programs

"If you feel 'burnout' setting in, if you feel demoralized and exhausted, it is best, for the sake of everyone, to withdraw and restore yourself."—Dalai Lama (https://teambuilding.com/blog/work-life-balance-quotes)

Abstract In this chapter we describe conditions (personal, program, organizational, and environmental/cultural moderators) governing the overall effectiveness of work-life balance (WLB) practices. Specifically, personal moderators include demographic characteristics (WLB programs are more effective for women, young adults, managers and corporate professionals, parents with pre-school children, and married to an employed spouse and with children) and perceptual/attitudinal/aptitude characteristics (WLB practices are more effective for those with low work-family self-efficacy, those with a positive attitude toward WLB programs, those who are favorably disposed to integrate work and family domains, those with management and planning skills, and those who are less fearful of being stigmatized). Programs moderators include program availability, large assortment with options, program informality, and programs imbuing sense of control. Organizational moderators include supervisor support, transformational leadership, and top management support. Environmental moderators include gender equality culture, human-oriented culture, individualistic culture, and an ICTs infrastructure with life domain border control.

10.1 Introduction

In this chapter, we will discuss the conditions that influence the general effectiveness of work-life balance (WLB) policies and programs. The conditions include: (1) personal characteristics, (2) program and organizational characteristics, and (4) environmental/cultural characteristics.

D.-J. Lee, M. J. Sirgy, *Organizational Strategies for Work-Life Balance*, Human Well-Being Research and Policy Making,
https://doi.org/10.1007/978-3-031-56314-0_10

Understanding the moderating effects of personal, program, organizational, and environmental/cultural factors is very important. Such understanding should help management do a better job at:

1. matching employees with the most optimal WLB program (effects of personal moderators);
2. modify programs to enhance their effectiveness and implement additional programs within the organization that can enhance program effectiveness (effects of program and organizational moderators); and
3. implementing programs that are congruent with the culture and environment in which the organization operates (effects of environmental/cultural moderators). See Table 10.1 for a summary of these factors.

Table 10.1 Summary of conditions influencing the general effectiveness of work-life balance practices

Moderating factors	Dimensions	Specific conditions
Personal characteristics	Demographics	More women (than men) More young adults (than mature adults), More managers and corporate professionals (than nonmanagerial and noncorporate occupations) More parents with pre-school children (than parents with older children) More married to an employed spouse and with children (than singles, divorced, widowed and no children
	Perceptual, attitudinal, and aptitude factors	Those with low (than high) work-family self-efficacy Those with a positive (than negative) attitude toward WLB programs Those who are favorably disposed to integrate work and family domains (than those who are unfavorably disposed) Those with management and planning skills (than those without these skills) Those who are less (than more) fearful of being stigmatized.
Program characteristics		Programs are perceived to be highly available (than unavailable) Programs are perceived as a large (than small) assortment with options Programs are supported more (than less) informally Programs that provide employees with a greater (than less) sense of control
Organizational characteristics		Supervisor support Transformational leadership Support from top management
Environmental and cultural characteristics		Gender egalitarian culture Humane-oriented culture Individualistic culture Information and communication technologies (ICTs) Infrastructure that can help control work-family boundaries

10.2 Personal Characteristics

This section reviews a set of personal l moderators affecting the outcomes of work-life balance programs. We grouped these personal characteristics into two major categories, namely demographics and perceptual/attitudinal/aptitude factors.

10.2.1 Demographics

Research has shown that WLB programs are more effective for: (1) women (than men), (2) young adults (than mature adults), (3) managers and corporate professionals (than nonmanagerial and noncorporate occupations), (4) parents with pre-school children (than parents with older children), and (5) married to an employed spouse and with children (than singles, divorced, widowed and no children).

First, WLB programs tend to be more effective for *women* than for men. Women often assume more caregiving responsibilities than men (Bureau of Labor Statistics, 2010), consider family benefits more important (Frone & Yardley, 1996), and express greater intention to make use of WLB programs than men (Butler et al., 2004). Studies show that WLB programs have stronger effects in samples that include more employees who are female, who are married/cohabiting, and/or who have dependents (Butts et al., 2013). Research also found that WLB programs had a stronger effect on the occupational commitment of women than the occupational commitment of men (Young et al., 2022). Through a survey of 293 information technology (IT) professionals, Young et al. (2022) examined the influence of gender and WLB on IT professionals' satisfaction with and commitment to their chosen occupation. Their results indicate that WLB was more salient for female IT professionals than for males when formulating their organizational commitment and job satisfaction. That is, gender moderated the relationship between WLB and occupational commitment such that better WLB had a more positive impact on women's occupational commitment than on men's. In addition, for female employees, the availability of work-life programs positively affects perceived organizational support and organizational commitment (Casper & Harris, 2008). Specifically, a study of 286 employees by Casper and Harris (2008) found that for female employees, the availability of work-family programs increases organizational commitment, irrespective of actual use. The study found that for women, the availability of WLB programs increases the perception of organizational support, which in turn facilitates organizational commitment. However, the study also found that for male employees, work-family programs serve to increase organizational commitment only when they use the programs. This implies that work-family programs have a greater impact on organizational commitment of female employees than that of male employees.

Second, *young adults* tend to benefit more from WLB programs than mature adults. Compared to older individuals, young adults tend to face greater demand at work (e.g., acquiring new skills and knowledge, choosing career paths). They also face greater family demand (e.g., setting up a family, raising young children), while having fewer resources (e.g., lack of experience, lower job status, lower pay, lack of job autonomy) to help them cope with work-family conflict (Bennett et al., 2017; Demerouti et al., 2012; Huffman et al., 2013; Reichl et al., 2014). Consider the results of a meta-analytic study conducted by Reichl et al. (2014). The study examined the effects of work-family conflict on burnout by testing the moderating role of age on the relationship between work-family conflict and burnout. The results indicate that the relationship between work-family conflict and burnout is stronger for young than mature adults. This is because young adults have minimal resources while being overburdened by high demand in work and family life. As such, it can be asserted that young adults need WLB programs much more so than mature adults.

Third, WLB programs are more effective for *managers and corporate professionals* compared to those with nonmanagerial and noncorporate occupations. Managers and corporate professionals tend to show greater satisfaction with family-friendly programs because their job-related tasks are often performed independently and flexibly (Swanberg et al., 2005). Workers who do have access to flexible work arrangements can be considered a more "privileged group of employees" (U. S. Department of Labor, 2002). The survey by the U. S. Department of Labor (2002) found that flexible schedules were more commonly available to White workers (30.0%) than to either Black (21.2%) or Hispanic workers (19.8%). In addition, employees in managerial and corporate occupations were more likely to have access to flexible schedule options, with 45.5% of executives, administrators, and managers able to modify their work hours in some form. In contrast, only 18.5% of employees in semiskilled occupations such as production, craft, and repair work, and 13.7% of operators, facilitators, and laborers had flexible schedules. Employees in lower wage-earning jobs have less access to flexible work schedules, while employees working in full-time, salaried, and daytime positions were more likely to have access to flexible work schedules.

Fourth, evidence suggests that work-life programs are most effective for *those with work-life conflict*. WLB programs tend to be valued resources for individuals predisposed to experience high levels of work-family conflict—via high levels of work demand and/or family demand (Davis et al., 2007; Hill et al., 2008). Research has shown that family-to-work conflict is greater for *parents with preschool children* and less so among employees with older or no children (Roehling et al., 2003). Hill et al. (2008) explored how the use and perceived value of work-life programs (part-time work, job sharing, flextime, and telecommuting) differ by gender and life stage. In this case, life stage is defined by the presence or absence of children and their ages. By analyzing a multi-company database between 1996–2006, they found a curvilinear relationship in differences between men and women in their use of workplace flexibility options. In Life Stage 1 (less than 35 years old and no children), there were no meaningful gender differences in the use of workplace flexibility programs. However, in Life Stage 2 (oldest child less than 6 years old), there were gender differences. Women were more likely than men to use part-time work, job sharing, flextime, and telecommuting. In Life Stage 3 (at least one child less than 6 years old and at least one child over 6 years old), women were even more likely than men to use these flexible work arrangements. In Life Stage 4 (no children less than 6 years old and at least one child over 6 years old), the differences between men and women were less pronounced. As we can see, women are more likely to value and use work-life family programs when they have young children. WLB programs tend to be valued resources for individuals predisposed to experience high levels of work-family conflict with a high level of role demands (e.g., parents with young children).

Finally, research also suggests that WLB programs are most effective for those with greater *family responsibilities*. Those with greater family responsibilities tend to benefit more from WLB programs as a resource than would those with fewer family responsibilities (Allen et al., 2013). That is, those with high family responsibility tend to experience work-family conflict and thus stand to gain more from WLB programs (Shockley & Allen, 2007). Employees who are *married to an employed spouse and have children*, tend to have greater family needs than those who are single, childless, or have a stay-at-home spouse (Swody & Powell, 2007). Shockley and Allen (2007) have suggested that WLB programs may be a more valued resource for individuals predisposed to experience greater work-family conflict via greater work and/or family demands. Individuals with greater family responsibility, such as parents, stand to benefit more from WLB programs than those with less family responsibility. Allen et al. (2013) conducted a meta-analysis which found that the effect WLB programs (e.g., flextime and flexplace) on family-work conflict escalates as the percentage of parents in the sample increases. That is, the results indicate that individuals with greater parental responsibilities stand to benefit more from WLB programs than individuals with less parental responsibility.

10.2.2 Perceptual/Attitudinal/Aptitude Factors

The second major category of personal characteristics—perceptual/attitudinal/aptitude factors—moderating WLB programs can be broken down into: (1) those with low (than high) work-family self-efficacy, (2) those with a positive (than negative) attitude toward WLB programs, (3) those who are favorably disposed to integrate work and family domains (than those who are unfavorably disposed), (4) those with management and planning skills (than those without these skills), and (5) those who are less (than more) fearful of being stigmatized.

First, evidence suggests that WLB programs tend to be most effective for those with *low work-family self-efficacy*. Self-efficacy refers to the belief in our own ability to manage work-family conflicts and successfully balance work and family roles (Basuil & Casper, 2012; Butler et al., 2004). Individuals with higher levels of work-family self-efficacy believe that they can competently handle the demands of work and family and may, therefore, perceive a reduced need for assistance from their organization to help cope. In contrast, those with low work-family self-efficacy are more likely to feel a greater need for WLB programs (Cho et al., 2022). Thus, one can argue that WLB programs are likely to be most effective for those with low work-family self-efficacy because these employees tend to experience high levels of work-life conflict.

Second, WLB programs tend to be most effective for those with a *favorable attitude toward work-family programs*. That is, employees are more likely to use WLB programs when they have a positive attitude toward their use (Butler et al., 2004; Lambert, 2000) and when they think that the use of the programs is unlikely to damage their prospect of promotion or relationships with co-workers and managers (Houston & Waumsley, 2003). Houston and Waumsley (2003) conducted a large survey of employees (n = 1724) on attitude toward work-family programs. The study results are as follows: (1) The majority of employees (72%) intended to use flexible working in the future if possible (women more so than men, and managers more so than skilled or semi-skilled workers). (2) Women feel more positively about flexible working than men. (3) Employees expressed strong expectations that flexible working would be good for both the employer and employee, particularly among female and managerial employees. However, the majority also disagreed that flexible working would lead to respect and promotion. (4) Positive attitudes were strongly associated with intentions to use flexible working. Employees who perceived greater personal benefits, better engagement with the organization, and fewer negative work outcomes expressed the strongest intentions to use flexible working practices. In summary, WLB programs tend to be most effective for those with a favorable attitude toward work-family programs because positive attitude is likely to lead to use of the programs.

Third, WLB programs tend to be more effective for those with those who prefer to *integrate work and family life domains*. In general, employees have different preferences for managing boundaries between work and family which influences how they perceived their work-family conflict (Beigi et al., 2018). Specifically, those employees with a high preference for life domain segmentation (e.g., prefer not to deal with work issues at home and conversely not deal with family issues at work) are less likely to use WLB programs such as flextime and flexplace (Ashforth et al., 2000; Beigi et al., 2018). High-segmentation employees (a rigid boundary between work and family domains) are not likely to enjoy the autonomy associated with flexible work arrangements, and consequently tend to perceive that the permeable boundary afforded by the WLB programs will increase (rather than decrease) work-family conflict (Beigi et al., 2018). In contrast, those with a high preference for domain integration (a permeable boundary between work and family domains) are likely to perceive greater value in WLB programs (e.g., flextime and flexplace) (Beigi et al., 2018).

Fourth, research has also shown that WLB programs are most effective for those employees with a *high level of time management and planning skills*. Employees enrolled in flexible work programs tend to face many distractions emanating from their non-work roles. Those with time management and planning skills (e.g., allocate/schedule time between their work and non-work roles efficiently) are better at extracting major benefits from WLB programs compared to those with little or no time management and planning skills (Azar et al., 2018). Time management and planning skills (e.g., planning, prioritizing, making to-do lists, and limiting the influence of interruptions) help employees use their time effectively while performing certain goal-directed activities. (Claessens et al., 2004; Douglas et al., 2016). As such, it is no surprise to find empirical evidence demonstrating that the positive effect of flexible work arrangements on job satisfaction is stronger for individuals with higher levels of time management and planning skills (Azar et al., 2018).

Finally, empirical research suggests that work-life programs improve employees' organizational commitment but only to the extent that employees feel free to use the programs with few or no repercussions (e.g., damaged career prospects, negative career paths) (Eaton, 2003; Thompson et al., 1999). Employees tend to feel reluctant to use WLB programs when they feel that they might be stigmatized for taking advantage of them. That is, employees, especially men, may not take advantage of programs in place due to *fear of social stigmatization* (Kossek et al., 2006). This may be due to gender roles being associated with the program.

10.3 Program Characteristics

Evidence suggests that WLB programs are most effective when they have the following program characteristics: (1) programs are perceived to be highly available (than unavailable), (2) programs are perceived as a large (than small) assortment with options, (3) programs are supported more (than less) informally, and (4) programs that provide employees with a greater (than less) sense of control.

10.3.1 Program Availability

WLB programs are most effective when they are perceived as being *highly available*. High availability of programs is related to positive work attitude (job satisfaction, affective commitment, and intention to stay) (Butts et al., 2013). This is because high availability of WLB programs symbolizes concern for the employees by the firm (Allen et al., 2013; Batt & Valcour, 2003) and increases perception of psychological control that can help alleviate work-family conflict (Kossek et al., 2006). Butts et al. (2013) conducted a meta-analysis that examined the relationships between the availability and use of WLB programs and job attitudes. The results indicate that the availability and use of WLB programs has positive relationships with job satisfaction, affective commitment, and intentions to stay. Further, tests of differences in effect sizes showed that policy availability was more strongly related to job satisfaction, affective commitment, and intentions to stay than policy use. Because policy availability may be perceived as a symbol of corporate concern for family wellbeing, employees may seek to reciprocate this concern by developing more favorable work attitudes. Thus, it can be said that WLB programs are most effective when they are perceived to be highly available.

10.3.2 Large Assortment with Options

WLB programs are most effective when employees perceive that the organization offers a *large assortment of programs with many options*. The positive effect of work-life programs on work attitude increases as the number of programs and options increases (Butts et al., 2013). That is, WLB programs are more strongly related to positive outcomes when there are multiple programs in place, rather than a single program (Arthur, 2003; Casper & Buffardi, 2004). This is because a combination of many programs is likely to better serve employee work-life needs (e.g., need fit) and multiple programs tend to reinforce one another (e.g., leave and childcare services) (Swody & Powell, 2007).

Both signal theory and systems theory suggest that multiple work-family support policies more strongly relate to positive employee outcomes compared to a single policy (Butts et al., 2013). Signal theory contends that signal effectiveness is enhanced by increasing the number of observable signals (Connelly et al., 2011). Thus, an organization that makes two distinct work-family support policies available sends two signals of corporate concern, which should result in more positive work attitudes than for an organization that offers only a single policy. Systems theory (Corning, 1998) suggests that increased value and synergies occur when multiple policies reinforce one another. For example, using both paid parental leave and on-site childcare may reduce a family's childcare costs and relieve family demands, resulting in more positive attitudes than if a single policy was used. Thus, it can be said that WLB programs are effective when employees perceive that the organization offers a *large assortment of programs with many options*.

10.3.3 Program Informality

WLB programs are most effective when they are accompanied by *informal support* within the organization. Research found that informal support (e.g., easy to take time off with short notice) is generally more impactful in reducing work-family conflict and stress than formal support (e.g., flextime and telecommuting) (Clark et al., 2017; Mennino et al., 2005). Specifically, Mennino et al. (2005) examined the impact of workplace characteristics and family demands on negative spillover between work and family life domains. The results indicate that an informal family-supportive workplace culture serves to reduce negative spillover across life domains, whereas the availability of formal work-family policies, such as dependent care benefits and flextime, do not. This implies that the workplace climate is more important than the availability of formal company policies in reducing negative spillover. In organizations with a family-friendly workplace climate, employees find it easier to balance their jobs and family because their employers acknowledge nonworkplace demands and do not penalize employees who attend to their lives outside of the workplace. Thus, it can be said that WLB programs are most effective when they are accompanied by informal support from the organization.

10.3.4 Program Imbuing Sense of Control

Research suggests that flextime is more effective than flexplace or other programs such as childcare services. Specifically, flextime is more strongly associated with reduced work-to-family conflict than flexplace (Shockley & Allen, 2007). This may be because flextime provides employees with a greater *sense of control* (Allen et al., 2013). Research also suggests that flextime contributes more to the perception that the organization is family-supportive than programs such as childcare services (Allen, 2001). The availability of flextime is more important than the actual use of the program because its availability can provide employees with a sense of control. For flexplace, however, actual use of the program rather than just its presence has a greater impact on reducing work-life conflict (Allen et al., 2013).

10.4 Organizational Characteristics

Research suggests that WLB programs are most effective given the following organizational characteristics: (1) supervisor support, (2) transformational leadership, and (3) support from top management.

10.4.1 Supervisor Support

Empirical evidence suggests that WLB programs are most effective when *supervisors are supportive* of their use. Specifically, WLB programs tend to be more effective when supervisors are aware of the programs and have a favorable attitude toward employee use of them (Casper et al., 2004; McCarthy et al., 2010). That is, supervisors must be accepting of the programs and their organizational benefits (Eversole et al., 2007). Supervisors must also be sensitive to the needs of their employees and buy into the instrumentality of the WLB programs. Research has documented the relative effectiveness of WLB programs when supervisors are sensitive to the work-family needs of employees and lend support to their use (Thompson et al., 1999). The effects of family support programs, albeit well-intended, tend to be quite marginal when they are not accompanied by supervisors' informal support (Behson, 2005). Thompson et al. (1999) developed a measure of work-family culture (i.e., the shared assumptions, beliefs, and values regarding the extent to which an organization supports and values the integration of employees' work and family lives) and examined its relationship to WLB programs, organizational attachment, and work-family conflict. Using survey data from 276 managers and professionals, they identified three dimensions of work-family culture: managerial support for work-family balance (i.e., managers are accommodating of family-related needs), career consequences associated with utilizing work-family benefits (e.g., family-related leaves of absence do not negatively affect subsequent performance ratings, promotions), and organizational time expectations that may interfere with family responsibilities (e.g., employees are not expected to take work home). As predicted, perceptions of a supportive work-family culture were related to employees' use of WLB programs. Both program availability and supportive work-family culture were positively related to affective commitment and negatively related to work-family conflict and intentions to leave the organization. In addition, through an analysis of national survey data of employees ($n = 3551$), Behson (2005) also found that informal forms of organizational work-family support are more useful than formal forms of organizational work-family support in explaining variance in employee affective, intentional, and behavioral outcomes. Thus, it can be said that WLB programs are most effective when *supervisors are supportive* of their use.

10.4.2 Transformational Leadership

WLB programs are more effective when they are overseen by *supervisors who are transformational leaders*. Family-friendly work programs produce higher levels of organizational commitment and reduced levels of work withdrawal when employees perceive their supervisors as inspiring, challenging, and individually considerate—as are transformational leaders (Wang & Walumbwa, 2007). This is because transformational leaders are likely to pay special attention to their subordinates individual needs (Avolio, 1999), are open to new and creative ideas about how to get work done (Bass, 1998), and encourage progressive and innovative ideas in terms of developing family-friendly programs (Perry-Smith & Blum, 2000).Family-friendly work programs produce the best personal and organizational outcomes when employees think their organization and their supervisors play an active role in addressing their work and family needs (Powell et al., 2009; Wang & Walumbwa, 2007). Wang and Walumbwa (2007) demonstrated the moderating effect of transformational leadership in the relationships between work flexibility programs and both organizational commitment and work withdrawal, and between childcare programs and work withdrawal. Thus, it can be said that the implementation of WLB programs that are overseen by supervisors who are transformational leaders are likely to be more effective compared to implementation by traditional managers.

10.4.3 Top-Management Support

The effectiveness of WLB programs is enhanced when *top managers are supportive* of their development and implementation. When top managers demonstrate support for WLB programs, evidence suggests that these programs produce higher levels of job satisfaction, as well as greater organizational performance (Ko et al., 2013). Top managers' responsiveness and support of work-family issues positively influences employee participation in family-friendly programs without concern about career prospects (Swody & Powell, 2007).

For example, Ko et al. (2013) conducted a study that explored the effects of top managerial support on a family-supportive workplace environment. They explained that sincere support from top management is crucial for the successful implementation of work-family programs as it is needed for symbolic reasons and to ensure proper resource provisioning (Bardoel, 2003; Karsten, 2006; Ngo et al., 2009). Managerial support has an important role in the effectiveness of WLB programs by encouraging employees to participate in the programs and by reinforcing an organizational culture that promotes a healthy work-family balance for employees (Thompson et al., 1999). Ko et al. (2013) used the 2010 Federal Employee Viewpoint Survey (FEVS) conducted by the U.S. Office of Personnel Management (OPM) to test these hypotheses. Their study results indicated that top management support positively moderated relationships between flexible work scheduling and perceived organizational performance (beta = 0.006, $p < 0.01$) and between dependent care programs and perceived organizational performance (beta = 0.007, $p < 0.01$). Thus, it can be said that the effectiveness of WLB programs is enhanced when top managers are supportive of their development and implementation.

10.5 Environmental/Cultural Characteristics

Research suggests that WLB programs tend to be more effective given the following environmental and cultural conditions: (1) gender egalitarian culture, (2) humane-oriented culture, (3) individualistic culture, and (4) an information and communication technologies (ICTs) infrastructure that can help control work-family boundaries.

10.5.1 A Culture of Gender Equality

Research has demonstrated that WLB programs tend to be more effective when the organization operates in a *society with a culture of gender equality*. Gender egalitarianism refers to the degree to which a culture minimizes gender role differences while promoting gender equality. In high gender egalitarian cultures there is less adherence to traditional gender roles—women's organizational roles tend to have more similarities in authority and status compared to men (Emrich et al., 2004; Lyness & Kropf, 2005). Cultures that are higher in gender equality have a higher proportion of women in positions of authority, more female participation in the labor force, and less gender segregation in employment (Powell et al., 2009). Cultures with high gender equality promote the use of flexible work programs by fostering the belief that such programs are an acceptable way for employees to pursue their goals regardless of gender (Peretz et al., 2018). The same societies value WLB programs (e.g., flexible work schedule) more than less egalitarian countries (Corrigall & Konrad, 2006). Thus, the positive relationship between WLB programs and their outcomes tend to be greater in organizations operating in countries with a high (than low) gender egalitarian culture (Lyness & Judiesch, 2008).

Lyness and Judiesch (2008) examined the relationship between WLB ratings and career advancement potential. Using the self-ratings, peer ratings, and supervisor ratings of 9627 managers in 33 countries, they examined the relationship between perceived WLB and career advancement potential. The results indicate that managers who were rated higher in work-life balance were also rated higher in career advancement potential than were managers who were rated lower in work-life balance. The results also indicate that work-life balance ratings were positively related to advancement potential ratings for women in high egalitarian cultures, but not for men in high egalitarian cultures. Thus, it can be said that WLB programs tend to be more effective when the organization operates in a society with a culture of gender equality.

10.5.2 A Humane-Oriented Culture

Research shows that WLB programs tend to be more effective in *societies characterized by a humane culture*. A humane-oriented culture is defined as the degree to which societies encourage and reward individuals for being fair, altruistic, friendly, generous, and kind to others (House & Javidan, 2004). Societies with a high humane orientation have a high level of expected social support, meaning that individuals are more willing to take responsibility for the wellbeing of others. In contrast, in low humane-oriented cultures, support for others is more limited and instead people focus on self-enhancement and self-sufficiency (Kabasakal & Bodur, 2004). People in a humane-oriented culture are likely to be sensitive to the wellbeing of others and encourage the provision of social support offered by WLB programs (Powell et al., 2009). Thus, the positive relationship between WLB programs and positive outcomes tends to be stronger in a high (than low) humane-oriented culture. In cultures with a humane orientation, people outside of the self, such as family, friends, community, and even strangers are important, people take responsibility for each other's wellbeing, and individuals are urged to provide social support to others (Kabasakal & Bodur, 2004). For example, people are more likely to assist each other materially and financially, socialize with each other, be empathetic, and share useful information. Consequently, the level of social support that serves to reduce work-family conflict will be greater in a society with a high humane orientation than in one with a low humane orientation (Powell et al., 2009). Thus, it can be said that WLB programs tend to be more effective in societies characterized by a humane culture.

10.5.3 An Individualistic Culture

Work-life programs are likely to be more effective in *individualistic* than collectivistic cultures. People in individualistic cultures experience a higher degree of work-family conflict because they usually receive less assistance with childcare from extended-family members. Research has shown that the positive relationship between work demand and work-family conflict is stronger for employees in individualistic cultures, much more so than those living in collectivistic countries (Spector et al., 2007). In addition, flexible work arrangements tend to complement individualistic traits; thus, they fit better in countries that value individualism over collectivism (Masuda et al., 2012). As such, organizations operating in countries high on individualism tend to promote the use of flexible work arrangements to satisfy personal needs (Peretz et al., 2018).

For example, Masuda et al. (2012) explored the availability of flexible work arrangements and their relationship with manager outcomes of job satisfaction, turn-over intentions, and work-to-family conflict across country clusters. Respondents of the survey were 3918 managers from 15 countries. Three country clusters were created. The Anglo cluster (n = 1492) included Australia, Canada, New Zealand, the United States, and the United Kingdom. The Asian cluster (n = 1213) included responses from managers in Hong Kong, Korea, Japan, China, and Taiwan. The Latin American cluster (n = 1213) included Argentina, Chile, Bolivia, Puerto Rico, and Peru. The results indicate that managers in individualistic countries (i.e., English speaking Western countries) were generally more likely to report working in companies that offered flextime, compressed working week, part-time work, and telecommuting compared with managers in collectivistic (i.e., Asian and Latin American) countries. This implies that adopting work-family programs is perceived as more important in individualistic cultures. In addition, the results show that flextime programs had positive outcomes in individualistic cultures, but not in collectivistic cultures (Masuda et al., 2012). Thus, it can be said that work-life programs are likely to be more effective in countries with an individualistic culture, much more so than in countries with a collectivistic culture.

10.5.4 An ICTs Infrastructure with Life Domain Border Control

Evidence also suggests that WLB programs are likely to be more effective when countries have *increased connectivity through information and communication technologies (ICTs) and control of work-family life domain boundaries*. Increased connectivity (e.g., phone, email, and other internet communications) can interrupt personal life and increase employee workload (Mazmanian et al., 2013). Increased connectivity also allows professionals to work in any place, at any time, increasingly workplace and schedule flexibility (Currie & Eveline, 2011). Thus, WLB programs become more important with the continual development and evolution of ICTs.

The increased prevalence and use of ICTs blurs the boundary between work and family (Currie & Eveline, 2011). In a study of Australian academics with young children, Currie and Eveline (2011) examined the impact of ITCs on their work lives. They investigated whether these technologies were beneficial or detrimental and found that the working conditions for Australian academics have deteriorated. The study revealed increased work intensity, longer working hours, and the intrusion of work into their private lives in a more fast-paced environment. The results indicate that many people felt that while having ITCs at home was of benefit to their work, their use came at a cost to their family life. The results also indicate that many people think it is important to establish clear boundaries between work and family life to maintain work-life balance. Thus, it can be said that WLB programs are likely to be more effective when the country has increased connectivity through information and communication technologies (ICTs) and controls of work-family life domain boundaries.

10.6 Summary and Conclusion

In this chapter, we discussed the conditions that influence the general effectiveness of WLB programs. These conditions include: (1) personal characteristics, (2) program/organizational characteristics, and (3) environmental/cultural characteristics. See Fig. 10.1.

We discussed these factors and how they work in some detail. Specifically, with respect to personal moderators, research indicates that WLB programs are more effective for: (1) women (than men), (2) young adults (than mature adults), (3) managers and professionals (than nonmanagerial and nonprofessional occupations), (4) parents with pre-school children (than parents with older children), and (5) married to an employed spouse with children (than singles, divorced, widowed and no children). These study findings suggest that management should be somewhat proactive in implementing WLB programs. One way to do this is by collecting information about employees and attempting to match programs to employees that would be the best fit. In other words, management is very likely to have in its database information about employee demographics which can be used to match WLB programs with selected employees based on their demographic profile. Employees identified

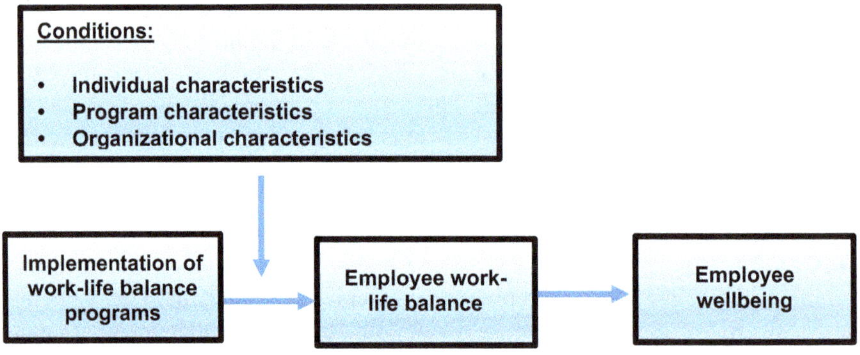

Fig. 10.1 Conditions influencing the effectiveness of work-life balance programs

as having any of the discussed demographic criteria (e.g., women, young adults, managers and professionals, parents with pre-school children, and/or married to an employed spouse with children) can be encouraged to apply for their preferred WLB program.

We also discussed how research involving perceptual, attitudinal, and skills-related moderators, the second category of personal moderators, can be used for the same purpose. We reported on the research suggesting that WLB programs are more effective for: (1) those with low (than high) work-family self-efficacy, (2) those with a positive (than negative) attitude toward WLB programs, (3) those who are favorably disposed to integrate work and family domains (than those who are unfavorably disposed), (4) those with management and planning skills (than those without these skills), and (5) those who are less (than more) fearful of being stigmatized. As such, management may decide to administer a survey questionnaire to their employees to gauge employees' level of work-family self-efficacy, attitude toward WLB programs, disposition toward integration of work and family domains, management and planning skills, and degree of fear of stigmatization. Management would heavily promote WLB programs only to those with low work-family self-efficacy, a positive attitude toward WLB programs, those who are favorably disposed to integrate work and family domains, those with management and planning skills, and those who are less fearful of being stigmatized.

With respect to program/organizational moderators, the research shows that WLB programs are most effective when they have the following characteristics: (1) programs are perceived to be highly available (than unavailable), (2) programs are perceived as a large (than small) assortment with options, (3) programs are supported more (than less) informally, and (4) programs that provide employees with a greater (than less) sense of control. As such, management should not offer only one or two WLB programs but, a large assortment and heavily promote their availability to employees. Supervisors should informally encourage their subordinates to explore the use of selected WLB programs, allowing the employees to explore the programs' benefits and possible costs too. Supervisors could also attempt to gauge the extent to which of the available programs can provide their subordinates with the greatest sense of control and promote those heavily to the selected individuals.

The research also suggests that WLB programs are most effective given the following organizational characteristics: (1) supervisor support, (2) transformational leadership, and (3) support from top management. What does this mean to management? It means that management should make it widely and clearly known that the organization fully supports employees who take advantage of WLB programs. Furthermore, top management should train their mid-level managers and supervisors to become transformational leaders. Transformational supervisors can be highly effective in promoting the effective use of WLB programs to their subordinates.

Regarding environmental/cultural moderators, evidence suggests that WLB programs tend to be more effective given the following environmental and cultural conditions: (1) gender egalitarian culture, (2) humane-oriented culture, (3) individualistic culture, and (4) an infrastructure replete with information and communication technologies (ICTs). Management should consider the cultural context and the country's level of ICTs in the development and implementation of the organization's WLB programs. In other words, WLB programs are likely to be more effective in certain countries—those characterized as egalitarian (in relation to gender), humane (in the way its government policies favor the disadvantaged and vulnerable members of society), individualistic (emphasis on nuclear, not extended families), and with well-developed ICT infrastructure. As such top management should encourage the development and utilization of WLB programs in their units or divisions located in countries that match these characteristics.

In sum, what we discussed in this chapter is very important. Based on the available evidence we discussed how certain personal, program, organizational, and environmental/cultural factors moderate the effectiveness of WLB programs. As such, the research findings should help management do a better job at:

- matching employees with the most optimal WLB program (effects of personal moderators);
- modify programs to enhance their effectiveness and implement additional programs within the organization that can enhance program effectiveness (effects of organizational moderators); and
- implement programs that are congruent with the country's culture and environment where the organization operates (effects of environmental/cultural moderators).

References

Allen, T. D. (2001). Family-supportive work environments: The role of organizational perceptions. *Journal of Vocational Behavior, 58*(3), 414–435.

Allen, T. D., Johnson, R. C., Kiburz, K. M., & Shockley, K. M. (2013). Work-family conflict and flexible work arrangements: Deconstructing flexibility. *Personnel Psychology, 66*(2), 345–376.

Arthur, M. M. (2003). Share price reactions to work-family initiatives: An institutional perspective. *Academy of Management Journal, 46*(4), 497–505.

Ashforth, B. E., Kreiner, G. E., & Fugate, M. (2000). All in a day's work: Boundaries and micro role transitions. *Academy of Management Review, 25*(3), 472–491.

Avolio, B. J. (1999). *Full leadership development: Building the vital forces in organizations*. Sage.

Azar, S., Khan, A., & Van Eerde, W. (2018). Modelling linkages between flexible work arrangements' use and organizational outcomes. *Journal of Business Research, 91*(October), 134–143.

Bardoel, E. A. (2003). The provision of formal and informal work-family practices: The relative importance of institutional and resource dependent explanations versus managerial explanations. *Women in Management Review, 18*(1/2), 7–19.

Bass, B. M. (1998). *Transformational leadership: Industry, military, and educational impact*. Erlbaum.

Basuil, D. A., & Casper, W. J. (2012). Work-family planning attitudes among emerging adults. *Journal of Vocational Behavior, 80*(3), 629–637.

Batt, R., & Valcour, P. M. (2003). Human resources practices as predictors of work-family outcomes and employee turnover. *Industrial Relations, 42*(2), 189–220.

Behson, S. J. (2005). The relative contribution of formal and informal organizational work-family support. *Journal of Vocational Behavior, 66*(3), 487–500.

Beigi, M., Shirmohammadi, M., & Stewart, J. (2018). Flexible work arrangements and work-family conflict: A meta synthesis of qualitative studies among academics. *Human Resource Development Review, 17*(3), 314–336.
Bennett, M. M., Beehr, T. A., & Ivanitskaya, L. V. (2017). Work-family conflict: Differences across generations and life cycles. *Journal of Managerial Psychology, 32*(4), 314–332.
Bureau of Labor Statistics. (2010). *www.bls.gov/opub*. US Bureau of Labor Statistics.
Butler, A., Gasser, M., & Smart, L. (2004). A social-cognitive perspective on using family-friendly benefits. *Journal of Vocational Behavior, 65*(1), 57–70.
Butts, M. M., Casper, W. J., & Yang, T. S. (2013). How important are work-family support policies? A meta-analytic investigation of their effects on employee outcomes. *Journal of Applied Psychology, 98*(1), 1–25.
Casper, W. J., & Buffardi, L. C. (2004). Work-life benefits and job pursuit intentions: The role of anticipated organizational support. *Journal of Vocational Behavior, 65*(3), 391–410.
Casper, W. J., & Harris, C. M. (2008). Work-life benefits and organizational attachment: Self-interest utility and signaling theory models. *Journal of Vocational Behavior, 72*(1), 95–109.
Casper, W. J., Fox, K. E., Sitzmann, T. M., & Landy, A. L. (2004). Supervisor referrals to work-family programs. *Journal of Occupational Health Psychology, 9*(2), 136–151.
Cho, E., Chen, T. Y., Cheng, G. H. L., & Ho, M. H. R. (2022). Work-family balance self-efficacy and work-family balance during the pandemic: A longitudinal study of working informal caregivers of older adults. *Journal of Occupational Health Psychology, 27*(3), 349–358.
Claessens, B. J., Van Eerde, W., Rutte, C. G., & Roe, R. A. (2004). Planning behavior and perceived control of time at work. *Journal of Organizational Behavior, 25*(8), 937–950.
Clark, M. A., Rudolph, C. W., Zhdanova, L., Michel, J. S., & Baltes, B. B. (2017). Organizational support factors and work-family outcomes: Exploring gender differences. *Journal of Family Issues, 38*(11), 1520–1545.
Connelly, B. L., Certo, S. T., Ireland, R. D., & Reutzel, C. R. (2011). Signaling theory: A review and assessment. *Journal of Management, 37*(1), 39–67.
Corning, P. A. (1998). "The synergism hypothesis": On the concept of synergy and its role in the evolution of complex systems. *Journal of Social and Evolutionary Systems, 21*(2), 133–172.
Corrigall, E. A., & Konrad, A. M. (2006). The relationship of job attribute preferences to employment, hours of paid work, and family responsibilities: An analysis comparing women and men. *Sex Roles, 54*(1), 95–111.
Currie, J., & Eveline, J. (2011). E-technology and work/life balance for academics with young children. *Higher Education, 62*(4), 533–550.
Davis, S. N., Greenstein, T. N., & Gerteisen Marks, J. P. (2007). Effects of union type on division of household labor: Do cohabiting men really perform more housework? *Journal of Family Issues, 28*(9), 1246–1272.
Demerouti, E., Bakker, A. B., Sonnentag, S., & Fullagar, C. J. (2012). Work-related flow and energy at work and at home: A study on the role of daily recovery. *Journal of Organizational Behavior, 33*(2), 276–295.
Douglas, H. E., Bore, M., & Munro, D. (2016). Coping with university education: The relationships of time management behavior and work engagement with the five factor model aspects. *Learning and Individual Differences, 45*(January), 268–274.
Eaton, S. C. (2003). If you can use them: Flexibility policies, organizational commitment, and perceived performance. *Industrial Relations, 42*(2), 145–167.
Emrich, C. G., Denmark, F. L., & Den Hartog, D. N. (2004). Cross-cultural differences in gender egalitarianism. In R. House et al. (Eds.), *Culture, leadership, and organizations: The globe study of 62 societies* (pp. 343–394). Sage.
Eversole, B. A., Gloeckner, G., & Banning, J. H. (2007). Understanding differential organizational responses to work/life issues: The role of beliefs and decision-making styles of chief executive officers. *Journal of European Industrial Training, 31*(4), 259–273.
Frone, M. R., & Yardley, J. K. (1996). Workplace family-supportive programmes: Predictors of employed parents' importance ratings. *Journal of Occupational and Organizational Psychology, 69*(4), 351–366.

Hill, E. J., Jacob, J. I., Shannon, L. L., Brennan, R. T., Blanchard, V. L., & Martinengo, G. (2008). Exploring the relationship of workplace flexibility, gender, and life stage to family-to-work conflict, and stress and burnout. *Community, Work and Family, 11*(2), 165–181.

House, R. J., & Javidan, M. (2004). Overview of GLOBE. In R. J. House, P. J. Hanges, M. Javidan, P. W. Dorfman, & V. Gupta (Eds.), *Culture, leadership, and organizations: The GLOBE study of 62 societies* (pp. 9–28). Sage.

Houston, D. M., & Waumsley, J. A. (2003). *Attitudes to flexible working and family life*. The Policy Press.

Huffman, A., Culbertson, S. S., Henning, J. B., & Goh, A. (2013). Work-family conflict across the lifespan. *Journal of Managerial Psychology, 28*(7/8), 761–780.

Kabasakal, H., & Bodur, M. (2004). Humane orientation in societies, organizations, and leader attributes. In R. J. House, P. J. Hanges, M. Javidan, P. W. Dorfman, & V. Gupta (Eds.), *Culture, leadership, and organizations: The GLOBE study of 62 societies* (pp. 564–601). Sage.

Karsten, M. F. (2006). *Management, gender, and race in the 21st century*. University Press of America.

Ko, J., Hur, S., & Smith-Walter, A. (2013). Family-friendly work practices and job satisfaction and organizational performance: Moderating effects of managerial support and performance-oriented management. *Public Personnel Management, 42*(4), 545–565.

Kossek, E. E., Lautsch, B. A., & Eaton, S. C. (2006). Telecommuting, control, and boundary management: Correlates of policy use and practice, job control, and work-family effectiveness. *Journal of Vocational Behavior, 68*(2), 347–367.

Lambert, S. J. (2000). Added benefits: The link between work-life benefits and organizational citizenship behavior. *Academy of Management Journal, 43*(5), 801–815.

Lyness, K. S., & Judiesch, M. K. (2008). Can a manager have a life and a career? International and multisource perspectives on work-life balance and career advancement potential. *Journal of Applied Psychology, 93*(4), 789–805.

Lyness, K. S., & Kropf, M. B. (2005). The relationships of national gender equality and organizational support with work-family balance: A study of European managers. *Human Relations, 58*(1), 33–60.

Masuda, A. D., Poelmans, S. A., Allen, T. D., Spector, P. E., Lapierre, L. M., Cooper, C. L., et al. (2012). Flexible work arrangements availability and their relationship with work-to-family conflict, job satisfaction, and turnover intentions: A comparison of three country clusters. *Applied Psychology, 61*(1), 1–29.

Mazmanian, M., Orlikowski, W. J., & Yates, J. (2013). The autonomy paradox: The implications of mobile email devices for knowledge professionals. *Organization Science, 24*(5), 1337–1357.

McCarthy, A., Darcy, C., & Grady, G. (2010). Work-life balance policy and practice: Understanding line manager attitudes and behaviors. *Human Resource Management Review, 20*(2), 158–167.

Mennino, S. F., Rubin, B. A., & Brayfield, A. (2005). Home-to-job and job-to-home spillover: The impact of company policies and workplace culture. *The Sociological Quarterly, 46*(1), 107–135.

Ngo, H. Y., Foley, S., & Loi, R. (2009). Family friendly work practices, organizational climate, and firm performance: A study of multinational corporations in Hong Kong. *Journal of Organizational Behavior, 30*(5), 665–680.

Peretz, H., Fried, Y., & Levi, A. (2018). Flexible work arrangements, national culture, organisational characteristics, and organisational outcomes: A study across 21 countries. *Human Resource Management Journal, 28*(1), 182–200.

Perry-Smith, J. E., & Blum, T. C. (2000). Work-family human resource bundles and perceived organizational performance. *Academy of Management Journal, 43*(6), 1107–1117.

Powell, G. N., Francesco, A. M., & Ling, Y. (2009). Toward culture-sensitive theories of the work-family interface. *Journal of Organizational Behavior, 30*(5), 597–616.

Reichl, C., Leiter, M. P., & Spinath, F. M. (2014). Work-nonwork conflict and burnout: A meta-analysis. *Human Relations, 67*(8), 979–1005.

Roehling, P. V., Moen, P., & Batt, R. (2003). When work spills over into the home and home spills over into work. In P. Moen (Ed.), *It's about time: Couples and careers* (pp. 101–121). Cornell University Press.

Shockley, K. M., & Allen, T. D. (2007). When flexibility helps: Another look at the availability of flexible work arrangements and work-family conflict. *Journal of Vocational Behavior, 71*(3), 479–493.

Spector, P. E., Allen, T. D., Poelmans, S. A. Y., et al. (2007). Cross-national differences in relationships of work demands, job satisfaction, and turnover intentions with work-family conflict. *Personnel Psychology, 60*(4), 805–835.

Swanberg, J. E., Pitt-Catsouphes, M., & Drescher-Burke, K. (2005). A question of justice: Disparities in employees' access to flexible schedule arrangements. *Journal of Family Issues, 26*(6), 866–895.

Swody, C. A., & Powell, G. N. (2007). Determinants of employee participation in organizations' family-friendly programs: A multi-level approach. *Journal of Business and Psychology, 22*(2), 111–122.

Thompson, C. A., Beauvais, L. L., & Lyness, K. S. (1999). When work-family benefits are not enough: The influence of work-family culture on benefit utilization, organizational attachment, and work-family conflict. *Journal of Vocational Behavior, 54*(3), 392–415.

U. S. Department of Labor. (2002). *Workers on flexible and shift schedules in 2001 (USDL 02-225)*. Author.

Wang, P., & Walumbwa, F. O. (2007). Family-friendly programs, organizational commitment, and work withdrawal: The moderating role of transformational leadership. *Personnel Psychology, 60*(2), 397–427.

Young, D. K., McLeod, A. J., & Carpenter, D. (2022). Examining the influence of occupational characteristics, gender and work-life balance on IT professionals' occupational satisfaction and occupational commitment. *Information Technology & People*, (ahead-of-print). https://doi.org/10.1108/ITP-08-2020-0572

Chapter 11
Recommendations for Implementing Work-Life Balance Policies and Programs

"You either walk inside your own story and own it or you stand outside your story and hustle for your worthiness."—Brené Brown (https://teambuilding.com/blog/work-life-balance-quotes)

Abstract In this chapter we make general suggestions regarding the implementation of work-life balance (WLB) policies and programs. In doing so, we discuss how to: (1) identify employees with greater need for WLB practices, (2) evaluate environmental circumstances for WLB practices, (3) design effective WLB practices, (3) facilitate the effective implementation of WLB practices, (4) provide management support for WLB practices, and (5) evaluate performance of WLB practices.

11.1 Introduction

Having discussed the moderators of work-life balance (WLB) policies and programs, we would now like to make general suggestions regarding the implementation of WLB policies and programs. In doing so, we will discuss how to: (1) identify employees with greater need for WLB programs, (2) evaluate environmental circumstances for WLB programs, (3) design effective WLB programs, (3) facilitate effective implementation of WLB programs, (4) provide management support for WLB programs, and (5) evaluate performance of WLB programs. See Fig. 11.1.

D.-J. Lee, M. J. Sirgy, *Organizational Strategies for Work-Life Balance*, Human Well-Being Research and Policy Making,
https://doi.org/10.1007/978-3-031-56314-0_11

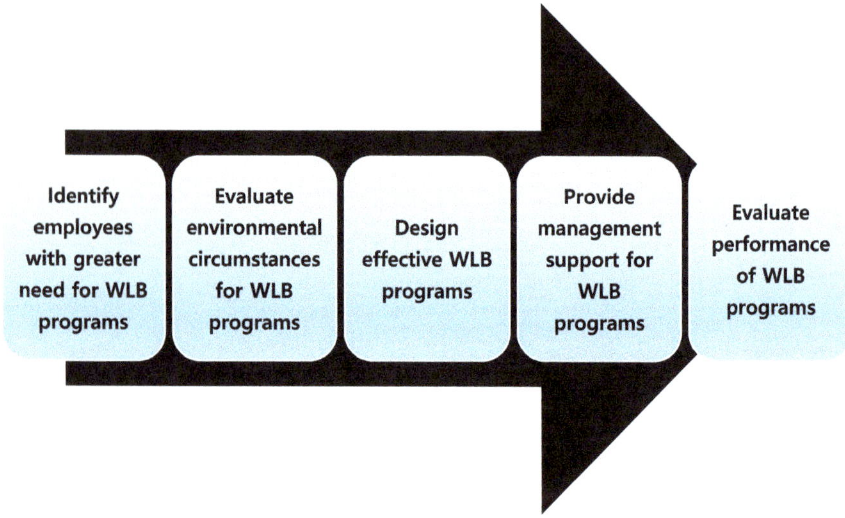

Fig. 11.1 Recommendations for designing and implementing WLB policies and programs

11.2 Identify Employees with Greater Need for WLB Programs

An important step to implementing WLB policies and programs is to evaluate and identity employees with a greater need for WLB programs. As such, we will discuss three categories of employees that can help HR directors identify these individuals: (1) individuals with needs related to specific WLB programs, (2) individuals with a specific demographic profile, and (3) individuals with certain psychographic characteristics. HR directors and supervisors should regularly interview employees with these characteristics to identify their WLB needs to develop WLB programs that meet those needs. It is also important for them to evaluate the urgency and importance of their WLB needs.

11.2.1 Individuals with Needs Related to Specific WLB Programs

In Chap. 3, this book described the WLB research related to five major sets of WLB strategies: (1) work-load management policies and programs, (2) flextime policies and programs, (3) flexplace policies and programs, (4) alternative job arrangements, and (5) family-care policies and programs. As such, management can identify employees based on their specific needs related to these five sets of WLB programs.

Specifically, certain employees may have specific needs related to work-load management. These employees have experienced significant work-related stress stemming from work overload. In other words, they have failed repeatedly to meet work demand because of certain aspects related to the job (e.g., the job requires too much time and effort exceeding the resources available to the employee) and certain personal aspects (e.g., they lack the proper skills and/or time and energy).

Some employees may have specific needs that best fit flextime programs. Consider an employee working 9 a.m. to 5 p.m. in a manufacturing plant. He is married and his wife works a similar schedule. His mother was recently diagnosed with an aggressive form of cancer requiring full-time care. As a result, he asked her to move in with him while she undergoes cancer treatment, and he can help care for her. As such, changing his shift to 6 p.m. to 2 a.m. would allow him to take care of his mother during the day while his wife would be able to take care of her during the evening. In this case, the flextime program seems a perfect fit, allowing him to take care of this urgent family situation.

What about flexplace programs? Consider a different case. An IT professional, whose work can be performed largely out of the office. The employee is a single parent to a young autistic child, requiring substantial personal time and attention at home. Allowing this employee to do her job from home goes a long way to helping her balance work and family demands. As such, the flexplace program is a perfect fit for this situation.

With respect to alternative job arrangements, consider the following situation. A fulltime administrative assistant working at a university who aspires to become an academic administrator. To do so, he needs to pursue an MBA degree, which is offered for very reduced tuition at the same university. However, he realizes that he cannot continue with his full-time job as an administrative assistant while completing the MBA program. The solution is to convince his department head to change his position from full time to part time—which they agreed to do.

Needs related to family-care programs are certainly a no-brainer. Consider the following example, an accountant in a consulting firm is expecting a baby soon. The WLB program that meets her needs in her situation is maternity leave. Her firm offers two options: (1) the traditional 10-weeks paid leave, or (2) 6-months unpaid leave. Her husband is an attorney who make a good income. They both decided that they can afford the 6-months unpaid option, and she is happy to have more time at home with her family.

11.2.2 Individuals with a Specific Demographic Profile

As discussed in Chap. 10, research has shown that WLB practices tend to be more effective for the following individuals with a certain demographic profile:

- women (more so than men).
- young adults (more so than mature adults).

- managers and professionals (more so than those in nonmanagerial and nonprofessional occupations).
- parents with pre-school children (more so than parents with older children.
- married to an employed spouse with children (more so than singles, divorced, widowed, and no children).

11.2.3 Individuals with Certain Psychographic Characteristics

Furthermore, as discussed in Chap. 10, research has shown that WLB practices are more effective for the following individuals with psychographic (i.e., psychological and lifestyle) characteristics:

- those with low (than high) work-family self-efficacy (i.e., those who are not adequately successful in meeting work and family needs without additional support).
- those with a positive (than negative) attitude toward WLB policies and programs (i.e., those who have expressed a favorable view of WLB policies and programs).
- those who are favorably (than unfavorably) disposed to integrate work and family domains (i.e., those whose attitude and lifestyle breaks down boundaries between work and nonwork domains and merge these domains, psychologically speaking).
- those with management and planning skills than those without these skills (i.e., individuals with these skills can manage better independently with little organizational direction and support).
- those who are less (than more) fearful of being stigmatized (i.e., those who care less about being viewed as "needy and dependent" on organizational support to meet their nonwork needs).

Once HR directors and supervisors have identified the WLB needs of these employees, they can develop a matrix reflecting what WLB needs are especially important for whom. They can then use the matrix in designing customized WLB programs.

11.3 Evaluate Environmental Circumstances for WLB Programs

Management should be able to take advantage of environmental circumstances that favor implementation of WLB practices. These circumstances are related to program affordability, cultural factors, and technological conditions. It is recommended that HR directors and supervisors evaluate both internal and external environmental conditions for WLB programs before designing and implementing such practices.

11.3.1 Circumstances Related to Program Affordability

Let's face it, WLB programs cost money. Many small organizations cannot afford them. Even many medium-size organizations are very selective in their WLB program offerings. However, most large firms, including government agencies, offer a large assortment of WLB programs and have policies in place. As such, if your organization is large enough and has the resources to develop and implement WLB programs, then don't hesitate to do so. The organizational and employee benefits of WLB programs are significant.

11.3.2 Cultural Circumstances

In Chap. 10, we discussed cultural moderators that influence the effectiveness of WLB practices. Evidence suggests that WLB policies and programs are more effective given the following cultural conditions: (1) gender egalitarian culture, (2) humane-oriented culture, and (3) individualistic culture.

As previously mentioned, WLB practices tend to be more effective when the organization operates in a society with a culture of gender equality. This means that the country has a culture that minimizes gender role differences while promoting gender equality. In high gender egalitarian cultures there is less adherence to traditional gender roles—women's organizational roles tend to be more similar to men's in relation to authority and status. In countries with low gender equality, management often treats men as the breadwinners and expects women to fulfill domestic responsibilities by staying at home to care for their families. Given that many WLB policies and programs tend to provide greater assistance to women than men, it is unsurprising that the effectiveness of these practices is stronger in organizations operating in countries with a high (than low) gender egalitarian culture. As such, firms operating in gender-egalitarian countries are encouraged to institute WLB policies and programs, much more so than firms operating in countries rated low in gender equality.

Research also shows that WLB practices tend to be more effective in countries characterized as humane. We defined a humane-oriented culture in terms of the extent to which individuals are encouraged and rewarded for being fair, altruistic, friendly, generous, and kind to others. People in a humane-oriented culture are more likely to be sensitive to the wellbeing of others and encourage the provision of social support for WLB policies and programs. As such, firms operating in humane-oriented countries are encouraged to institute WLB policies and programs, much more so than firms operating in countries rated low in humaneness.

Moreover, research also indicates that WLB practices are likely to be more effective in countries characterized as having a culture that is more individualistic than collectivistic. We explained in Chap. 10 that people in individualistic countries tend to experience a higher degree of work-family conflict because they usually cannot obtain family care assistance from extended-family members. Certain WLB programs such as flexible work arrangements tend to complement individualistic traits; thus, they fit better in countries that value individualism, culturally speaking. As such, firms operating in individualistic countries are encouraged to institute WLB policies and programs, much more so than firms operating in collectivistic countries.

11.3.3 Other Environmental Circumstances

There are other environmental circumstances that influence the effectiveness of WLB policies and programs. Consider the quality of Information and Communication Technologies (ICT) infrastructure. There are certain WLB policies and programs that are dependent on good ICT infrastructure such as flextime and flexplace programs. Economically developed countries tend to have a good ICT infrastructure, compared to less-developed countries. Simply put, WLB policies and programs are likely to be more effective in countries with good ICT infrastructure, compared to those with poor infrastructure. As such, organizations operating in countries with good ICT infrastructure are encouraged to institute WLB policies and programs, much more than for firms operating in countries with poor ICT infrastructure.

11.4 Design Effective WLB Programs

Throughout this book we discussed five major sets of WLB programs: (1) workload management programs, (2) flextime programs, (3) flexplace programs, (4) alternative job arrangements, and (5) family care programs. We also discussed how these programs should be implemented. Let's briefly discuss each in more detail.

11.4.1 Work-Load Management Programs

As discussed in Chap. 5, there are at least four ways to implement workload management programs: (1) reduction of workload, (2) provision of mutual help, (3) work smarter, and (4) minimization of workload during off-time.

Specifically, examples of activities to reduce workload include the following:

- setting realistic deadlines and planning work activities; accordingly, and
- establishing a standard range for employee performance that is attainable and sustainable with reasonable engagement and effort and reducing overtime.

Examples of activities to provide mutual help include the following:

- designing work to foster high social support.
- cross-train employees to be able to share the workload.
- reward helping behavior.
- foster a culture that prioritizes care.

Examples of activities to work smarter include the following:

- valuing quality over quantity or speed and allowing employees to perform to the best of their abilities.
- allowing for a measure of job control or discretion over employees' work and performance.
- evaluation based on results, not face time.

Examples of activities to minimize workload during off-time include the following:

- creating and fostering a culture of healthy work practices (e.g., no job demand or no job-related communications during off-time); and
- leave control for time off work.

11.4.2 Flextime Programs

Management can develop individually set schedules and provide workers with discretion over when, where, and how long they work. As discussed in Chap. 6, flextime policies and programs can be implemented through: (1) flexible work time, (2) compressed work week, (3) absence autonomy, and (4) an open rata system.

The goal of flexible work time policies and programs is to allow employees to choose arrival and departure times that best fit their needs within the workday. For example, employees can select different starting and finishing times for each day (working from 9:30 a.m. to 6 p.m. instead of 8:30 a.m. to 5 p.m.).

With respect to compressed work week, management can allow employees to make their workweek fewer than 5 days. This may entail working longer shifts for fewer days per week, rather than the traditional 5-day workweek consisting of 8 h per day for 5 days. An employee can have every Friday off by working 10 h per day for 4 days (e.g., 4/10 schedule) or have every other Friday off by working 9 h per day over 2 weeks (e.g., 9/80 schedule).

Absence autonomy refers to allowing employees to take time off when needed and make up the time off on another day. For example, employees can take a break during the work week to attend a school function or doctor's appointment and make up time lost later in the week.

The open-rota system is a self-scheduling shift program that provides shift employees with a measure of ownership and choice over their work-rest schedules. That is, employees select their preferred shifts, and then collectively decide and implement a monthly work schedule which takes into account individual preference.

11.4.3 Flexplace Programs

As discussed in Chap. 7, flexible workplace policies and programs can take several forms: (1) telecommuting, (2) working from home, (3) e-working.

Telecommuting means that employees perform all or part of their work at a location outside of a physical office. It could be any place—a coffee shop, a hotel, home, a satellite office located in a more convenient place, etc.

Working from home, or homeworking, is work conducted specifically from one's own home. Homeworking is any paid work that is carried out primarily from home for at least 20 h per week.

E-working means online working with locational flexibility—remote working using information and communication technology such as videoconferencing.

11.4.4 Alternative Job Arrangements

As discussed in Chap. 8, alternative job arrangements allow for more control over the quantity of work. Here are at least four types of alternative job arrangements: (1) part-time work, (2) job sharing, (3) career breaks, and (4) contract work.

Offering access to part-time jobs and part-year work allows employees to voluntarily choose their labor intensity and work time without penalty. Part-time workers are workers who work less than 35 h per week with fixed a schedule. Relatedly, a large percentage of part-time workers are on-call workers and seasonal employees.

Job sharing means that a full-time position is shared by two employees who each work part-time hours, which means that both employees also share a single salary and the same benefits. Job sharing brings a broader range of knowledge, skills, and experiences to a position and provides cross-training and skill enhancement opportunities for each partner.

Some organizations offer alternative job arrangements for their employees by permitting career breaks without losing one's job (i.e., sabbatical). In some cases, management offers opportunities such as part-time and job sharing and treats those as regular career breaks. Career breaks are not held against the employee for promotion and career advancement within the organization.

Contract workers refer to workers who work for themselves based on a short-term contract. They are hired to apply their knowledge and skills based to a specific and usually very short-term project. Rather than a salary, they are paid by the hour or project, which a client specifies in a written contract before the work begins.

11.4.5 Family Care Programs

As discussed in Chap. 9, family care programs include: (1) childcare and eldercare programs, (2) family-leave policies and programs, (3) time-off policies and programs, (4) assistance programs and policies, and (5) other services.

Many companies provide access to childcare and eldercare facilities, in some cases to both part-time and full-time workers. Many also have childcare and eldercare facilities on site.

Family-leave programs include maternity leave (employment-protected leave of absence for employed women directly around childbirth/adoption), paternity leave (employment-protected leave of absence for employed fathers at or in the first few months after childbirth), parental leave (employment-protected leave of absence for employed parents, which is often supplementary to specific maternity and paternity leave periods), and home/child care leave (employment-protected leaves of absence that sometimes follow parental leave and that typically allow at least one parent to remain at home to provide care until the child is 2 or 3 years of age).

Time-off programs include time off for personal and professional development, paid vacations and sabbaticals, and accrued days off.

With respect to assistance policies and programs, some organizations provide information, consultation, and educational services about family care. Some even provide financial assistance and access to home networks that employees can use at work (e.g., remotely control home temperature, remotely control home appliances). Many companies also offer other family care services such as dry-cleaning services, employee counselling, postal and mailing services, onsite fitness facilities, and healthy food options. Some organizations provide health-related assistance such as voluntary, work-based programs that offer free and confidential assessments, short-term counseling, referrals, and follow-up services to employees who have health-related problems.

11.5 Facilitate Effective Implementation of WLB Programs

Research suggests that the effectiveness of WLB programs can be significantly increased if management takes measures to enhance the match of WLB programs with employees. We already discussed how this match can be exercised in the previous section related to identifying employees with greater need for WLB programs (Chap. 10). However, much more can be done to enhance fitness and promote various programs.

11.5.1 Enhance the Need Fit

Management should provide employees with enough flexibility in choosing WLB programs that best fit their personal needs and life circumstances. As discussed in Chap. 10, research has shown that there is a great deal of individual differences in the wellbeing effectiveness of various WLB policies and programs. In other words, certain WLB policies and programs impact employees differently. The explanation seems to involve an employee's sense of control. That is, because of individual circumstances, one WLB program can be more effective than another because that program imbues the employee with a greater sense of control.

If so, the question that arises is how to enhance an employee's sense of control in relation to their selection of WLB programs. The answer is twofold:

1. Provide various optional programs that employees can choose from. That is, offer a large assortment of options, and make these programs available to all employees. Then help employees select the program that matches well with their personal needs.
2. Customize each program to each employee (e.g., details of WLB program duration, time, place, work conditions, etc.). That is, management should make adjustments to a selected program to enhance the WLB need fit for each and every employee.

11.5.2 Inform and Educate

Research has shown that WLB programs are most effective when employees are informed and educated about the organization's offerings (see Chap. 10). That is, management should provide consultation, education, and information services to help their employees become more aware and knowledgeable of the organization's policies and program availability. This can be done through periodic WLB seminars and workshops organized and directed by HR personnel.

11.6 Provide Management Support for WLB Programs

Management support for WLB policies and programs is reflected through a supportive organizational culture. As discussed in Chap. 10, supportive organization culture refers to the shared assumptions, beliefs, and values regarding the extent to which an organization supports and values the integration of employees' work and family lives. In a supportive organizational culture, top management, supervisors, coworkers, and employers all provide social support by providing needed resources and imbuing the workplace with positive social interactions.

There are still many organizations that do not provide support for family-friendly programs. In those less-supportive organizations, there is an unwritten rule that one can't take care of family needs on company time. In such organizations, employees who prioritize their family or personal needs over their jobs face disapproval, and they are expected to handle their family responsibilities independently with minimal support from their employer. They often must choose between advancing in their career or devoting attention to their family or personal lives. They may not take advantage of family-friendly policies because they perceive that doing so will have negative career consequences. There are still many people who think that an employee who uses flexible work hours is less committed to their job and less suitable for promotion—despite no differences in perceived capability compared to other employees not using a flexible schedule. Thus, it is not sufficient for an organization to simply offer family-friendly benefits to employees. It is necessary to provide managerial support for family-friendly benefits and ensure that use of work-family benefits does not negatively affect an employees' career.

How exactly can organizations encourage a supportive organizational culture for WLB programs? They can do the following: (1) demonstrate a positive attitude toward WLB policies and programs, (2) display strong managerial and social support for WLB policies and programs, and (3) ensure fairness implementing WLB policies and programs. Also see Box 11.1 for practical recommendations.

Box 11.1 For Practical Recommendations from Industry Practitioners About Managerial Support

There are several ways managers can provide support to help their employees achieve good work-life balance:

Remind your team to unplug: Encourage your team to leave their laptops and work phones at home when they go on vacation. You may think it doesn't need to be said, but they will appreciate the gesture.

Give employees space to connect: Organize virtual happy hours, birthday parties, book clubs, and other opportunities to connect socially.

Educate employees on their benefits: Remind your employees that sick leave and part time off are part of their compensation.

Check in with direct reports: Make time during your check-ins to ask about their wellbeing. You may have to read between the lines for what's not being said. Missed deadlines or a lack of responsiveness can indicate poor work-life balance.

Be aware of company culture and norms: Try not to normalize an "instant messaging" culture. Make it clear that messages sent on off-hours don't require immediate attention. Avoid interpreting responsiveness as engagement.

Respect working hours: Don't schedule meetings before or after work hours. This can be particularly tricky when working across different time zones. Encourage your employees to end work at a designated time each day. Check in with team members you notice consistently working after-hours.

Source: Adapted from https://www.betterup.com/blog/how-to-have-good-work-life-balance

11.6.1 Demonstrate a Positive Attitude Toward WLB Policies

Top executives should demonstrate a positive attitude towards family programs—such as publicizing their positive beliefs about work-family balance (e.g., norms on working hours; norms on using family benefits) through seminars and educational courses. In addition, executives should reinforce the expectation that there are no negative career impacts from using family programs and work to dispel the misconception that family program users are not serious about their career. It is important for organizations to build a culture of flexibility to achieve work-life balance.

11.6.2 Managerial and Social Support for WLB Policies

Management can provide managerial and social support for work-family programs. Supervisors and middle-management executives should use every means possible to provide employees with moral support—show they care for the wellbeing of their employees and demonstrate empathy and understanding towards those using family benefits.

Furthermore, management can encourage employees to look after one another. This means that management rewards employees that show initiative and support their co-workers, especially co-workers participating in WLB programs.

11.6.3 Ensure Fairness in the Implementation of WLB Policies

It is important for management to ensure fairness in terms of employee access to and ability to use WLB programs. Managers should be fair and not show favoritism in responding to employees' personal or family needs.

Another issue involving fairness is the stereotypic perception that employees taking advantage of WLB programs are likely to suffer career setbacks. That is, their chances for promotion and career development would be significantly diminished. Management should ensure that such stigmatization does not occur. This can be done through information disseminated by the HR department as well as discussion about this topic in WLB seminars and workshops conducted by HR personnel.

11.7 Evaluate Performance and Improve WLB Programs

To further enhance the effectiveness of WLB policies and programs, management should conduct periodic evaluations of the WLB policies and programs in place and make adjustments based on the feedback. As such, we will discuss two major topics related to evaluation, namely conducting annual reviews and measuring the impact of the WLB policies and programs in place.

11.7.1 Annual Reviews

WLB policies and programs are designed to help employees achieve balance in their lives, which in turn should enhance employee overall wellbeing. As such, target goals should be set based on current data about employee WLB and wellbeing, and a procedure should be developed to monitor employee WLB and wellbeing to gauge progress towards the goals. HR and other top-level executives should be involved in setting target goals.

We advise that HR directors establish a review committee to launch a review process and make recommendations to top management about possible changes (e.g., delete certain indicators, add others). The review committee serves a good purpose. It not only identifies needed changes in the organization's WLB policies and programs but also enhances organizational citizenship. It does so by allowing managers and employees to become actively involved in the review process. And in some ways, this citizenship (sense of camaraderie and belonging) helps maintain commitment of management and support of labor unions and other key stakeholders in the organization.

The review committee should be directed by the HR director (or representative of the HR department) and composed of representatives from top management (e.g., CEO or CEO representative), key personnel involved corporate social responsibility, the Public Relations Department, employee associations (e.g., labor union), and other key personnel from legal counsel. Further, it is advisable to have an industrial/organizational psychologist on this committee who would administer periodic employee surveys to gauge the level of employee WLB and wellbeing over time.

What should be reviewed? We can break down the review elements in terms of processes that can be captured through a checklist. Here is the checklist:

- Were the resources needed for developing and implementing WLB policies and programs identified and used?
- Did the management of WLB programs include key representatives from the organization such as the HR director or representative, CEO or representative, key personnel involved corporate social responsibility (CSR), the Public

Relations (PR) Department, employee associations, legal counsel, and an industrial/organizational psychologist (expert on WLB research)?

- Was input from representatives of the stakeholder groups accepted by the HR director or shut out?
- Was a subject-matter expert (i.e., the industrial/organizational psychologist) consulted?
- Was the employee WLB and wellbeing measures selected based on accepted and well-established criteria?
- Were best practices for data collection and management (related to the administration of employee WLB and wellbeing surveys) used?
- Has the reporting been done regularly, in a manner friendly to key constituents (HR, CEO, CSR, PR, employee association, legal counsel, …)?
- Were communication tools related to WLB (e.g., websites, social media, publications) used and tracked?
- Have steps been taken to ensure sustainability of the organization's WLB policies and programs?

Another method of the review process can be administered by answering the traditional five interrogatives: what, why, when, where, and who.

What?

- Did the metrics of WLB quantify values, conditions, outcomes, and results important to all the organization's employees?
- Were the metrics developed through consensus-building?
- Did the metrics of WLB reflect balance of life domains in terms of input (time balance, role engagement, and fit between needs and resources)?
- Did the metrics of WLB reflect balance of life domains in terms of output (role effectiveness, role satisfaction, and minimal role conflicts)?*Why?*

- Was the employee WLB survey helpful in telling a story of where the employee's WLB is today compared to its past?
- Was there dialogue and debate among the key constituents that led to identifying important issues in employees' WLB?
- Was there dialogue to determine strategies to improve employee WLB and wellbeing, and identify resources to implement the WLB policies and programs?*When?*

- Were the employee WLB surveys (administered periodically) helpful in plotting historical trends and alerting the need for improvement of conditions fostering employee WLB?
- Were long-term and annual goals and targets established periodically, and progress measured and reported to key constituents?*Where?*

- Were the surveys explicitly defined in terms of geographic location of employees?
- Was the data compared with other comparable surveys of employee WLB?
- Were the surveys conducted in ways that ensured voluntary employee participation (e.g., confidentiality) and accessibility (e.g., online survey)?*Who?*

- Were employees (or representatives of this constituency) able to provide input on the design of the survey questionnaire?
- Were other key constituencies (or their representatives) involved?

11.7.2 Measuring the Impact

Many organizations do not engage in any systematic evaluation of their WLB policies and programs. They should do so to be more effective. Their reluctance may be related to the difficulty in measuring the impact of WLB programs. What should these impact measures be? Below is a *hierarchy of effects* related to the impact of WLB policies and programs, namely awareness, knowledge, attitude, and action.

Awareness

Awareness can be measured subjectively through a survey directed to employees that is conducted periodically (once a year or so) in which sample respondents are asked the following question: "Are you aware of the organization's WLB policies and programs?" A 3-point scale with the following response categories can be used to capture responses: "I am not aware at all," "I am a little aware," "I am very much aware."

Knowledge

Knowledge of the organization's WLB policies and programs can best be measured subjectively by the same survey used to capture awareness. Knowledge goes beyond awareness to capture specific information about the organization's WLB policies and programs. Example survey items include: "Are you aware of the fact that the organization offers flextime in the form of compressed work week?" A "Yes-No" response scale can be used to capture responses.

Attitude

Attitude can also be captured by the same survey. Examples of survey items may include: "Do you have a favorable or unfavorable opinion of compressed work as an important element of the organization's WLB policies and programs?" Responses can be captured on a 5-point scale: "very favorable," "favorable," "neither favorable nor unfavorable," "unfavorable," "very unfavorable"; or "Do you believe that the organization's compressed work week is making a difference in achieving better work-life balance?" Responses can be captured using the following 3-point scale: "making a big difference," "making a little difference," and "making no difference."

Action

Finally, *action* can be measured using objective indicators (e.g., number of people taking advantage of each WLB offering over time) and the WLB index (e.g., WLB scores summarized within the organization over time).

Performance Evaluation and Change Management

We then evaluate the overall impact of WLB programs through the following checklist:

Impact on employees:

- Did the WLB programs reduce work-life conflicts of employees?
- Did the WLB programs reduce role stress of employees?
- Did the WLB programs increase the personal health of employees?

Impact on the firm:

- Did the WLB programs enhance job satisfaction of employees?
- Did the WLB programs enhance morale and productivity of employees?
- Did the WLB programs reduce absenteeism and time off from work?
- Did the WLB programs increase work productivity?

Change of WLB impact over time:

- Did the impact of WLB programs on the employee improve over time? If so? Why?
- Did the impact of WLB programs on the firm improve over time? If so? Why?

11.8 Summary and Conclusion

In this chapter we discuss general suggestions regarding the implementation of WLB policies and programs. In doing so, we discuss how to: (1) identify employees with greater need for WLB programs, (2) evaluate environmental circumstances for WLB programs (3) design effective WLB policies and programs, (3) facilitate effective implementation of WLB policies and programs, (4) provide management support for WLB policies and programs, and (5) evaluate performance of WLB policies and programs.

Specifically, we discussed how to identify employees with greater need for WLB programs. In this vein, we discussed three categories of employees that can help HR directors identify employees with greater need for WLB programs: (1) individuals with needs related to specific WLB programs, (2) individuals with a specific demographic profile, and (3) individuals with certain psychographic characteristics.

With respect to individuals with needs related to specific WLB programs, we described five major sets of WLB policies and programs: work-load management, flextime, flexplace, alternative job arrangements, and family care. With respect to individuals with a specific demographic profile, examined the following demographic segments: women (more so than men), young adults (more so than mature adults), managers and professionals (more so than those in nonmanagerial and nonprofessional occupations), parents with pre-school children (more so than parents with older children), married to an employed spouse with children (more so than singles, divorced, widowed, and no children). Finally with respect to individuals with certain psychographic characteristics, we showed how WLB policies and programs are more effective for those with low (than high) work-family self-efficacy, those with a positive (than negative) attitude toward WLB policies and programs, those who are favorably (than unfavorably) disposed to integrate work and family domains, those with management and planning skills (than those without these skills), and those who are less (than more) fearful of being stigmatized.

Following this discussion, we discussed how to take advantage of circumstances that affect the success of WLB programs. To do so, we elaborated on research exploring how program affordability, cultural factors, and technological conditions influence overall effectiveness. We highlighted the finding that many small organizations do not offer WLB programs because the costs with these programs are prohibitive. Primarily only medium and large organizations can afford them. We also discussed how culture influences overall effectiveness of WLB policies and programs, specifically: gender egalitarian culture, humane-oriented culture, and individualistic culture. We also highlighted the fact that many of the WLB programs in place are dependent on good ICT infrastructure.

We then discussed how to develop and implement WLB policies and programs by examining five major sets of WLB policies and programs: (1) work-load management policies and programs, (2) flextime policies and programs, (3) flexplace policies and programs, (4) alternative job arrangements, and (5) family care policies and programs. With respect to work-load management policies and programs, we described four methods: reduction of workload, provision of mutual help, work smarter, and minimization of workload during off-time. Regarding flextime policies and programs, we described four methods of implementation: flexible work time, compressed work week, absence autonomy, and an open rata system. Concerning flexible workplace policies and programs, we described several forms: telecommuting, working from home, e-working. Regarding alternative job arrangements, four types were described: part time, job sharing, career breaks, and contract work. Finally, with respect to family care policies and programs, we touched upon childcare and eldercare programs, assistance programs, family-leave programs, time-off programs, and assistance services.

Then we examined how to facilitate implementation of WLB policies and programs. Here, we discussed how to enhance the employee-WLB program fit and how to inform and educate employees about the organization's WLB offerings. Specifically, in relation to how to enhance fitness, we suggested that management should provide a large variety of programs with numerous options that employees can choose from and the ability to customize each program to each employee. In relation to how to inform and educate employees about the organization's WLB offerings, we highlighted suggestions related to periodic WLB seminars and workshops organized and directed by HR personnel.

We then discussed how to provide management support for WLB policies and programs. In doing so we focused on three issues: demonstrating a positive attitude toward WLB policies and programs, managerial and social support for WLB policies and programs, and ensuring fairness implementing WLB policies and programs.

The final topic of this chapter focused on how to evaluate and improve WLB policies and programs. In this vein, we discussed two issues: conducting annual reviews and measuring the impact of the WLB policies and programs in place. With respect to annual reviews, we advise that a review committee be formed. The committee should be directed by the HR director (or representative) and composed of representatives from top management (e.g., CEO or CEO representative), key personnel involved corporate social responsibility, the Public Relations department, employee associations (e.g., labor union), and other key personnel from legal counsel. We also advised the recruitment of an industrial/organizational psychologist. We then elaborated on the review elements (e.g., "Were resources needed for developing and implementing WLB policies and programs identified and used?" "Was the employee WLB and wellbeing measures selected based on accepted and well-established criteria?" "Have steps been taken to ensure sustainability of the organization's WLB policies and programs?"). We also reframed the review checklist in terms of answering the traditional five interrogatives—what, why, when, where, and who.

We then discussed how to periodically measure the impact of WLB policies and programs through a hierarchy of impact measures that include awareness, knowledge, attitude, and action. That is, employees would be surveyed periodically and asked questions such as "Are you aware of the organization's WLB policies and programs?" "Are you aware of the fact that the organization offers flextime in the form of compressed work week?" "Do you have a favorable or unfavorable opinion of the compressed work as an important element of the organization's WLB policies and programs?" Unlike the previous measures, *action* can be measured using objective indicators (e.g., number of people taking advantage of each WLB offering over time).

To conclude, we would like to emphasize to the reader that good management and higher productivity do not come at the expense of WLB. In today's management of medium-size and large organizations, effective WLB policies and programs are imperative to organizational health and prosperity.

Tony Blair, the former Prime Minister of the United Kingdom, once asserted that "The UK has shown it is possible to have flexible labor markets combined with [...] family friendly policies to help WLB [...]. The result has been higher growth, higher employment, and low unemployment."[1] This assertion is a resounding fact. We hope that readers of this book will take it to heart.

[1] Toby Helm and David Rennie, "Blair attack on 'out-of-date' Chirac," *Daily Telegraph*, March 3, 2005, http://www.telegraph.co.uk/news/main.jhtml?xml/news/2005/03/25/weu25.xml&sSheet/news/2005/03/25/ixnewstop.html.

Author Index

D.-J. Lee, M. J. Sirgy, *Organizational Strategies for Work-Life Balance*, Human Well-Being Research and Policy Making,
https://doi.org/10.1007/978-3-031-56314-0

Subject Index

D.-J. Lee, M. J. Sirgy, *Organizational Strategies for Work-Life Balance*, Human Well-Being Research and Policy Making,
https://doi.org/10.1007/978-3-031-56314-0

Printed in the USA
CPSIA information can be obtained
at www.ICGtesting.com
CBHW060254170724
11581CB00013BA/57

9 783031 563133